Ahead of the Class

Ahead of the Class

MARIE STUBBS

JOHN MURRAY
Albemarle Street, London

© Marie Stubbs 2003

First published 2003
by John Murray (Publishers) Ltd,
50 Albemarle Street, London W1S 4BD

3 5 7 9 10 8 6 4 2

The moral right of the author has been asserted

A catalogue record for this book is available from the British Library

ISBN 0-7195-6335-6

Typeset in Adobe Palatino 11/14 pt by
Servis Filmsetting Ltd, Manchester

Printed and bound in Great Britain by Clays Ltd, St Ives plc

For Bill, always my best teacher, my family, Sean and Tracey, and the staff and children of St George's School

Contents

While this book is the true story of St George's, some names of individuals and details of incidents have been altered where necessary in order to protect the identities and sensibilities of all the children, parents and staff concerned.

Acknowledgements

There are certain people without whom this book would never have been written. My thanks go to Anne Simpson of the Glasgow *Herald*, who first encouraged me to tell this story; to Felicity Rubinstein, my literary agent, who suggested that I write the book and provided support and encouragement throughout the process; to Jean Ritchie, whose energy helped me to organize a mass of material and get the book on course. A very special thank-you goes to Hazel Wood for her outstanding literary skills. Without Hazel the book would never have been published.

Special thanks also to Caroline Knox, my editor at John Murray, whose professionalism and lively interest in the book kept me on track; to Antony Wood for his exemplary copyediting; to Caroline Westmore of John Murray for all the practical help and good sense which kept me sane; and to Paul Clements, who took the jacket photograph.

1

The Call

March 2000

'Chill man. Don't go there.'

The speaker is a large youth wearing a baseball cap, over-sized trousers and a torn black sweatshirt. He's rolling a fat wad of chewing-gum around his mouth, which he keeps open. He can't be more than sixteen, but there's the shadow of a dark moustache on his upper lip. He towers over me – not difficult as I'm only five feet three, with a couple of extra inches added by my high heels.

He returns my gaze insolently for a second or two, then turns and saunters away across the playground. I've asked him to pick up a ball of paper he's thrown on to the ground. His reply throws down something else: a challenge. He has no intention of obeying me, and he wants to make that plain, not just to me but to anyone else who's listening.

As I watch his retreating back my heart is thumping slightly, but I'm not alarmed. His response is certainly challenging – that politically correct word we use in education for behaviour that is outside the normal range. But in my thirty years of teaching I've dealt with many pupils who were spectacularly outside the normal range, and I'm not thrown by yet another.

As he saunters away I become aware that someone else is watching me curiously – a tall, well-built girl with vividly streaked hair wearing enormous hoop earrings and only the slightest semblance of a school uniform.

'Would *you* like to pick that up?' I ask her.
'F— off, man,' she replies.
Welcome to St George's.

I'd been on holiday in Scotland with my eldest daughter Nadine and her three children when my mobile rang. 'Turn the television down, please, Grandma can't hear,' I said to the eldest, lively seven-year-old Vanessa, who was lying engrossed, her chin in her hands, watching cartoons. Somewhat unwillingly she reduced the sound by a few decibels and as the squawks of Tom and Jerry receded I could just make sense of a message to ring Tony Mackersie, the Director of Education for the Catholic Diocese of Westminster. I was puzzled. I hadn't had contact with him for over a year and couldn't imagine why he'd want to talk to me. My relationships with some of the Diocese's officers had been mixed.

When I got through to him and heard what he wanted I was stunned. He was asking me to come out of retirement to help turn round St George's Roman Catholic Secondary School – the school where the head teacher, Philip Lawrence, had been murdered in 1995. The school, he told me, was now on Special Measures – the government term for the especially close monitoring given to a failing school – and for two years had been in such straits that it had now been temporarily closed. The Head and the Deputy Head had left, and it was two months away from possibly being closed down permanently.

As Tony Mackersie spoke, a picture came back to me of the likeable man in a smart suit and bow tie I'd met once at a head teachers' conference. 'I'm Philip Lawrence from St George's, Maida Vale,' he'd said, holding out his hand with a smile. 'And I'm Marie Stubbs from The Douay Martyrs, Ickenham, out there in the sunny suburbs,' I said, and we both laughed. We talked briefly and I liked his warmth. Then he moved purposefully off across the room and was lost in the crowd. When I heard that he had been knifed to death in front of his own pupils I was appalled, like everyone else in Britain, and particularly those of us in the same profession. The Lawrence family dominated our thoughts and prayers at that time, and we still think of them.

I must confess, however, that until I got Tony Mackersie's phone call I hadn't given St George's itself much thought. Since I'd retired six months previously, after thirteen years as Head of Douay, I'd been enjoying myself. Almost the first thing I did was to say to my hairdresser, 'Steve, turn me into a blonde.' 'Don't be ridiculous Marie,' Steve replied in his usual straightforward way – but I was serious. I'd always wanted to try being a blonde, but it hadn't seemed quite suitable for a sensible headmistress. Next, with a sense of achievement, I bagged up all my practical navy blue and black work suits for the charity shop and went shopping for some trendy sports tops and trousers. I enrolled for a course in botanical drawing and started swimming regularly and going to the gym. What with all this, plus a fascinating trip to Japan with my husband, and the fun I was having with my grandchildren, it was hard to remember how I'd ever found time to go to work, though I still felt too energetic to be truly retired.

A few days later I was back at Marks & Spencer's trying on sensible suits, and phoning Steve for an appointment to turn me back into a serious brunette. I'd said yes to Tony Mackersie. 'I'll need a couple of other people I can trust to come and work with me,' I said. 'I'm a team player. I don't believe in the superhead concept.' The problems at St George's, he told me, were largely to do with behaviour and the challenges of having a large number of children whose first language was not English, but behind his careful words I picked up a strong sense of a school in chaos. I was to be given four terms to turn it round. It felt a bit like a military emergency – I was going to be parachuted into a school I'd never seen and knew almost nothing about at only a few days' notice. I had one week to prepare myself. I was to start on 6 March.

At one level I thought I must be mad. My family certainly did and my mother was understandably worried. Up in Scotland she'd been reading horror stories in the papers about London gangs and stabbings and seriously wanted to know if I was going to be given a flak jacket to go into school. 'I shan't sleep at night, Marie,' she said to me during one of our evening phone conversations. 'You're sixty now, and at your age you should be having a quieter life.' Everyone seemed to be joining in the chorus – friends, family, the carpark attendant at our flat. Nice Father Burns at St George's, the Oxfordshire parish where we spend weekends, told me he would pray for me and was going to say a special Mass.

I was touched, but after a while a professional irritation began to creep in. These were just naughty children after all, I thought, who needed to be pulled into line, and we adults were the people who should be doing it. It's often the pupils who get the blame when things go wrong in a poor school, and I felt the pupils at St George's had taken enough of the blame already. I felt rather as you do when you come home to find your children have had a party. I wanted to go in there and help them tidy things up.

But could I do it? Glasgow girls are famously tough and feisty. 'Well,' I told myself, 'you're from Glasgow, you've had thirty years in teaching, and remember – you survived The Centre.' The Centre was a residential unit outside London for teenage girls between fourteen and sixteen with severe behavioural and emotional problems, where I was in charge of education. The girls came with histories of drug-taking, living on the streets, criminal convictions for theft and violence, and chronically deprived family backgrounds. It was here that an angry pupil held a piece of glass to my throat and threatened to cut me. And it was here that I got to know Susan, a desperately unhappy girl who, like others at The Centre, habitually cut themselves with anything they could find in order to get attention.

Susan would take her bloodstained bandages off in my English Literature classes and call out: 'Look what I did, Stubbsy.' 'That's boring, Susan,' I'd force myself to say. 'Put your bandages back on. If you drip blood on your essay you'll be in big trouble.' 'If I was dead and in my grave,' she once said to me, 'you'd be looking down yelling "Have you done your homework?"', wouldn't you Stubbsy?' 'That's right,' I said and gave her my severest look, at which we both burst out laughing and she put her bandages back on. I often wonder how her life unfolded – she was a talented girl.

So after The Centre I wasn't afraid of dealing with distressed and disruptive pupils. Most important, perhaps, my time there confirmed my belief that, whatever their problems, children can still be inspired by a good education. I couldn't sort out the mess of these girls' lives, but I could make sure they left The Centre with something positive. I'll never forget the broad, slow smile on the face of a plump, pretty teenager who had been living rough, when she first managed to read a whole sentence. Or the whoops of delight from some of the brighter girls when they learned they'd passed a handful of O Levels.

The Douay Martyrs School, a large comprehensive three times the size of St George's, where I spent thirteen years as head, was a different proposition, and it was here that I was able to put my ideas for developing a good school into practice. I have a distinct vision of what a good school should be like. I feel it should have the best features of a good independent school, a good grammar school and a good secondary modern school all rolled into one. I believe the state sector should provide, free of charge, a really exciting and, you might say, patrician education. At Douay I introduced Latin and Greek as well as Mandarin, and encouraged the development of a choir which became well-known internationally. I also wanted the children to have good manners – to know how to use a knife and fork correctly, to speak clearly and politely when they addressed teachers. Some might call this snobbish but I think it's a very Scottish perspective: 'the lad o' pairts' – believe in yourself, work hard, and the world can be yours. By the time I retired, Douay had received a glowing report from Ofsted, the government schools inspectorate, and not long after was given Beacon status, which singles it out as one of the best schools in Britain. I was very proud of what I and the staff there had achieved together.

Opening my 'nostalgia file' brought it all back: my management ideas, photos, press-cuttings, letters, cards. I'd been thinking that these would gather dust in the filing cabinet until the day when I'd be able to throw them out, but now I flicked through them, sorting out the ones that might be useful. As I thought of Douay I became more and more certain about the two people I needed for my St George's Task Force. Sean Devlin and Tracey O'Leary were two of my three excellent Deputy Heads at Douay and I sometimes thought we were like the Three Musketeers. I knew that if I could get Sean and Tracey with me for St George's, everything would be all right.

I turned the situation over in my mind. I knew that both of them were more than ready to head their own schools and would begin looking for new jobs that summer, but I'd have to be sure that if the new Head at Douay released them now she'd be given proper financial help to replace them. I also knew that we'd built up a very big and highly skilled management team, so she was well supported, and it would also give her the chance to bring a couple of people of her own choice into her team.

'Are you sitting down Sean?' I said when I rang him, less than a week before I was due to start. 'I'm going to drop a bombshell.'

I'd acted as Sean's mentor during the term after my retirement, when he was Acting Head at Douay, so we'd kept in touch. I pictured him now, sitting back, cradling the phone on his shoulder, with his legs crossed and his arms behind his head the way I'd seen him so many times. With his slim but athletic frame, ready laugh and twinkling eyes, Sean is a charming personality, but he is also a financial wizard, has the heart of a lion and is ferociously determined to get results. When I'd done there was a bit of a silence – Sean always thinks before he speaks. Then I heard him take a deep breath. 'Well, I won't say no, Marie. I'm going to think about it. I'll talk about it with Dorothy' – his attractive and clever Ugandan wife, who was then his fiancée – 'and ring you back.'

When he told me next day he'd 'decided to have a go' I was jubilant. 'I'd really like Tracey to come on board too,' I said.

'Would you talk to her? I think she'd find it easier coming from you.'

Tracey is an inspired English teacher with a special talent for dealing with overwrought children. At Douay Sean and I always called her room 'the decompression chamber', a room where angry and out-of-control children would be listened to, spoken with, and gradually calmed down. She is a passionate advocate of children, too, with a clear understanding of the importance of ensuring that every one of them has a quality education. With her soothing aura, her lovely speaking voice, her lively way of dressing and the confidence with which she carries herself, I knew what a reassuring presence she'd be in this difficult situation. I also knew that her literacy expertise was just what we needed. So when I heard her clear voice on the phone saying 'I've thought about it and I'd like to join you', I knew we were in business. Now all I had to do was to persuade the Westminster Diocese and Westminster LEA, who jointly shared responsibility for St George's.

2

Could It Get Any Worse?

Second half of Spring Term, 6 March to 14 April

The taxi draws up in Lanark Road outside a low, off-white building. Tracey, Sean and I sit for a moment taking it in. Like a lot of Fifties architecture it has a somewhat temporary look about it. Opposite is a graffiti-plastered building called the Paddington Boys' Club, and just along the road are tower blocks of council flats. I guess that a lot of our pupils come from these. On the other side of the school, where the tops of red buses can be glimpsed moving along behind the high wall of the playground, is Maida Vale – a contrasting world of luxurious apartment blocks and large, security-protected houses with price tags in the millions. Unlikely that many of our pupils come from these, I think, but who knows.

We climb out of the cab and walk towards the two large metal gates at the entrance which open on to an electronically-operated front door. Peter Clare, the Chairman of the School Governors, a large, balding man with a rather bustling manner, arrives with us. He presses a buzzer and almost immediately 'I'll be right wid ya,' an Irish voice crackles on the intercom and Mick Chamberlain, the schoolkeeper, appears.

Peter Clare introduces us. 'You're very welcome to St George's, Lady Stubbs. Mr Devlin and Miss O'Leary too, o'course,' says Mick, in a quaintly formal way. I like the look of him with his fresh friendly face, high cheekbones and bright blue eyes. 'Glad to meet you Mick,' I say. 'The school buildings are very important to me. I'd like to have a talk about them with you later on.'

'Ah, Lady Stubbs,' he laughs, 'I can see you're a woman after my own heart.'

This all feels encouraging, and we follow Mick into the school, a large set of keys clanking against his hip as he walks. At the end of a short passage we arrive in a high, square, glass-ceilinged atrium, with doors off it that are all tightly closed. The air is stale and lifeless. I feel as if I'm in a museum, except that there's nothing to look at. What is this place for? I wonder. Straight ahead of us through the atrium are gates leading into the playground, and beyond the playground the sinister-looking big black gates, so beloved of the press, that lead into Maida Vale. I ask Mick if we can go into the playground. I want to see the school as the children must see it each morning when they arrive. It's a bleak, empty place, a large expanse of tarmac pitted and crusted with chewing gum. To the left is a small enclosed concrete area with a bench, surrounded by an iron fence and some shrubs. This is the Philip Lawrence Memorial Garden. The three of us stand in silence before the plaque, which is visible from the road and bears the simple inscription: 'Love Never Ends'.

We continue our tour of the empty, silent school. The children are on their compulsory break until tomorrow, and our footsteps echo uncomfortably through the long corridors as Mick leads the way, opening doors here and there. The building forms a T-shape, with the atrium and its corridor leading to three corridors of classrooms stacked one on top of the other and linked by grey concrete stairways. The school hall is at one end on the ground floor, the gym on the top and the chapel and library in the middle. The chapel, like the library, is well-carpeted and neatly furnished but feels uninspiring to me, with very little on the walls except a plaque bearing the names of previous heads. Walls everywhere are painted a uniform, washed-out magnolia and the paintwork a dreary brown, and there are very few posters or noticeboards. I wonder why my shoes seem to be sticking to the floor and looking down I realize the carpets are matted with chewing-gum – ugh! The place isn't really dirty – Mick sees to that – but I feel somehow a miasma of exhaustion and despair hangs over it.

Behind it all though, it's not a bad building. In my mind's eye I can see how it would be transformed by hanging plants and bright, upbeat colours. I have a sudden, nostalgic flashback to the state convent school where I was educated, with its reassuring, all-pervading smells of polish and fresh flowers. 'I'm just not having this!' I think, Sean is looking around in his optimistic, good-humoured way, and Tracey also seems cheerful. 'It's got possibilities,' she says as we finally stand together in the atrium. 'What about getting some quick posters done at Prontaprint for a start?' We all agree. We jot down our ideas, and although we come up with different things, there's one message we all want to give the children: 'Welcome Back.'

Most of the classrooms are locked, but finally I find one that's open and it's not encouraging. Although it's the middle of term there are few displays on the walls and it's hard, from the look of the room, to know what subject is being taught there. There is a collection of battered tables covered with inky childish scrawls, and some of the chairs are wobbly. There's no whiteboard, just a chalky old-fashioned blackboard. If this room depresses me, just poking my nose in, I think, how must it feel to be a child coming into it day after day? The three of us look at one another and we don't need to say anything.

We finally manage to locate the toilets on the ground floor, just where the doors open in from the playground, but they're locked. There are locked doors everywhere. No wonder Mick has such an impressive bunch of keys. He issues us each with a set and warns us not to forget them. They're obviously an integral part of life at St George's.

For a moment I feel dispirited again. We've arrived just after lunch, having spent the morning at a packed press conference at Westminster City Hall that raised my adrenalin and made me uncomfortably aware of how deeply the story of St George's has embedded itself in the national psyche – first with Philip

Lawrence's death and then with the decline of the school into Special Measures for the past two years. A lot of the national press, radio and television stations were there, and I sat on the platform under bright television lights, facing rows of journalists. I was not alone on the platform, but it was me the questions were fired at. I've been interviewed by journalists before about school events, but now I was being interrogated about a school where I had so far met none of the pupils or parents and none of the teachers apart from one – a slim, lively woman called Ariadne Lish who was present as teacher governor when I was interviewed about the job at Westminster Council Offices.

'Why have you taken this school on?'

'What makes you think you can do it?

'What will you do about the violence?'

'How will you deal with the terrible attendance?'

These were difficult questions, and I felt an unpleasant edge to them. I was determined to be positive and to avoid criticizing the children who, it occurred to me, must be only too used to reading dire things about themselves in the press. It was not a St George's pupil who killed Philip Lawrence, but by association St George's pupils had been characterized as thieves, vandals and gangsters. I realized that it was casually assumed they brought knives and other weapons to school. I felt sure the attitudes of neighbours and pupils from other schools must be deeply demoralizing and depressing for everyone connected with St George's – children, teachers and parents.

'What will you do about chronic lateness?' I was asked. 'I'll buy alarm clocks for any children who are persistently late,' I said quickly. 'You're the leader of a Task Force, so what will your title be?' someone else wanted to know. 'I'll be known as Headmistress,' I said, determined to signal a return to good old-fashioned manners. I used the idea of Lent – a period of reflection in the Catholic calendar before the rebirth of Easter – to tell the journalists what I intended to do. 'We will reflect, then work positively,' I said. 'This is the perfect time for St George's to go forward as a Catholic school.'

After a quick sandwich lunch, which I found somewhat hard to swallow in the company of my interrogators, it was time to leave for the school. I was pleased to find the media so genuinely interested. But I also realized that whatever I do at St George's is going to be monitored not just by the education authorities but by the press, which will always be on the watch.

After our brief tour of the building, and a quick introduction to my PA, Dot, a small, cheerfully energetic woman who, to my amusement, greets the Chairman of Governors with the words 'allo Trouble!' we head for the hall, where he has arranged for us to meet the staff. We're all nervous: we know this first meeting is crucial. We're only too aware how difficult the past few weeks must have been for them, as well as for the children. They are likely to be confused, upset and anxious about their jobs. We stand outside the door for a moment. I can see that Tracey's hand is tightly clenched round the papers she is holding and Sean looks graver than I've ever seen him. We've all made a special effort to look smart and businesslike. I'm wearing a pinstripe Marks & Spencer suit, and, thanks to Steve, my newly cut and darkened hair is shining. Sean has on a dark suit and a cheerful tie. Tracey's long brown curls are tied back and in her well-cut black suit she looks younger than her years.

I suddenly feel very protective of both of them and wonder what on earth I've got them into. Whatever happens here, I at least can walk away at the end of it, but they've both put their careers on the line. They're such a talented pair, so loyal and energetic. Such fun to be with too – we're always laughing when we're together, which is one of the reasons I need them so badly.

I remember all the wonderful things Tracey organized in the English department at Douay – poetry evenings, magazines, competitions. She came to Douay as quite a new young English teacher, but it became clear immediately how gifted she was, and when our head of English tragically died I made her head of department. Because she was so young there was a certain amount of opposition in the staffroom, but I never regretted it, and the more she did, the happier I was. She had such warmth when dealing with children and parents, but she could also be tough; her sensitive, artistic appearance could be deceptive. 'Don't mess with Miss O'Leary,' I would say to the children. 'She's the iron hand in the velvet glove.'

Sean and I, it's true, didn't always see eye to eye when he first arrived at Douay after teaching for fourteen years in Papua, New Guinea, where he became head. It only took me a short while, though, to realize what an inspiring teacher he was, and how brilliant at restoring discipline and dealing with administrative problems, as well as getting on well with other staff. Sean keeps everything in perspective, never gets ruffled, and we've developed a deep respect and liking for one another.

'Is my hair sticking up?' I ask Tracey, tugging down my suit jacket. 'All right, let's smile now and look cheerful. We need to make a good first impression.'

I take a deep breath and push open the door. The hubbub of conversation dies, and we are facing a sea of expectant faces. Tables have been arranged around the hall and the staff are sitting in groups. In the first few seconds I notice some handsome, powerful-looking black women, and one in particular, a statuesque figure in bright, elegant clothes who is sitting like a grande dame, calm and attentive. There's a pretty blonde, bright-eyed girl with a ponytail, and among the blur of faces I think I glimpse some facial jewellery and – surprisingly among all the suits and woolly jumpers – someone in a very short top half-hidden beneath some sort of cardigan. A slender, elegant, regal-looking woman of Arabic appearance says a friendly 'Good afternoon', and I'm relieved to spot the slight figure of Aradiane Lish, the teacher governor. Her questions at my interview impressed me and showed me that she genuinely cares about the school.

There are fewer men. Their body language looks to me defensive. One sits back with his arms crossed, gazing at the ceiling, another seems to be the leader of a small group in one corner. One or two don't make eye contact with me at all. We are greeted by David Edwards, who was brought in last September as temporary Deputy Head by the Council's consultants Nord Anglia. I note the Welsh lilt in his voice: another member of the Celtic fringe, I think. I hope the staff won't feel overwhelmed.

There are 35 teachers in all and my first impression of them as a group is that they are like the school buildings – exhausted and magnoliaed over. There's a trapped, wary feeling in the room, and I understand it. My predecessor left precipitately, and now they have me foisted on them. They've spent the last week coming into a school without any pupils in it, which must have been eerie and dispiriting, especially since some of them will remember the tragic death of Philip Lawrence and all the sadness it brought.

I introduce the three of us as lightly as I can. 'I'm Marie Stubbs,' I say, 'and I'm very pleased to be with you at St George's. My two colleagues here, Sean Devlin and Tracey O'Leary, worked with me for many years at The Douay Martyrs School in Ickenham, which has 1,500 pupils, and they're both highly experienced Deputy Heads. We've all chosen to come to St George's because we feel it is an extremely worthwhile community, and we're concerned that teachers here should have been having to work under such strain and that children, for whatever reason, should be having such a difficult education, when it is every child's right to have a good one. We want to give them hope, to give them back their future.

'I know it's a very complex situation, but the past, as they say, is another country. As professional teachers all of us, I'm sure, want to help the children go forward and win the struggle with Ofsted to get the school off Special Measures. As for myself, I'm pretty much an aged grandmother who's come out of retirement to help turn the school round. I'm probably far too old to be doing this kind of thing, so I hope you'll all be very nice to me.'

My words are met with silence. Now Sean steps forward to say his bit. His voice is firm and he speaks briefly. 'I teach economics,' he tells them. 'I'll be taking some of the classes who would like a practical application for their subject, and I also hope to sort out the school's finances. I'm looking forward to working with you all.' One or two staff bridle, others look interested.

When Tracey stands up I see a flicker of curiosity on some of the faces. Who, they're clearly wondering, is this attractive, quietly authoritative young woman with the tanned skin and long brown hair? 'I'm an English teacher and I'm interested in how children learn,' she says in her well-modulated London accent that's quite a contrast to mine and Sean's. 'Helping you to keep your classes learning is what my job will be. I'm looking forward to working with you and the pupils to create a really good school.'

'Have you read the reports we spent all last week writing for you?' a gruff male voice demands.

It's the first time I've heard anything about them and I feel wrong-footed, but I bluff my way through: 'No,' I admit, 'but I'm very much looking forward to reading them.' An audible wave of annoyance runs round the room. It must seem that I haven't bothered to read what my staff have to say. I wonder why these reports haven't been passed on to me and make a mental note to ask David Edwards. When they're brought to me later I find they are full of the kind of gripes and moans I've encountered before in schools that are functioning badly. I take on board some of the points and who made them, then hastily consign the reports to my 'Not to be Opened for a Year' tray.

The feeling of the questions the teachers ask me is not so much hostile as weary and dispirited. 'Well,' I say finally to end the proceedings. 'I'm very much looking forward to meeting each of you individually. Please do drop into my office, or stop me when you see me looking around the school today.'

Outside the door, our guard down once more, we look at one another in dismay. I suppose there is some childish part of each of us that was hoping we'd be welcomed with open arms as the saviours of St George's. After all, I have left my comfortable retirement, and Tracey and Sean have both given up prestigious jobs to come here.

'Well, that was cheerful. We were as welcome as traffic wardens,' says Sean.

'That really didn't feel right, did it?' says Tracey.

'Well,' I say firmly, 'let's ignore it. People are often different when you get them alone. Let's wander round and meet them one at a time.'

I really am eager to talk to the staff and get a feel for what it's been like to work at St George's. The information isn't long in coming. Some teachers catch me sitting in my office – a bleak, sparsely-furnished room off the atrium with dozens of files ranged around the walls – and some bump into me in the corridors and on the stairs as I walk around from time to time getting the feel of the school.

'Well, if you really want to know what it's been like here, Lady Stubbs,' says one, 'there were fights every day, sometimes really serious, with children ending up in hospital. One teacher went to separate two boys who were fighting and had to jump out of the way when she realized they were carrying a broken bottle and a jagged piece of metal. Both those boys ended up in Casualty having stitches.'

'Don't think these are nice kids who only need a kind social worker,' another one warns me. 'There was one girl who pushed a table over in class, went out and got a dustbin and threw it at another girl. A young supply teacher was taking that class and she's refused to work here again. We haven't seen her since. That's the kind of thing that happens here.'

The catalogue continues. A picture emerges, whether based on reality or not, of physical attacks on teachers, threats to the Head, noisy, unco-operative children who commonly engage in theft and vandalism and take no notice of instructions, older pupils who roam the corridors whenever they like and who are often abusive to staff. One teacher says that there's been 'an unsettled, often frenetic feel to the school', despite the best efforts of many staff.

After a meeting with the pastoral staff, Sean returns with depressing statistics. Attendance figures are down to 70 per cent (anything below 90 per cent is a cause for grave concern and in itself is a warning light to Ofsted). It's been difficult to recruit staff to work here, which is not surprising, and the staff who are here have probably been under such strain that sick leave has become an acute problem. On most days in January 2000, two months before my appointment, only 20 of the 35 staff were in school, so I'm told.

Together Sean and Tracey meet the staff to gauge their morale and get their perspective on the school. The picture they relay to me reflects some of the points made by staff in their written reports: low staff morale, a lack of teamwork between departments, a large number of young and inexperienced teachers led by a tired middle management who have not been able to motivate them and who seem to have been unconvinced by any new ideas or suggestions for change from the previous Head. Apparently one teacher described the children as 'scum' to an Ofsted Inspector. Another warned an Inspector it was dangerous to stand in the stairwells 'because the kids spit on you.' (To me that word 'kids' says it all. It's a disrespectful word, and I never allow it to be used in my schools. I usually refer to the children as 'young people', Sean, with his overseas teaching background, says 'students', and Tracey prefers 'pupils'.) This depressing picture seems to have developed over the last few years, according to the staff.

My own impression is that many of the teachers see us as Babes in the Wood, quite unprepared for the horror we're about to face. But behind all the weariness and cynicism I can also feel a genuine professional concern for the children, and I find the staff nicer as individuals than in a group. I ask them to call me Marie, because I suspect there are a few who might like to use my title as a weapon, giving it a contemptuous emphasis. So I'm at pains to show how down-to-earth I really am.

There are plenty of down-to-earth requests. Everyone wants more textbooks, and I tell them to see Sean and order what they need.

'What do I do about kids who lose their exercise books,' someone asks me helplessly. 'Half my class have lost theirs.'

'Order some new ones,' I say, 'and then we'll try and sort out with the young people why the exercise books seem to be disappearing at such a rate of knots.'

The two union representatives seem to be powerful figures within the school, and have already asked to meet me. I don't hurry into agreeing dates to see them. I want to speak to all my new staff individually, to get to know their thoughts, opinions and worries, before I start hearing representations on their behalf. I want them to help me with my job of getting the school on track.

About mid-afternoon, Sean and I decide to take a proper look at the staff room. Just as a kitchen is the heart of a home, the staff room is the heart of a school and I can tell a lot about a school from a good look at the staff room. In some schools I've worked in it is a no-go area for the Head, and in one there were actually self-appointed 'gatekeepers' sitting by the door, monitoring who was going in and out. I always felt it was like Ancient Rome: if you got the thumbs up you were welcomed in, but the thumbs down meant you were cold-shouldered. Wherever I've worked, I've always wanted to be part of the staff room. It gives me a sense of what people are feeling, and what's going on, though I realize it wouldn't be appropriate for the Head to be in there all the time. But I won't allow myself to be excluded. I don't like no-go areas.

The staff room is empty, but it speaks volumes. There's an electronic code to open the door, but I'm not surprised to hear from Sean that the children have worked it out, so the staff don't feel secure. It's a cramped, low-ceilinged, poorly lit room with a small, nicotine-smelling smokers' area at the back. Blue lockers line one wall and on another there is a noticeboard with scrappy bedraggled bits of paper with cheerless notices about detentions and union meetings. The carpet is stained, the chairs are battered and uncomfortable-looking, the cups on the draining-board of the sink unit are ingrained with ancient tea and coffee stains, and the tea-towels look as if they need a good wash. All my housewifely instincts are aroused. There's not a plant, not a poster.

Sean and I survey the room gloomily. 'What happened to that government plan for improving staff rooms then?' says Sean.

He laughs at my expression as I survey the scene. I feel like pulling on my rubber gloves and getting it cleaned up right away. How totally depressed and undervalued the staff must feel if this is the only place they have to come to after lessons. I realize later, however, when I make a comment about it to one of the teachers, that I must be careful. 'Well, it's our staff room and we like it that way,' he mutters. The message is clear: 'Keep out, this is our territory.'

'The gloves are off but the Marigolds are on,' I tell Sean with a laugh. 'The place needs a good makeover.'

'Marigolds?' Sean stares at me for a moment as if I've taken leave of my senses.

'I can see you don't do a lot of washing up in your house,' I tease him.

As we're leaving the staff room, we stop to speak to a silver-haired, nicely made-up older lady who comes clicking along the corridor on heels even higher than mine. She introduces herself as Maggie Worley, one of the site staff. She stares at me in undisguised astonishment when I ask if there is anyone to make tea and coffee for the teachers. 'Oh you must be joking, Lady Stubbs,' she says. 'They do it for themselves.' Maggie's own role, it appears, is somewhat broad, including dusting, locking and unlocking doors, and 'anything else Mick and you need doing', but I'm taken with the humorous look in her eye and as she click-clacks briskly away on her high heels I somehow feel better for having met her. I sense she and Mick will both be allies in helping me make the school a more cheerful place – just like my wonderful schoolkeeper Margaret at Douay, I think with a twinge of nostalgia, remembering those happy days.

I'm aware that my next important call is the school office, which is in a room opposite mine off the central atrium. The office is the nerve-centre of any school, and the way it functions is another indicator of how well the place operates. I introduce myself to the three office staff. They seem to find it hard to communicate their concerns and seem jumpy and distracted. There's almost an atmosphere of suppressed panic in here, and my requests and questions seem to be met either with a look of resignation or in a chippy, slightly aggressive way. I sense the staff are not happy in their work, and are quite naturally anxious about the future, and I feel for them.

They're certainly not helped by their working conditions. As everywhere else, the office is dreary, painted the familiar drained magnolia, with long computer and telephone cables stretching and looping from desk to desk but apparently with no way of transferring calls from one to another. The effect, if it weren't so desperate, would be comic. Important calls are already coming in from the press and from social workers and we stumble from phone to phone, trying to discover which one they've come through to. 'Talk about the Land of the Long White Cloud,' mutters Sean. 'This is the Land of the Long White Wires. Not quite as spiritual as New Zealand, eh?'

There are masses of paper lying about the office, but it seems remarkably difficult to unearth any real information, and the LEA so far hasn't provided me with any kind of starter-file. I don't know when I'll ever have time to plough through the dozens of files in my own office. I am not keen on lots of paper. I'm with the American Admiral Metcalf who growled when inspecting a new frigate with a cabin devoted to filing cabinets: 'We don't shoot paper at the enemy do we?'

I ask for a breakdown of pupil numbers – how many children there are on the school roll, how many in each class, how many have special educational needs, how many are gifted or talented. I also ask for all the Ofsted reports. I gaze bemused at the acres of colour-coded filing systems, and when I learn that the last three meetings of the Governors' finance committee have been cancelled because it was too difficult to get together the information, I see warning lights. What are the priorities here?

I make it clear to the staff, in as friendly a way as I can, that I'll be looking into the workings of the office. It's not their fault that they've been working in a crisis situation, but we simply have to sort all this out. The office itself needs rethinking for a start. I turn to the great organizer. 'Over to you Sean,' I say. 'Audit the office's needs, please, and report by the next team meeting.'

Sean has been talking to the teachers about the electronic registration system, and isn't happy with what he's heard. The Bromcom system we've inherited has a good record in many other schools, and St George's has paid out a large sum of money to lease it. All the staff have been issued with laptops to record attendance, but we're told these have been broken or stolen. The staff 'borrow' one another's, and in a few cases pupils have been using them to fill in their own attendances. Pupils who have left the school are still on the system, and the folders in which the Bromcom returns should be filed can't be found.

'Oh, throw them all in a cupboard and get some good-old fashioned school registers,' I say impatiently, and Sean lifts a quizzical eyebrow: 'We can't Marie – the school's spent a lot of money on them.'

'OK Mr Devlin, then they're your baby,' I say.

'Hello, are you the new Head Teacher?' The young policeman politely removes his helmet as he steps into the atrium. 'Well, I like to be called Headmistress because I'm an old fuddy-duddy,' I reply and he laughs.

He's come to discuss an incident that occurred on the day before the school was closed two weeks ago, when, it seems, a dozen of the staff's cars were vandalized. Was it an angry gesture, I wonder, from pupils who felt they were being locked out? Whatever the reason, it was appalling behaviour. The culprits have been identified, and the police need to take statements from the owners of the cars, which is quickly arranged. Sean and I both travel by tube, but my thoughts fly immediately to Tracey's little sports car which is one of her great loves. I hope it's going to be all right here. The children involved have been told not to return to school and since this all happened before our arrival, strictly speaking we have no jurisdiction. But I intend to send out a clear message about our standards. I believe exclusion is an absolute last resort, but I'm willing to use it when necessary.

I'm delighted by this opportunity to meet one of the local police. It gives us a chance to start building contacts with them, which I hope will increase over the next few months. I want the police to become a normal, everyday part of school life, not just people who arrive to investigate a crime. I can tell that the young PC is pleased when I tell him I hope we can arrange some workshops on topics like drugs, and racism, and relationships with the community.

I'm a little surprised to be told that the local police haven't been invited into St George's. I believe in making use of whatever help is available, and I know that the more the local community is involved in a school, the easier it is for the Head to deal with complaints. We all have the feeling, even from this first day, that St George's has been functioning in its own little bubble, completely out of touch with the community outside – always a recognizable mark of a school in trouble. There are apparently no arrangements for work experience worth mentioning, and to our eyes at least, a rather limited careers programme.

'I feel like a doctor who's being asked to treat a patient without having access to his medical records,' I say to Sean as we walk slowly up Lanark Road to Maida Vale tube that evening some time after seven.

'We'll be all right. The patient will survive,' says Sean cheerfully. 'We'll take it steadily.'

My legs are aching as we wait for the train – I must remember to bring in a pair of flat shoes tomorrow to keep in my cupboard at school. As I open the door of the flat the phone is ringing. It's Hilary, my middle daughter, anxious to know that I'm home in one piece. Then there's a call from my mother. I try to play down the day's difficulties, but she's not fooled. 'You really are too old for all this stress you know,' she says severely. My *mother* telling me I'm too old!

I put a ready-cooked meal into the oven. My husband William, who always gets his priorities right, presses a gin and tonic into my hand, I kick off my shoes, sink back and close my eyes. I know there's a phone call I need to make, and I'm not exactly looking forward to it.

Father George Dangerfield, who was for many years the priest teacher at Douay, is a complete original, a delightful, in my opinion somewhat eccentric man who has always remained apart from the 'politics' and general camaraderie of the priests in the Archdiocese of Westminster. He's also one of the best and most charismatic teachers I've ever encountered, able to interpret the teachings of the church in an anecdotal way that children immediately respond to, and appeal to their sense of the theatrical with his liturgy and his spectacular vestments – embroidered for him, I believe, by nuns in the Netherlands – which, I've always teased him, are truly the Armani of the vestment world. Over the years we'd always worked together well. So I was furious when Father George did actually carry out one of his many threats to resign, just before an Ofsted inspection, and I vowed, in the heat of the moment, that I would never speak to him again. Typical Celtic behaviour on my part.

But I need Father George now. St George's, it seems to me, is really not the Catholic School it should and could be and the Ofsted Inspectors have highlighted this concern. There are few services that involve the children, little in the way of religious displays on the walls, and the children don't appear to be engaged in any sort of charitable activities. There's a rhythm to the Catholic year that I love and which seems wholly missing. As well as being a gifted teacher, Father George is able to give children a sense of the numinous that they badly need. So I must swallow my pride and try to put the past behind us. The gin and tonic helps.

Strangely enough, he doesn't seem surprised when he hears my voice. He tells me he was working in his room earlier on when his mother called him to say I was on television, and he watched my morning press conference on the news. We discuss the situation at St George's.

'I badly need your help here,' I say. 'You know I think it's some kind of message from Above that you and the school share a name.'

We laugh a bit, and talk about old times. 'Will you do it then?' I say finally. 'You couldn't manage to come tomorrow, could you, at eight o'clock, to be there for the first Assembly? I know you're an early bird.'

'I don't think I have a choice, do I, Marie? It's God's will. I'll be there before seven' is his characteristic reply.

When my alarm clock rings at 5.30 next morning I'm already awake, after one of those nights when you're not quite certain whether you've been to sleep at all. Images of Sean and Tracey kept running through my mind as I tossed and turned, fear that if I make a mess of things they're going to suffer, and thoughts of the parents, staff and children who are going to suffer too. And it's all going to be so public, with the media spotlight constantly on us. Everyone's going to know about it – family, friends, past colleagues, people in the educational world. Whatever reputation for competence I have gathered over thirty years could be destroyed.

I take special care with getting dressed, choose some silver jewellery, dry my hair for slightly more than the usual three minutes. I know that I mustn't let any of my private anxieties show – uncertainty is catching. I sit up very straight on the tube, tell myself that I've been here and done all this before, and say a quiet prayer for help. I must be moving my lips, for gradually I become conscious that the people who populate the tube at this time of the morning, the sleepy-eyed office cleaners and manual labourers, are staring at me curiously.

I change at Baker Street on to the Bakerloo line, get out at Maida Vale tube, which is beginning to look familiar, and walk briskly up a deserted Lanark Road, thankful that I've got my comfortable flat shoes ready for later in my bag.

It's a grey, cold morning, and the low school buildings look even less welcoming than they did yesterday. Sean must have been up even earlier than me. I find him already in the office he and Tracey are to share, one door away from mine, and he tells me he's been in since six. Tracey and I both arrive together at about seven. We have a quick discussion, then quickly get down to pinning up the posters in bright primary colours that we had printed yesterday. We put *Welcome Back* posters where the children will see them when they first arrive and pin the others at strategic points along the corridors: *Respect Each Other, Walk Don't Run, Talk Don't Shout, Get to Lessons on Time, Wear Correct Uniform, Put Rubbish in the Bin.*

As so often, I'm grateful for my initial training as a primary school teacher: primary schools know the importance of interesting wall displays, whereas some secondary schools still have long, blank, dismal corridors. Posters engage children's attention, and these will help reinforce all our messages about what is and is not acceptable behaviour.

At Tracey's suggestion we've had the posters printed not just in English, but with Arabic, Spanish, Portuguese, Farsi and Yoruba translations underneath. I know that more than half the children at St George's speak English only as a second language – some of them speak very little, so I'm relieved to learn we have teachers and support staff who can speak the main foreign languages. Tracey astonished me yesterday by showing me a list of the 52 languages other than English spoken by the pupils, a number of which I have never heard of before. I try to spell them correctly.

This is the list, in order of how many pupils speak each: Arabic, Portuguese, Farsi, Spanish, French Caribbean Creole, Yoruba, French, Ibo, Swahili, Twi Fante, Hindi, Albanian, Amharic, Russian, Bengali, Luganda, Italian, Polish, Somali, Greek, Urdu, Turkish, Kurdish, Idoma, Tagalog, Ga, Maltese, Shona, Tigrinya, Pashto, Mongolian, Bulgarian, Ewe, Mandarin, Slovak, Rwanda,

Cantonese, Sinhalese, Konkani, Slovenian, Serbian, Krio, Bemba, Mende, Hausa, Tamil, Malaysian, Dinka, Oromo, Tonga, Swedish, Wolof. The last five languages apparently have only one speaker each.

It's like having a big slice of the world under one roof. I find it an extremely exciting prospect and I long to create the conditions where all these children from such varied backgrounds can learn together and play together, and get to understand and respect one another's cultures. 'I feel I'm going to learn a lot here,' I say to Tracey as we pin up the last of the posters.

She nods but says cautiously: 'Yes, but this number of languages is going to be a big difficulty. It takes years to learn a language fluently you know, and most of these children have been learning English for a lot less than that.'

I'm also very much aware that there are children in the school who have nobody, not a member of staff nor even another pupil, who speaks their language. I imagine how frightening and isolating that must be if their English isn't good, and I'm already wondering what I can do to make things easier for them.

As we sit talking over a cup of coffee in my office, we decide we need a motto, a tag, something to hang on to which symbolizes our efforts, that we can use on notepaper, posters and press releases. After a lot of discussion we finally decide on 'Moving Forward Together in 2000'. It may be a cliché, but it seems to sum up the situation. For some time the school has been static, not working together, and I want to get across the idea that we are making progress, as well as that we all, teachers, pupils and parents, need each other to take the school forward.

'OK, that's it,' I say. The only problem I can see is: will we have the *energy* to keep moving forward for the rest of 2000?' and the other two smile rather wanly. I realize that the school I have taken over is seen by some as a school of last resort, filled with the refugees and children with special needs who have failed to get in anywhere else. They have told me so. Sean has learned from an English-as-an-Additional-Language teacher that a lot of St George's pupils come and go, moving from country to country with their families, who can't get settled anywhere, snatching little bits of education for a few months wherever they land. This is something none of us has encountered before. I want to welcome these children, but how on earth will we be able to help them?

'A good many of these sixteen-year-olds have been in the school for less than a year,' says Sean. 'Apparently these poor students' families just pack their bags and disappear for all sorts of reasons. And sometimes the same children just turn up again in school a few months later.'

It's nearly 8.30, and for some time I've been hearing the familiar sounds of children arriving though I can't see out into the playground from my window as the dusty Venetian blind seems permanently lodged in the down position. Cries of 'Hey man,' and 'Chill man' rise above the chatter and laughter and remind me I'm in the inner city now. I like the feel of it.

We've decided to stagger the children's return, and today we have only the Year 11s in, aged fifteen and sixteen, the oldest group in the school, which doesn't have a sixth form. I'm especially concerned about these children, who have only another term and a half to go before they leave and who are just about to take their GCSEs. I can't imagine what this unsettled period must have been like for them. They are the only children left in the school who will remember Philip Lawrence, some of them have lived through all the traumatic years since his murder, and my heart really goes out to them.

We look for Mick, and he and I go round the assembly hall, making sure everything's in order. It is the same room where we met the staff yesterday, but then I was too preoccupied with their faces and their reactions to take in the detail of the room. I'm pleasantly surprised. It is a large panelled hall with good lighting and a stage. A statue of the Virgin Mary gazes from a niche above our heads, with pink plastic flowers set to the right and left of it. All is clean and tidy. I ask Mick to make sure there are enough chairs for every pupil to sit down, which I think is important for their dignity and comfort as adolescents.

I'm delighted when Father George, looking his usual shining and immaculate self, appears in the atrium, closely followed by the tall thin figure of Monsignor Harry Turner, Episcopal Vicar for Central London. I'd been hoping that the Diocese might be in touch to suggest that a representative be present at this first, important assembly, but by last night I had heard nothing, so I contacted Monsignor Harry myself through Canon John McDonald, my Chairman of Governors at Douay. This is a Catholic school, and I feel the presence of these two symbolizes something very important – something enduring that transcends all the worries about finances and buildings and exam results.

Again Tracey, Sean and I stand anxiously outside the hall. The behaviour of Year 11 and their response to us is crucial, because it will provide a template for the rest of the school. We walk purposefully into the hall and stand at the front. The buzz of conversation dies as Sean calls everyone to attention.

'Right, Year 11, settle down now. We don't have any time to waste. You've all had an extra week off school, which I hope you've made good use of, since you all have your GCSE exams coming up soon. As you know, I'm Mr Devlin, and this is Miss O'Leary. We're your new Deputy Heads, and we'll both be checking up on your course work.' As ever, I admire the slight hint of menace he is able to inject into his friendly words.

Then Sean introduces me with a clear 'Now stand for your Headmistress' and I move forward, deliberately clicking my heels on the wooden floor, to stand near the front row. I sweep the room's four corners with a determined glance – a technique that pulls all the children into my audience. The only sounds to be heard are the muffled sounds of the kitchen staff preparing lunch behind the screens which hide the kitchen. They're a wonderful-looking bunch of children, a rich mixture of races and physical types, some watching me with undisguised interest, others, inevitably, making it clear from their stance that they feel they have better things to do. I speak in an even tone, which nevertheless carries to the back of the hall:

'I'm going to say "Good Morning" to you, and I expect all of you to say "Good Morning, Headmistress" to me.' I pause, then raise my voice to boom out 'Good Morning, Year 11.' The change in decibel level takes them by surprise – some of them actually jump nervously – but it works. 'Good Morning, Headmistress,' they chorus. I know then that I have a good chance of dealing with them successfully. It will be tough, but it can be done.

'We have a new motto,' I tell them. 'It is "Moving Forward Together in 2000"'. This means the past is over, and our school, of which I'm so proud to be Headmistress, is going to be a place where we will all pull together, learn, enjoy events and outings, and start clubs. And, for Year 11 only, there will be a very special event which we will organize together: a May Ball.'

A May Ball for leavers was something I started at Douay and it worked so well for ten years that I don't see why we can't do it here. Sean and Tracey agree. Leaving school is such a huge event in young people's lives, and for these young people especially, who've had so much to contend with and so many blows to their self-esteem, I want it to be marked by some rite of passage, some-thing that will make them feel good about themselves.

'We're going to celebrate the end of your time at St George's,' I tell them confidently. 'We'll all work together to come up with an exciting programme and we'll be holding the event at a top London hotel.' There is a gasp, and a ripple of excited chatter. Those who can't speak English well look at the specialist teachers, who translate for them. As to the staff, however, I can see from their faces that some of them think I'm mad. It's not the kind of thing that happens at St George's. They can't believe that these 'kids' will ever behave well enough to attend a formal social event in a formal hotel setting. This is going to be mayhem, I can hear them thinking. I don't think so, but I know a lot of work will have to go into organizing it if we're going to pull it off. To my relief a few staff smile and look pleased at this idea.

I really do believe in a Heineken effect where children are concerned: we must reach the parts that ordinary approaches cannot reach. The May Ball, I feel, will do that, and the excitement of planning it, I hope, will spill over into co-operation with us over the grind of academic tasks.

'And now,' I say, 'shall we ask God to help us in our work together? We're extremely fortunate today that a very special priest, Monsignor Harry Turner, has come to share our service with us.'

Mgr Turner, who has been sitting quietly at one side, gets up and greets the children. They listen, clearly fascinated, as he describes to them his own schooldays in the East End of London, and exhorts them to take our motto seriously and move forward in 2000. He leads us all in prayer, and the Year 11s on the whole seem quiet and reflective. I feel it is important that each assembly includes a blessing, because St George's is a faith school, and having a spiritual element in school life is vital. No matter that two-thirds of the children are not Catholic (the non-Catholic proportion normally expected by the Diocese is no more than ten per cent). From now on I want St George's to observe the church calendar, and we will start each morning with a prayer, making sure that all the children feel included.

After the prayers I say: 'Right, now I want to meet every one of you, and shake hands with you.' I've decided to do this because I want to try to make personal contact with each one of these children. But I've never done anything like it before, and I'm aware that it could misfire and make me look foolish.

They stand up, one row at a time, and come out to meet me. The first boy towers over me, but he avoids my eye, looking sheepishly down at the ground. His hair is cut in an exaggerated French crop, long on top and short at the sides.

'Good morning,' I say. 'Would you look at me while we shake hands? I think you've got a brilliant hairstyle, by the way.' He blushes a little, but he lifts his head and looks me in the eye for a moment.

Ariadne Lish, who is their Head of Year, introduces each pupil by name and I shake hands with every one in turn. They really are a striking bunch of youngsters, but I notice that some of them seem to have very little regard for the uniform rules. St George's has rather a becoming uniform – grey skirt or trousers, black blazer, white shirt and black and red tie. Some children have the odd token bit of uniform thrown in, but some are in denims, baggy trousers, trainers, baseball caps, and lots of jewellery. Most of them are chewing gum: I can see why the carpets are so sticky. As the girls wait to meet me, their appraising glances lay down a peculiarly feminine challenge. I know that every detail of my makeup, hairstyle and clothes will be dissected later on. I can see my role with these girls will be a combination of mother figure, professional friend, and also someone who can enjoy the fun of talking about fashion and makeup with them. Some of the boys look surly, awkward and suspicious.

I am grateful to Ariadne for helping me to get their names right, because many are difficult to pronounce. I remember once at another school hearing a teacher laughing at pupils' foreign names and saying that he would never be able to get his tongue around them. I felt it was discourteous, even racist: these children don't have a lot, but they do all have a name and an identity. I say something different to each one, something positive, and most importantly, I say it with a smile. Smiles are infectious: they smile back.

It's a pleasure to be working with Ariadne. She's such a positive presence, with her open face and merry smile, and I like the respectful way she introduces each child. She has a wonderfully scrubbed look, as if she's just got out of the shower, and the way she dresses, in a simple white top and a pair of beautifully cut trousers, matches her character. Such a good role model for the children, I think. This issue of appropriate dress is one I know I'm going to have to take up at the next staff meeting, but I'll need to do it carefully. A lot of the staff, I'm sure, will think me an old fogey, but to me it's one of those small but important things that set the whole tone of a school. I feel that teachers should look like

31

teachers, so that the children know where they are, just as I think it helps hospital patients if nurses actually look like nurses, and air passengers if pilots look like pilots.

When the last children have returned to their seats, looking, I must confess, somewhat stunned at this personal introduction to their new Headmistress, I hand over to the Deputy Heads. The Head, whilst being accessible and friendly, must retain a certain distance, I feel – a suggestion of Miss Jean Brodie doesn't go amiss at the start. So I leave the hall with a certain theatrical dignity, sweeping out with my chin held high.

I stand outside and hear Sean announcing that we are going to appoint prefects and library monitors. Tracey speaks to Year 11 about becoming actively involved in the running of the school and asks for volunteers to attend a meeting that day to discuss how St George's could be improved. We've agreed that it's vital, if we are to break down the 'us and them' culture, to give these older children a sense that they have responsibility. It sounds as if the idea has gone down well and I'm pleased to see that they leave the hall in an orderly manner.

When they spot me, I am bombarded with questions. 'What's this about prefects Miss?' 'Can I be a prefect Miss?' 'Will we get badges Miss?'

'Why are you called *Lady* Stubbs?' someone asks me. I knew this was bound to come up sooner or later. 'It's because the Queen knighted my husband for his work in education,' I explain to the knot of children who are still hanging around me.

'Did you go to Buckingham Palace, then?' asks someone. 'Yes,' I say.

The questions come thick and fast. 'Did you have a cup of tea with the Queen?' 'Was Lady Di there?'

'Come along now,' I say, refusing to be distracted from the job in hand. 'Lessons, lessons. You mustn't be late.'

When I return to my office after the assembly the newspapers have arrived, and I'm astonished at the amount of space devoted to our arrival at St George's. A lot of the coverage seems to be focused on me personally: I'm described as a 'glamorous granny', and my high heels come in for a few mentions. What do people expect a Headmistress to look like in the year 2000, I wonder? Margaret Rutherford? The piece that disappoints me most, however, is one in a national newspaper suggesting that the job should have gone to a man. 'Well, everyone's entitled to their opinion. I'm not changing my sex now,' I say to Sean and Tracey with a giggle.

At breaktime I hear a teacher shouting 'Out! Out! Out!' as he herds a group of children towards the stairs. Mick is standing in the corridor, keys at the ready, and I go across to thank him for setting out the hall so neatly. 'Sorry, Lady Stubbs,' he says, flustered, 'I'll be wid' you in a minute. I've just got to lock all the doors.' I realize he is locking all the classrooms, and I follow him downstairs where he locks the doors to the playground, with the children on the outside. He tells me he does this every break and lunchtime: the children are not allowed on the premises, even if it's blowing a gale, pouring with rain, or blanketing them with snow.

Teachers talking together in the atrium look surprised when I ask Mick to unlock the playground door. Sean, Tracey and I put on our coats and go out on to the windswept tarmac, where one wary-looking teacher is shivering against a wall. Knots of girls are huddled together under the large overhang of the school building and there's a lot of shouting from some boys who are kicking a football around rather aimlessly. I remember hearing that an Ofsted Inspector was told by one teacher not to go out there without a flak jacket, but most of the children are friendly, clamouring around me for attention and hanging on to my elbow, tugging at my coat and holding my hand. There are only a couple of unpleasant moments, when I confront the boy who drops litter and the girl who tells me to 'F — off.' They glower as I say 'Hello.'

As I'm standing surrounded by children, I notice two girls at the far side of the playground scrabbling to get footholds on the crumbling brick perimeter wall. Then they lever themselves over it like lightning and disappear towards Kilburn High Road. I must confess that I'm taken aback – I'm not used to such blatant behaviour. The playground is certainly not appealing, but 'bunking off' is no solution. Break is ending and I hurry in and send Sean after them. He catches up with the two culprits, they are returned to school and calls are made to their parents. This is a problem we've got to address, and address quickly.

Outside the school walls I'm well aware that there is a gang culture, to which I already suspect some of our pupils belong: we've already connected some of the graffiti 'tags' and symbols on local walls with the doodles in their exercise books. I've got to make sure that we keep gang rivalries and enmities well away from school premises.

In preparation for the big event of the day, I retire to one of the small staff toilets which I've decided I'm going to appropriate for my own personal use. This may seem selfish, but I feel it's important to the staff that the Head does not overhear the kind of chit-chat that inevitably goes on between them in the cloakroom, and I badly need my own retreat where I can repair the ravages of the day and think about things for a few minutes without fear of being interrupted.

It seems extraordinary that an Ofsted Inspection should be scheduled for our second day here, but I realize the date was set before the crisis decision to replace the Head and bring in a Task Force. I am out hovering on the steps to greet the two Inspectors when they arrive. I have to admit that my heart sinks as they stride into the entranceway, their Ofsted identity passes dangling on chains round their neck. I take them into my office. Graham Ranger, who is in charge of monitoring progress at St George's, must be as nonplussed as I am about the radical changes that have taken place at the school since their last visit in 1999. He's a friendly, fresh-faced Northerner with a professional and focused approach to the school's problems. He understands that it is unreasonable to expect us to have made any impression yet and he decides they will spend just today in the school and talk us through his report at the end of the day.

Year 11 go about their business pretty well on their first day, though we soon realize you can't assume at St George's that telling the children something once will be enough. You have to say the same things over and over and over until you are bored with the sound of your own voice, and hoarse too. 'Please walk. Did you hear what I said? Please *walk*. It's dangerous to run in the corridor,' I hear Tracey and Sean calling over and over again.

The afternoon flies by, much of it spent listening to various staff about their urgent needs: some of them have practical worries about the shortage of books and equipment, old desks, an acute lack of chairs in some classrooms. Others want to tell me about individual pupils they regard as impossible. The procession is continuous, and my head aches. Finally Father George appears in my office, worried because he doesn't know where he's going to get ashes for tomorrow's Ash Wednesday service in the chapel. 'Oh, please don't ask *me*!' I feel like saying. It seems such a small thing, but then I remember my grandmother saying that if you take care of the small things the big things will take care of themselves. I feel guilty at my own irritation and offer him a cup of coffee whilst we look at options together. Eventually Father George arranges to collect some from St James's Church in Spanish Place, where he sometimes helps out as a supply priest.

When Sean, Tracey and I finally sit down with the Inspectors we're prepared for the worst, and we certainly get it. We're told that the school is 'at the bottom end of limited progress', which makes me think of one of the outer circles of Dante's hell. St George's is a school on Special Measures and this 'limited progress', they say, after two years at this level, makes them gravely concerned about the state of the school. Since the last Inspection four months ago, the state of the school has hardly improved at all.

The grim litany continues. In one third of all lessons the pupils dictate the pace, not the teachers. Almost all lessons are disrupted. Only 20 per cent of the teaching is good, and in some subjects there is no good teaching at all. Literacy teaching is poor, and there is an urgent need for a literacy programme. The Religious Education, English, Maths and ICT curricula fall short of what is required. In some lessons the work is too easy. There are problems with bullying and attendance.

Former management is seen as having been over-involved in day-to-day matters. This is something we've already been told about by the staff – any discipline problem was apparently referred upwards, and at times the atrium was filled with as many as sixty pupils queuing for attention because they had thrown a pencil or looked the wrong way at a teacher. For some of the staff the way to deal with problems seems to have been to push them out of the classroom and on to the Head, creating chaos in the atrium and a breeding ground for trouble.

The Inspectors describe the whole management of the school, especially in relation to timekeeping, the dining hall and movement between lessons, as a major cause of concern. They conclude that the school needs to be more self-evaluative and self-critical.

I thank Graham Ranger, though there aren't many surprises in what they've told us. They tell us they will be back on the 20th of the month, which gives us eight working days – a terribly short time for us to achieve anything at all.

Afterwards Sean sits looking grave. 'For the first time I'm seriously wondering whether I've made a mistake,' he says. It's unlike Sean to be less than buoyant, and his mood affects all of us. Silently Tracey goes into the office they share and comes back with a bar of chocolate. Without a word she divides it between us. We eat it thoughtfully. 'Well,' says Sean finally, 'We *are* a Task Force. We wouldn't be here if things were going all right. We musn't allow ourselves to be down for more than five minutes and one bar of chocolate!' Sean smiles – the old smile. I immediately feel better.

In a way it's a relief to have the school's deficiencies described so clearly. I don't suppose any teaching staff relishes Ofsted Inspections, but I do believe in an external monitoring system for schools. Ofsted Inspections have become much tighter than they were when the system was first introduced: what would have slipped through five years ago will be weeded out today. I simply feel that we could have been given a little bit longer to get started on our mammoth task – but you don't argue with Ofsted.

The three of us finally get away at ten pm, and I'm so exhausted that I fall asleep on the tube, waking by some miraculous instinct when I get to my stop. When I get in I'm almost too tired to eat, and I've barely collapsed into bed, it seems, before the alarm wakes me again.

Next morning I run into Sean on the tube platform at Maida Vale and we climb the steps together. There is a newspaper kiosk outside the station, which does a brisk trade at this time of the morning. There's a small knot of teenangers hanging around it, and I recognize a couple of girls from St George's. 'That's our Headmistress,' I hear her telling the others.

A powerful voice calls out: 'Hey, Madame, can you come here a minute?' I turn and see a large man, whose voice has an Arabic sound to it, waving at me from the cramped space behind the counter of the newspaper kiosk. His piles of morning papers are weighted down to stop the wind that whips up from the station from whisking them away. While he carries on selling he gives us a rundown on what he thinks of the pupils of St George's.

'Madame, if you're the new Headteacher you've got a *big* job. You've really got some problems. The kids round here, they steal from me, they're rude, they spit, they fight in the station.'

All I can do is smile and reassure him: 'I shall make sure that none of the children in *my* school ever behaves like this.' I say these words loudly, so that the St George's children clattering up the stairs behind us can hear.

'Good. You think you can change things, Madame?' he answers. 'Then I wish you luck – you need it.'

'Isn't it enough to have Ofsted, the Education Authority, the Diocese, and the press monitoring us? Now we've got the

37

newspaper-seller too!' says Sean, rolling his eyes, as we walk up the road together.

It's cheering to find my youngest daughter Fiona, who is a primary school teacher, waiting for me in the atrium with the family's latest contribution to our success – 200 laminated posters printed with our new motto, which she's dropping off early for us. They're in a selection of eye-catching primary colours, and Sean and Tracey start pinning them up right away.

A smiling Dot presents me with a heap of mail that also cheers me up. After all the publicity, the cards, letters and phone calls of support are flooding in, some from people I knew in the distant as well as recent professional past, others from complete strangers. There is a touching message of hope from Gerard Curran who was the first Head of St George's when it opened in 1956. He has been retired for 25 years. There are letters from ex-pupils, including an army chaplain, and from ex-teachers. A message from the Education Secretary David Blunkett arrives in the same post as one from a nun in Ireland who has no connection with the school or me, but says she is praying for us. A retired Inspector who inspected my primary school classes when I was a newly qualified teacher in Carlisle arranges for me to receive a huge plant to cheer up my office. Someone I have not seen since I was eighteen sends a card saying: 'You were such a strong character you were going to go to the good or the bad – I'm glad you chose the good.' Hm, a bit cheeky, I think, but I know what he means. I was always something of a rebel, which may be why I understand naughty children.

There are even donations. The Malaysian Students Association sends £100 and my friends Lord and Lady Alexander of Weedon send a generous cheque. Mick staggers in with a vast box of goodies from McDonalds: the little toys and games they give out in their restaurants. We decide to use them as rewards for good work, for good attendance, punctuality – anything that deserves celebrating. I suspect some of these children aren't used to being given things. The value of the prize is irrelevant: it is the fact that we are telling them they are worth something that counts.

One letter I receive comes from Denis, a former Inspector for the Inner London Education Authority who met me in a tough, failing inner city school where I was a deputy head.

'Among that demoralized management team you were the only one to show belief in the children and in the power of the school to help them,' his letter says. 'As a result the children responded to you, and to you alone. The assemblies I saw were a shambles, unless you were in charge when they became orderly, purposeful and – unbelievably in that defeated atmosphere – positive and indeed spiritually meaningful. If you don't carry it off at St George's that will only attest the more strongly to your courage in the attempt. But I powerfully hope that you do.'

I feel tears springing to my eyes as I read this. So many people are putting such faith in me, and I feel the weight of all these expectations. 'No fool like an old fool,' I say to a former colleague who phones. Already I'm feeling like a very tired sixty-year-old – and this is only Week One. I'm also, I must confess, feeling secretly bewildered that among all these thoughtful messages there is nothing from the Diocesan Education Board. They, after all, are the people who have invited me in to deal with this crisis situation, and Sean, Tracey and I might have hoped for some expression of support from the Chairman of the Education Board, Monsignor Barltrop, at this very difficult stage. But there is nothing, not even a phone call. 'Oh well,' I think philosophically. 'All in good time. After all, he's a very busy man. I just hope he's praying for us, that's all.'

I'm touched again when at breaktime my oldest daughter, Nadine, turns up with what she calls 'Mum's starter pack'. This consists of a cafetière, two mugs, a tray, a crate of bottled water, some oatcakes and a huge bunch of daffodils. She also brings me a computer mousemat with a quotation from Oscar Wilde on it: 'We are all in the gutter, but some of us are looking at the stars.'

*

All through the first week, as day-by-day more children return to school, we repeat the Welcome Back assemblies. Attendance figures are up to 75 per cent – fuelled perhaps by curiosity to see the new Head. At each assembly I shake every child's hand, and to the younger age groups I explain that, historically, people shook hands with one another to demonstrate they had no weapon in their hand.

'Of course I don't have a weapon,' I say, 'but I've got something else for you. It's a challenge – to make the most of your school, and all the exciting chances school can give you.' Standing in front of rows of these large, volatile adolescents makes me somewhat tense about meeting their expectations, but I know I mustn't show it. I have a *Lord of the Flies* attitude to children: they'll take you over if you don't get there first. It's vital to seem strong and fearless, even if it's all an act. In an important sense, schools survive on the good will of their children. It must be earned and kept daily. I need to engage the attention of children who are not used to sitting still and listening.

A very old friend of mine, Canon John McDonald, gives the blessing at this first week's assemblies. Canon John, pleasant and silver-haired, is the parish priest of a Covent Garden church and chaplain to the acting profession – which I tell him includes me, after my performances at these assemblies. He's also a trained social worker and extremely supportive, and I'm anxious to get him on to the Board of Governors if he has the time to contribute.

Father George assists Canon John with the prayers and blessings, and I'm delighted to see him making his presence felt in the school in his own inimitable way. He connects wonderfully with the children, whatever their background or religion, often wandering out into the playground to talk to them at break, and yesterday one of the younger boys pointed to him and said to me quite spontaneously: 'Father George, him good man.' I can tell that the staff like him too. It's impossible, really, not to respond to cheerful, teasing Father George.

*

During this first week a meeting is arranged to introduce the Task Force to the parents. The Director of Education, John Harris, and several of the Governors are expected, and Sean, Tracey and I stand waiting to welcome them in the atrium after school. What happens when they arrive takes me aback. Though they shake hands with me, they appear to completely forget about Sean and Tracey and sweep on into the hall where the parents are waiting, making me feel as though St George's is not a school on Special Measures but has been awarded Beacon Status.

This seeming slight to Sean and Tracey puzzles and irritates me, and I make a point of seating them with me and John Harris, a small, anxious-looking man, on the platform, while the Governors are in the front row. The fact is, I'm surprised by the Governors' attitude. The parents have turned out in force, and while the faces turned towards me are of many different nationalities, the emotions I see on them are universal – anxiety for their children, a wish to help them succeed and to know how best to do it. In my book these parents and children have been badly let down, and I feel the least the Governors can do, as the body responsible for the school, is to apologize.

I start to speak immediately. 'I'm very pleased to be here with you this evening,' I say. 'I'm greatly looking forward to helping your children and to working with you – we regard parents as very important partners and I plan that there will be many more opportunities for us to have meetings and get together. I don't wish to talk about what's happened in the past, I want to go forward and that will be our motto in the future.' Then I introduce Sean and Tracey and they describe how they plan to help the children.

The parents' response is heartwarming. They tell us how glad they are that we are here, how anxious they've been about their children and how eager they are to help us sort things out. Afterwards I hear specific worries about bullying, about books not marked and homework not set. Some of the parents whose English is poor or non-existent seem simply bewildered by the situation. Altogether I have the impression of a thoroughly nice group of people who have not, in the past, been as involved in the life of St George's as they would have wished. Whatever our problem is in the future, I foresee it's not going to be the parents.

'Hurry, or you'll be late,' I say to three Year 8 girls who are dawdling along the corridor when they should be in class. 'F—off man,' one of them mutters under her breath – quietly, but I suspect I'm meant to hear. I see it's the big girl with streaked hair who swore at me in the playground on the first day. The other two start to move marginally faster but the large girl ambles behind them, insolently refusing to quicken her pace. I ask Ariadne about her. Her name is Debbie and Ariadne tells me she's a bright girl who has fallen behind because of her attitude and her bad attendance record. 'Debbie, Debbie,' I muse. 'I've met you so many times before, in all my schools – a poor attender but a girl with great personality and potential.' She reminds me of a group of girls I met on my first day at Douay. They were clacking along the road towards the school on white stilettos and with bare legs, and one of them shouted to me: 'Are you the new Head then?' When I said yes they burst into raucous laughter and one of them shouted: 'We'll have you.' No you won't, I thought, I'll have *you*, and you'll be in tights and full school uniform before very long. They were too – and smiling. Nice enough girls once they learned who was boss.

Another girl I'm concerned about, but for very different reasons, is a slight shy girl in Year 11. She's from Somalia, and I will call her Rachel, an anglicized version of her name. Tracey tells me that Rachel came to this country entirely alone two years ago and that she no longer knows where her mother and her brothers and sisters are. Her father she knows is dead. She seems to have been placed on her own in bed and breakfast accommodation in Kilburn.

Clearly there's a community of families there who keep an eye on her, and of course she has a social worker, but the tragedy of her situation haunts me. She has a sweet, shy smile, but understandably she's quite withdrawn, and because she's a serious girl, more concerned with her schoolwork than with boyfriends or socializing, it seems she doesn't have many friends in school. When she arrived in England she spoke no English at all, but she's clever and she's picked it up fast. She understands better than she speaks, and can follow lessons pretty well. I just want to give her every chance I can for her GCSEs and Tracey is trying to arrange some extra help for her.

I feel such a responsibility for children like this. Rachel's circumstances mirror those of many refugee pupils at St George's who have arrived in Britain unaccompanied, knowing nobody, and whose only real support is Social Services. They have to get themselves up for school in the morning, manage their own benefits, look after their own food. None of them is more than sixteen and some are only thirteen or fourteen. They're living in a foreign land, surrounded by people who speak a language they barely understand and they have huge worries about what's happening to the families they've left behind in Kosovo or Rwanda or one of the other troublespots across the globe. I can't help but think of my own daughters when they were that age, living a happy protected life in a normal family.

And yet, Tracey points out, it's amazing how philosophical these children seem to be. After all they've been through they're used to surviving, and for many of them it's a luxury just to have a roof over their heads. They're used to being on the move, and mostly they're here for only a few months before they're settled elsewhere. But while they're here we have to fit them in somehow and do our best to help them. For many pupils St George's represents the only point of stability and hope in their lives.

For Tracey, reading the social work reports here has been an eye-opener. Some of the children at St George's are living in cramped housing where they don't have their own beds. A lot of them have nowhere to do their homework. Yesterday, in the small playground, she tried to calm down a child who was running around and causing havoc, and he told her that he's not allowed to play or make a noise at home because the family live in bed and breakfast accommodation and they'll be evicted if they cause any problems. No wonder he has to let off steam in school. Many of our children have to look after younger brothers and sisters in the evenings while their parents are out at work, a lot of them have part-time jobs – not just for pocket money.

I've realized it is best never to refer to a pupil's mother or father. Now I always say: 'Who looks after you at home?' Very often the answer is not 'My Mum' or 'My Dad' but 'My Auntie', 'My Nan' or some other relative, a foster carer – or 'Don't know' is the answer in a few cases, which we try to investigate quickly.

Compared to the adolescents I've dealt with at my previous schools, where teenage romances, the latest fashions, the newest music and the next set of exams are the main worries, a great many of the children here are very mature young people leading very complicated lives. The other day I heard one of the teachers say with patronizing sarcasm, 'I'd have thought you could give a *bit* more time to your homework.' I know this is quite the wrong approach. Some of these youngsters are dealing with bigger problems than most of us have ever had to face, and have shown extraordinary strength of character and courage in surviving.

On the other hand, I admire the way some of the staff have developed a 'tough love' approach to these youngsters. From my experiences with the the Centre girls, I know it's important not to treat these pupils any differently from the others. They've still got to do their homework, dress in school uniform and get to school on time. There's no point in adding to their disadvantage – they, of all the children, need structure and education to counterbalance the poor cards life has dealt them. But if there's a school tie missing, I'm going to make sure there'll always be a spare one in the welfare assistant's drawer. If there is nowhere at home to do homework, there's going to be a place where they can to do it in the school building. I want to provide them with a strong but unobtrusive system of support. We will become their professional friends.

*

Sean, Tracey and I spend much of the first week walking round the school, watching how it functions. Sean points wryly to a group of children chattering away on their mobiles under a sign saying 'The use of mobile phones is strictly forbidden in school'. Every day after lunch, when lessons should have begun again, I see groups of children standing around talking and laughing. They are noisy, larking about, ignoring the electric bell that has signalled the start of school. Some of them mooch aimlessly towards the classrooms, some show no sign of going to lessons.

'Put those mobile phones away please. You should be in your classrooms! Now! Hurry please! No drinks, no toilet, no chatting!' I hear myself saying the same thing many times a day. Some children scatter when they see us, but Sean and I have worked out a pincer movement, with one of us on each of the two staircases that link the floors at either end of the corridors, so that if they run away from me, they go full pelt into Sean. I'm determined these children aren't going to get away with avoiding lessons or wasting precious time.

In one classroom, a supply teacher is writing on the blackboard, and looks alarmed and indignant when I come in and stand quietly inside the door. There are children sitting on the radiators. Many are wearing their coats. There's a group of girls at the back who are clustered together chatting, looking into makeup bags, showing no interest or involvement in the lesson. 'Put that make-up away – *now*,' I say sharply. They jump, turn round, then pack it sheepishly away and turn towards the teacher. I nod to him and leave.

'I know what St George's reminds me of sometimes,' I say to Sean, 'a youth club, with some lessons now and then. The young people come here to meet their friends and socialize. Their time-keeping is awful: they arrive late, spend ages moving from one lesson to another, and then walk in and out of them in a completely random way.'

I've noticed that some of the staff are also pretty lax about the start of lessons, walking into classrooms anything up to ten minutes late because they've been lingering over cups of coffee and chatting. I decide that the moment has come to address this at one of the early-morning staff briefings I hold three times a week. There's some surprise when I bring it up, and I realize that most are almost unaware they are doing it – it's simply become a habit, part of the lackadaisical, laid-back atmosphere of the school. 'Ofsted will never take us off Special Measures if lessons are late and fragmented, and the atmosphere is so casual,' I say. 'And besides, it's unprofessional, as we all know.'

I also tackle the issue of dress, as tactfully as possible. I'm not worried if teachers dress with individuality, even eccentricity, provided they take trouble and can bring it off, because I think that's enriching for the children. It's clothes that are inappropriate that I'm against. To my surprise some teachers come to school in flip-flops which, in my old-fashioned way, I consider to be quite unsuitable.

'I've noticed some very odd versions of the school uniform, and a lot of the children aren't wearing proper school uniforms at all,' I say. 'I'm very anxious to provide good role models and I think it would give a very useful message if we were all to make a special effort to dress formally when we're in school. I would also like footwear to be secure and sensible, because I'm concerned about the safety implications. I dress like an old fuddy-duddy headmistress in school, but you should see me at the weekend!'

Most of the staff, in fact, dress perfectly suitably and some, like Khadija, who is head of Modern Languages, are extremely elegant. Khadija, who was once a model, is a tremendous character and always looks as if she's stepped straight out of an expensive Parisian boutique.

I catch Tracey's eye and she smiles at me. Tracey never looks anything but attractive, but she's what I'd call an 'arty' dresser. She's always gently trying to erode my dress code and she and I have had silent battles over the years, about which we laugh a lot.

At the beginning of the second week we start to compile a draft Action Plan for Ofsted, whose next visit is only a week away.

Writing it is a kind of torment. Late on Monday night, when we're all jumpy from too much caffeine, Sean says suddenly: 'All this feels like fiction. We're writing a Plan for a school we have very little data about, there seems to be very little infrastructure, we don't know the children, and we don't know the staff.' I realize we need help, and fortunately I'm able to co-opt an old friend and colleague of mine, Pauline Hoey, who is now working as a freelance Ofsted Inspector. Pauline has been a Special Educational Needs inspector in Hillingdon, and she agrees to help us with the Special Needs part of our Action Plan, since this is one of the aspects of St George's highlighted as most in need of improvement. I'm also able to bring in John Whately and David Soulsby, two highly experienced and friendly former LEA and Ofsted Inspectors who give us invaluable professional advice, though we're all aware that the Action Plan has to be ours, and that we are responsible for making it workable.

In fact, from being a real bind, the writing of the Plan eventually turns out to be a very inspiring exercise. David and John help us to clarify what we really want to do, and I decide to start by summarizing on the front page our vision of what the school will be like on the day it comes off Special Measures: 'A school where vision and mission are realized through effective strategic planning, clearly defined objectives and active learning, contextualized by the ethos and tradition of the Catholic Faith.' The following 60 pages will describe how we plan to arrive there.

Throughout the week Sean, Tracey and I are staying at school till ten and eleven at night. The face that looks at me in the mirror each morning is pasty and drawn, with two furrowed clown-lines on either side of the mouth, and I can tell that my family are beginning to feel anxious. Tracey's family and friends are concerned about the hours she's working, and Sean says Dorothy is worrying too – and if Dorothy is worrying, that really is a bad sign. She's highly intelligent, and one of the calmest people I've ever come across, centred and wise.

When the first draft is at last completed it all sounds wonderful, but next morning I feel I'm receiving a message from Above when I open my paper and read some words by Ferdinand Mount, the political historian, who has studied why some government regimes last longer than others. He calls the long-lasting ones 'survivor regimes' and argues that they 'do not usually arrive in office with any detailed set of plans stretching over years, or, if they do, the plans have speedily to be rewritten under the pressure of events.' The first need of survivor regimes, he believes, is 'to communicate a sense of confidence and to establish stability. Characteristically, they will then develop a rolling agenda.'

I stick the cutting on the noticeboard in my office. Action Plans are all very fine I know, but it's how we respond to day-to-day events that will really matter. The Action Plan can't possibly encapsulate everything we plan to do.

In contrast to the writing of the Action Plan, my first meeting with the School Governors does nothing to lift my spirits. Ofsted, I tell them, has described St George's as being 'at the bottom end of limited progress' and I am seriously concerned about the state of the school. I describe in detail the dreadful attendance, poor behaviour and low staff morale, the parlous state of the school's finances, the lack of essential teaching materials, the absence of vital data and of a proper administrative infrastructure – in short, of all the mechanisms for maintaining a good school.

After painting this devastating picture I pause. In my anxiety and naivety, I suppose, I am expecting that the Governors' response will be one of dismay, and of willingness to leave the past behind and do all they can to help me in turning St George's round. While I appreciate that the story of St George's is a complex one, I feel this is the least I can expect from the body responsible for running the school, and it would immediately show me that I have their understanding and support. But there is barely time to draw breath before the Chairman thanks me and suggests the meeting now moves on to sorting out the various committees. I'm flabbergasted.

I can't let them brush aside such serious issues. The children deserve better. Their future is what is at stake.

'Before we move on to other business,' I say, 'do the Governors wish to respond to the points I have just made?'

'Are you criticizing the Governors, Marie?' a Governor asks me, bridling.

'That would be most improper,' I answer as sweetly as my rising temper permits. 'What I'm asking is, are the Governors minded to respond to the serious issues I have raised about the school?' I glance at Sean and Tracey. Sean looks furious, and Tracey looks appalled.

There is an embarrassed silence. 'I think you're telling us off,' says one finally, trying to make a joke of it.

'No,' I say. 'But I would like to emphasize that the Governors are the responsible authority and we should all be aware of the gravity of this situation.'

There's a lot more paper rustling, but no one speaks and we finally turn to other business. It's a moment of revelation. It seems to me that the Governors and I are not singing from the same hymn-sheet – though I tell myself that it's the end of a long day, that perhaps I'm overreacting and that they have been through a difficult time too.

I think, with a real anguish, of the wonderful Governors I left behind at Douay – the friendly Colonel Hendricks who would come in and have a chat with children who needed chivvying up, David Adams, the British Rail personnel chief who helped us so sensitively with personnel matters, Lorraine Savidge, the wise parent Governor who brought common sense to many issues, the efficient way the finance and other committees were run. All those Governors, the excellent Chairmen, Mgr Arrowsmith and Canon John were part of our school family, friendly, professional and totally focused on the interests of the child. What they had, above all, was an understanding of life which it is impossible to teach. They never simply rubber-stamped decisions. We respected one another professionally and intellectually and they were always there with counsel and support. How I wish they were here now.

When I see the minutes I find that my report is barely mentioned. I ask the Clerk to formally record my concerns about the school and to attach my report as part of the record of the Governors' Meeting.

We hold a staff meeting to discuss the new and more detailed Mission Statement that Sean, Tracey and I have drawn up for the Governors, who are after all responsible for the school. It consists of sixteen points underlining our commitment to the pupils, to the Catholic faith, to the parents, and to increasing our links with the community. I know this is a crucial psychological moment. When you start looking at your Mission you are looking at the very nature of what you do – it's as fundamental as asking a hospital to consider the nature of caring for patients. To me it is an essential practice. Every organization should do it from time to time, because it's easy to lose direction and start acting out of expediency.

I'm aware that I'm asking the staff to consider what St George's is actually about and why we are here, and I'm not surprised that some of them appear resistant, because it's very demanding, especially for a school that has lost its way. When an institution is under stress it's natural for people to feel threatened and to cling to what they know, but in a crisis such as this there's little time for analysis and reflection. Whoever is in charge must lead, so I push the Mission Statement through. There is nothing in it that anyone can really object to, though one or two of the Governors feel it's too long and detailed. But by spelling everything out, I know I have a supportive structure for driving through the Action Plan. Better a lot of detail than the previous vacuum, I think angrily.

'They're off!' Sean calls to me as he comes hurrying in from the playground one lunch hour. 'They're going over the wall!'

'Who are? What's going on?'

It appears that a large number of our Year 11 pupils have decided that, although they quite like the Task Force, they have no intention of letting it interrupt their normal lives, which means they plan to spend the afternoon mooching with friends in Kilburn High Road. We've seen the odd child disappear over the wall before, but this is a mass breakout: when we check the registers we discover that about twenty of them have gone AWOL. We can't do anything until next day, because by the time they are spotted going it is too late to catch them.

'Well, the gloves are off,' I say to Tracey. 'They've played our game for a week, but now they're letting us know that they want life to continue the way it was before we came.'

'We'll just have to let them know that's not the way it works now,' says Tracey.

So the following day we are ready with a list of names, and these children are brought to my office to discuss what happened.

''s not just us. Lots of people do it,' somebody mutters.

'I don't care how many people have done it before,' I say. 'If you're going to learn, you have to be in school. I'm sending letters home to your parents, and you're all going to catch up with the work you've missed in detention. I'm going to prove to you, though, that school can be fun. Got that – FUN.'

At this they look at me in disbelief.

'Look cheerful, and try and sit still. It's only a photograph, you're not going to the dentist!' I'm talking to one of the youngest girls who can't seem to stop fidgeting while her picture is taken. I've brought a professional photographer in to take a picture of every child in the school. My daughter Fiona has offered to spend next weekend mounting them in large year group displays, which will be put up on the walls nearest the main entrance. It's a way of telling the children that this is their school. They're all very taken with the idea, and there's a lot of titivating before the pictures are taken.

When the pictures are mounted there's a great deal of jostling and laughing as they look at themselves. One girl comes and asks me if she can have a reshoot, as she had a bad spot on the day it was taken. 'You can hardly see it,' I say, peering at the picture. 'Just imagine though if you were Kate Moss. Then it would really matter. Anyway, it looks like a beauty spot and shows up your nice complexion.'

I sympathize with her teenage angst about her appearance. I'm not looking so good myself. In moments of stress Sean tends to bring out the chocolate, and what with that and school dinners all the weight I managed to control at the gym is creeping back. Sometimes, as I travel home on the tube with couples who are obviously on their way out for the evening, I dream about having some kind of normal life again. Well, I tell myself, next year . . .

Sean and Tracey have a meeting with the Teaching Union representatives. It seems we've arrived at St George's with a reputation for bullying unions. This really isn't fair. I think our record proves that we do our best work with them. It's just that if co-operation proves impossible, we make sure we win – professionally, of course! – for the greater good of the children and staff. I acknowledge that unions have an important role to play in negotiating terms and conditions for their members and helping with serious professional issues, but I don't believe this extends to the day-to-day running of a school. There's a danger of creating a version of Dickens' Circumlocution Office in *Little Dorrit*, wasting everyone's time and doing nothing for the children's education.

Thirteen years ago, when I arrived at Douay, I found myself up against a highly unionized workforce, and I battled against all the petty rules and regulations they tried to impose on me. I had hate mail pushed under my office door, and one evening I left work to find that photographs of me, with horns and a tail added, had been pasted to the headlights of my car. I knew the children had had nothing to do with this. It must have come from the staff. It was at the end of a long, difficult day, and I felt like weeping. Eventually I won most of the staff round, and those who couldn't accept what I was doing left. It was a long, lonely campaign, exhausting, debilitating and sometimes frightening, but it put steel into my soul.

Now it looks as if Sean, Tracey and I have been given a poor press, which may explain why the staff here have seemed so suspicious. Word has apparently gone round that we harass people and make them do things they don't want to do. Like other dysfunctional schools, St George's, I've realized, has an unhealthy gossip level, with tittle-tattle taking up energy that should be going into better things.

Sean and Tracey tell me they've learned that the staff feel discipline in the school is a huge problem, that they have not been helped with it, that there is a culture of pupils not doing what they are told, and that they feel many of the worst behaved pupils should be excluded. I'm not surprised by all this, though it's too sadly familiar. 'It's somebody else's fault' is a typical approach to problems in any failing organization.

Somehow, I tell myself, I have to sell my dream for the school to the staff, weave it into their consciousness in a million different little ways so that they gradually absorb and accept it. I know they badly need encouragement, and inspiration, and it's my job to provide them. If I feel daunted (and I frequently do) I must never let it show. It's the law of the jungle: if other animals get a sniff of blood from a wounded tiger, they go for the kill, so even if you are crying inside, as a Head you must never let your staff see it. That's my philosophy, anyway. I simply put on more makeup and force myself to smile. Sometimes, at the end of the day, my face actually aches.

I have a meeting with some of the Heads of Year, good, enthusiastic teachers like Ariadne, Tonya Frost who teaches Art, Harvi Ghudail from Science, and Eve Churchward, a lively PE teacher. I've had an idea for tackling the problem of children roaming the corridors when they should be in lessons. I suggest giving passes to the teachers to be issued to pupils who have a legitimate reason for leaving a lesson. The passes will be colour-coded, to prevent forgeries. This means that any child not in class can be challenged by any member of staff and returned to class if appropriate.

They're enthusiastic, and when I say that I plan to send letters home to the parents of children not in class, one of them suggests sensibly that we get standard letters printed in the main languages of the pupils, so that the parents will understand. We decide the letters will be individually stamped and posted, not put through the St George's franking system, which would allow pupils to recognize them when they land on the doormat at home. You have to be a jump ahead of children in my view. In fact the system immediately proves phenomenally successful, with many parents phoning in to tell us that they had no idea of what was going on and are furious that their children are missing school.

My next idea causes rather more ripples in the staff room. For several days some words from a statement by the Sacred Congregation for Catholic Education have been running through my mind: 'From the moment of entering a Catholic school, a child should have the impression of entering a warm and loving environment which respects the individual's freedom. The religious image of the school should recreate or replace, if necessary, a pleasant and happy family atmosphere which is rich in both human and spiritual facilities.' I suppose I tend to see things in practical, black and white terms, and I can't see how locking children out into a cold playground, let alone giving them a poor education, can be reconciled with such a statement. At one of our early morning briefings I say: 'I'd like to stop locking the children outside every lunch and breaktime. May I please have your agreement to open up the school?'

There are shocked looks, and one or two of the staff start to tell me that they don't think it will work. One shakes his head sorrowfully, as if he is dealing with innocents. It's all part of a kind of bunker mentality, where the children have come to be seen as a threat and the staff take refuge in the staff room. We promise that

we and the senior staff will personally supervise the new arrangement. Whilst sympathetic to the staff's anxieties, the children
come first I feel.

When the children are told they're to be allowed into school
during breaks they seem as astonished as the staff. For the first
few days Tracey, Sean and I are everywhere, putting our heads
round the doors of classrooms and watching the stairs for signs of
trouble, but in fact because everybody now has more space, the
arrangement works remarkably well and helps to defuse the situation in the playground. I can see how much the children enjoy
standing around chatting in the atrium – allowing them near the
staff offices clearly makes them feel trusted and valued.

A week later, I get a letter from a girl in Year 11 that makes me
sure the effort is worthwhile:

Dear Headmistress, I welcome you to our school and hope you
enjoy your time here. I also thank you for giving up your retirement time to come and save our school. I feel that the school has
improved and gone up already. It was a good idea to let everyone
in the atrium because it makes all the pupils more welcome. It is
also really nice of you to let the pupils have their say in things. I
also know a lot of pupils like you because you are a really good
person to talk to. Love from Mila. P.S. I hope you like working with
us and being the head of our school.

As well as opening up the doors of the school, I also open up
the blinds. When I first arrived the blinds in my office windows
were down, and I always had to keep the light on. Now I get
Mick to haul up the blinds which means that the children wandering round the side of the school at break or dinnertime can see
in. I'm not worried: there is nothing going on that I mind them
seeing. At first the novelty intrigues them and some, particularly
those with behaviour problems, come and knock on the
windows. One boy gives me a V sign, which I pretend I don't see.
Later I tackle him and ask menacingly: 'Did I *imagine* a rude sign

to me made through the window by you?' He denies it, but gets the message.

Within a few days the children are bored with peering in and don't bother me any more, but I often get a smile and a wave as they go by. It takes me a few days, however, to convince Mick that I want the blinds open all day: every time I leave my office he pops in and closes them again. We compromise. I agree that he can close them every evening, as long as I can have them open all day.

'Oh, you are a determined woman, Lady Stubbs!' he says, smiling.

'*Never*, Mick,' I say.

Of course, opening the blinds also helps me keep an eye on the playground, where we are still facing problems.

One lunchtime in our second week I hear ragged shouts which unify into a chant: 'Fight! Fight!' I look out of the window of my office, where I'm snatching time to do some phoning while I eat a quick snack at my desk, and see a crowd of children swarming towards one corner of the playground. Sean has heard the shouts too, and we're both quickly out of the door and making towards the scene, Sean moving more quickly than me, as I have a rule never to run unless there is a real crisis. I learned this from The Centre: appearing calm is three-quarters of the battle, whatever you feel inside.

Two big fifteen-year-olds are embroiled in a vicious fight: kicking, swearing, thumping, grabbing one another's hair, there are no rules. As I arrive I move the children who are blocking my way to one side: they're so used to fights that they instantly create their own ring, three or four deep, around any promising-looking scrap. This is their entertainment, their excitement, and they do everything they can to prevent it being broken up before they have a chance to egg the antagonists on.

I'm too angry to feel afraid. I manage to take one of the youths by the arm and Sean gets a grip on the other one. We speak to them quietly and they separate quite easily: there's no need for brute force – the shock, I think, of being physically restrained by a sixty-year-old grandmother is quite enough. The boy whose arm I have hold of looks surprised and even rather embarrassed. 'Get outa my face', he mumbles at me, but he makes no attempt to shrug me off. The other boy is red-faced and furious, and goes on swearing loudly for a moment or two after Sean moves him away. As soon as they're both quiet I tell them to go to my office and wait for me. The watching crowd begins to ebb away. It's all over in minutes. I know the school is waiting to see what will happen next.

'These boys' parents are going to be told about this, and the same will go now for anyone else who gets into a fight,' I say loudly. 'I won't have this kind of thing happening in the playground and I'm sure you don't really want it either.'

It is only as I walk towards the school that I realize my heart is pounding and my pulse is racing. It's not just the natural adrenalin rush of finding myself pitched between two aggressive teenagers: it is also the realization of how desperately bad it would look to the LEA and the media if this kind of thing were allowed to get out of hand. For the sake of the children and the name of the school we've got to stamp it out. We set up meetings with the boys and their parents, and it's agreed that they will do detention after school and will be carefully monitored by Sean over the next two weeks.

One afternoon, just as the children are about to leave, Sean comes into my office looking anxious. 'I think we may be in for a bit of trouble,' he says. 'There's a gang of boys hanging about outside the gates. I think it's one of the elder brothers and his friends come to settle scores.'

I think about it for a moment. I know it's a dangerous situation and inflaming it could make things worse. I go out into the playground and walk across to the main gates, picking up a few pieces of litter as I go in a studiedly casual way. I can see the group of tough-looking characters outside, joshing with one another and from time to time kicking and rattling the gates.

'Hello boys,' I say pleasantly when I'm within a few yards of them. 'I'm afraid if you're wanting something I can't help you at the moment. I'm extremely busy, so I'd be grateful if you'd move on.'

They seem surprised to be addressed so civilly.

'Just hanging out man,' the leader says with a smirk.

'Well,' I repeat politely, 'I'd be grateful if you'd move on quickly now. I'll be back in five minutes to check, because I'm a very bossy teacher.' I give them a friendly look and walk back across the playground in a leisurely way. All my training at The Centre tells me I must avoid any kind of confrontation.

'They're still there,' Sean reports five minutes later. We decide there's nothing for it but to call the police, and within minutes a squad car arrives. When we look out again the gang has disappeared, though I'm only too aware that it may not be the end of this particular story. But it's all part of getting the message across that violence and gang culture are no longer part of the culture at St George's.

Fighting isn't the only problem we still face in the playground. I often see knots of boys hanging round by the school walls. They seem to be playing a game that involves throwing coins to the wall, and I begin to wonder what they're doing.

'They're gambling,' Sean tells me.

'Gambling?' I associate gambling with cards and dice.

'Yes, they throw a coin down and then bet on who can land another coin closest to it. It seems to be an obsession with some of them, I've seen them playing it in Lanark Road, and down in the tube station. As far as I can make out, it seems to involve the bigger boys taking money off the smaller ones.'

'We can't allow it,' I say. 'I want you to warn them all in assembly that their money will be confiscated if they do it, and we'll give anything we get to charity.'

It only re-emphasizes to me how little there is for the children to do in the playground. One lunchtime I ask Paul Ainsworth, the

Technology technician, to come and see me. I have already realized how professional and capable Paul is. He's a tall, reserved man in his thirties and when I tell him what I have in mind he's clearly astonished.

'If I give you £200 from the Governors' Fund would you go over to B&Q or somewhere and spend it on the playground?' I ask him. 'I'd like every year group to have a quiet area with a table where they can read and eat their sandwiches, or just sit and chat, so we need five tables and plenty of chairs and benches. And can you get some big fairly indestructible plants in pots to separate the areas off and create a nice atmosphere? I want every age group to have their own space, so the older children can't bully the younger ones.'

Paul is very taken with the idea, and goes straight off to B&Q, returning to report that the furniture and plants will be delivered at the end of the week. I also ring Jim Doyle, a painter of great flair and imagination who did a lot of work for me while I was at Douay. I discuss our problem with him, and he agrees to come in during the weekend and work his magic on the playground with jazzy zigzag shapes and lines for basketball and football. He adds his own artistic flourishes, including a yellow desert island surrounded by blue sea, and by Monday morning he's transformed it completely from the ugly, pitted tarmac yard it was before. The Chairman of the Governors has a contact who provides us with five more massive concrete flowerpots at no charge, and we fill them with childproof plants too, mainly attractive conifers with small bright annuals planted around them. I smile my thanks to Mr Clare with genuine warmth. I also order basketball nets, and we buy a supply of footballs and basketballs.

'*Wicked!*' is the children's verdict when they see their new playground on Monday morning. 'Are those benches for us to sit on, Miss?' one little girl asks me.

'Of course. They're for when you want to sit and chat, or read, away from all the noise.' I firmly believe that both boys and girls need protected 'quiet areas' in the playground.

The boys in particular are thrilled to have nets, and we're aston-ished by how good they are at getting balls through them. They're so gloriously physical, I think, as I watch them leaping and turning, we must keep them involved in sport. I give them a few laughs when I join in: I used to play netball, and they're all very amused at the way I stand still and shoot for goals. The whole playground watches us, and they cheer wildly when I manage to get one through the net.

We decide that the balls will be kept in the Deputy Heads' office, and handed out to children who queue for them at break and lunchtimes on a first-come first-served basis. Rushing to reach the queue first to get one of the balls becomes a favourite ritual. We keep an eye on the queue: in the first few weeks there is a bit of bullying, with older boys pushing to the front, but when we make clear that this is not acceptable, it stops. We lose a few balls: they are accidentally kicked over the wall or occasionally smuggled out of school.

'I suppose it's probably a big thing round here to have your own basketball,' says Tracey, always keen to understand and explain.

We also unlock the Philip Lawrence Memorial Garden. I feel he would have wanted the children to be allowed to sit quietly in this little oasis.

'It'll get vandalized,' one of the teachers warns Sean. 'They'll ruin it. It's an insult to his memory to let them in there.'

'I think it's a tribute to his memory that I trust them not to damage,' I tell the staff.

One afternoon Nadine calls in with her three-year-old daughter Sophie. It feels like a perfect opportunity to show the children just how much I do trust them. 'I'm going to take Sophie for a walk around the playground if that's all right with you,' I say to Nadine.

'OK, Mum. If you think it's safe out there, it's safe,' she says. 'But I'll be here watching you out of the window,' she adds cautiously.

'Nothing to worry about. I'll keep hold of her hand,' I say.

As we walk out we are immediately the focus of a lot of atten-tion. Children crowd round, and little fair-haired Sophie handles the situation with aplomb. She's quite happy to go off, hand-in-hand with me and one of the older girls, on a tour of the play-ground. 'Miss, can she have some of my chocolate?' 'Miss, can we take her into the memorial garden?' She is spoiled and fussed over, and meanwhile I am sending out a very clear message: the playground is a safe and happy place where I am delighted to bring my little granddaughter. My vanity is flattered, too: several of the children ask if she is my daughter.

Every day I spend some time in the playground, and the children love chatting to me. They are quite uninhibited about touching me, taking my arm, peering closely at my earrings, and fingering my silver charm bracelet, which particularly fascinates them. They want to know the story of how I acquired each charm, and they ask me if I am going to get any new ones.

'Yes, I'm going to get a champagne bottle when St George's comes off Special Measures!' I tell them, 'And I hope that's going to be soon.'

There are still unresolved problems left over from before my arrival. One afternoon, for example, I have to meet the parents of two girls who were involved in a particularly vicious brawl a few weeks before my arrival, with both of them ending up needing medical treatment. Both families are very bitter about it, and it looks as though the whole affair may end up in court. I've asked both sides to come in and meet me and there is a very uncomfort-able atmosphere in my office as both girls and their parents sit glaring at one another. I draw on my best mediating skills.

'You do realize what will happen if there's a court case?' I say. 'It will take months to come to court and during that time it's going to be difficult for Jeanie and Jo to get on with their lives. It's bound to be traumatic and there's always the possibility of a cus-todial sentence and criminal records. What they should be doing is concentrating on their Standard Attainment Tests. I think it would be better for both of them to have a good SATs record than a criminal record, don't you?'

The families look uncomfortable, but when coffee and biscuits arrive they gradually loosen up and start to talk. 'I never really thought we'd be able to talk about it like this,' says one of the mothers. 'I just thought there was nothing for it but to go to court and I didn't think you'd want them back in school.'

'I do want them back in school,' I say. 'We're certainly going to keep a close eye on them, and if there's any more trouble we may have to deal with it differently. But I'm hoping this has taught them both a real lesson. Now perhaps they can get on with learning and enjoying themselves in sensible ways, which is what they're supposed to be here for.'

The meeting ends with everyone agreeing to let the matter rest. The two girls look sheepish, but agree to apologize, though I notice they avoid looking at one another as teenagers do.

The violence in the playground certainly hasn't disappeared completely, but by the second week I begin to feel a different atmosphere. There's only the odd skirmish now, whereas we've been told that before we came there were one or two fights a day. Fights will occasionally break out in any school, however well run, but our secret is that we intervene, physically if necessary, before they get out of hand and some of the other staff are beginning to follow our example. The children have already stopped gathering round: they know there will be no show to watch. When they say 'What's happened?' I say in a bored way: 'Only some silly boys. Miss O'Leary will call their parents and sort it out. They need to start growing up.' This message is repeated endlessly by the three of us. Fighting is boring and childish.

Most of the children don't really like the fighting any more than we do, and they're quickly on our side. 'There's going to be a fight over by the Music Room,' a boy mutters to me one lunchtime. 'Jim and Carlos are calling each other names.' Children pick these things up faster than we can, and sure enough, under the Music Room windows two Year 9 boys are swearing at one another in a way that's bound to end in a fight.

'OK you two, what's this all about. Break it up,' I say. And they do stop, growling at one another like two separated dogs.

Warnings are always given furtively: the children never rush up to say 'Miss, Miss, there's going to be a fight, Miss,' which is what would happen in most other schools. But we can tell that they're beginning to enjoy the new atmosphere.

'It's cool, being able to play games,' one of the younger boys tells me. 'Watching fights is fun sometimes, but it gets a bit boring.'

The new prefect system is helping. The older children are loving being given responsibility and wear their badges with obvious pride, knowing they are part of the school's authority. They decide to organize litter patrols, and I see them insisting that other children get rid of chewing gum, and even telling them how stupid fighting is.

Sean, Tracey and I are all very aware, though, of the extremely volatile situation at St George's. I was brought up near the East end of Glasgow, and as a teenager I would often walk home through the city from dances at midnight. It's made me very streetwise, and I know how important it is in a difficult situation to keep the temperature down.

When children pour out of school in huge groups it can easily be a flashpoint, and during these first weeks we orchestrate the end of each afternoon carefully. We've asked our two nice young community police constables Wayne and Laura to be there regularly outside the school gates, giving a huge message to everyone that troublemakers won't be tolerated, and we let the children out into Maida Vale in small groups. Sean, Tracey and I are always at the school gates, hanging around in an apparently inconsequential way, joshing with the children and getting them to hurry on home. So far we've had no problems, and I think the children themselves are beginning to find this ordered exit at the end of the day very reassuring.

Setting off the fire alarm in schools can be a wonderful game. Each time, the school has to be evacuated into the playground while the Fire Brigade comes to check. Even when one is sure it's a hoax, schools can never afford to take any chances. The whole procedure can take an hour out of the school day, especially as all the children have to be counted back in again, and there's always a lot of pushing, shoving and jostling.

Thinking about preventing what has seemingly been a problem, I say to Sean: 'Let's get those new security cameras installed – and quickly. The present ones just aren't effective.' The cameras record what's happening in the corridors and staircases, so we can identify any culprits who are setting off the alarms. I warn the children about the new system at assembly.

'Life's too short to spend hours standing in a chilly playground because one person has been foolish enough to set off the alarms. It is not only a stupid thing to do, it's dangerous and it wastes the Fire Brigade's time,' I tell them. 'It's a waste of your time too when you could be in the classroom learning. From now on, Mr Devlin is going take the videos from the cameras home every evening and check them all.'

Afterwards Sean laughs. 'They must think I've got a really sad life if I've got nothing better to do at home than watch hours of security videos!' But we do all watch some of them, and they are always there as a record in case anything goes wrong.

During this second week we start going into classrooms to observe lessons. With Ofsted's next visit looming, I want to be able to discuss the relative strengths and weaknesses of my staff.

'Stand up, please. You must stand up when your Headmistress or any other important visitor comes into the room,' I tell a classroom full of reluctant fourteen-year-olds. The teacher looks as surprised as they do, but they do eventually all stand. I'm still shocked by what I see in some of the classes: children wearing overcoats and baseball caps, reading magazines, flicking bits of paper around, sitting on radiators and desks instead of on chairs.

'Don't you think letting them wear coats in class gives out the message that everything is very casual?' I ask one teacher later over a cup of coffee. 'No wonder they're not paying attention to the lesson.' 'That's what these kids do,' comes the reply. Once again,

I'm up against the fact that some of the staff regard the St George's children as a race apart, intrinsically different from pupils in well-run schools. But I also see some exciting teaching by staff with natural flair and ability. And there are others who are struggling, but are trying hard and need support and encouragement.

My main concern is for the Year 11s. They've had such a rough time with all this year's upheavals, and their GCSEs are now only a matter of weeks away. Most won't expect more than one or two A–C grade passes, if that, but I'm anxious for us to do what we can. 'We must draw up their Learning Plans straightaway,' says Tracey, 'and identify the subjects they need to concentrate on for their revision. It's late, but it can still make a difference.'

I intend all children in the school to have Learning Plans which will go forward with them through the school, listing their achievements, their attendance records, their first language, their home country, their hopes and ambitions. But I can see Tracey's point: the Year 11s can't wait, even a few days.

There's still a lot of scuffling going on inside the school building. On 17 March, the end of our second week, there is a set-to on one of the staircases, with at least a dozen boys involved in one way or another. Sean and some other members of staff quieten them down and bring the main culprits into the atrium, where we leave them to cool off before talking to them.

Then I bring them into my office and offer them a cold drink. 'Now, boys,' I tell them. 'If my grandchildren behaved like you did just now I'd be very disappointed, because the oldest of them is seven, and I expect them to be able to keep their tempers if they're annoyed.'

The message gets through. I spend twenty minutes going through what happened with the boys, and at the end they shake hands.

'I'm going to arrange for you to have a talk with Mr Devlin,' I say. Sean is excellent at talking with teenagers in an unembarrassing, man-to-man way about the difficulties of growing up. Many of these boys have no adult role models, no one with whom they can talk things over. I know that one of the things St George's badly needs is a regular school counsellor, and I add yet another item to my mental shopping list.

'Fanks, Lady Stubbs,' one of the boys mumbles on the way out.

'We're moving forward together, even grooving forward together, but not fighting forward together,' I say with a smile, and they all laugh.

It's Friday, and today we have in fact got one of the best role models I can think of coming into school. One of the first phone calls I made when I got here was to Lincoln Crawford, an old friend and one of the best-known black barristers in the country. 'What we need here is aspiration,' I told him. 'I'd love it if you'd come in and tell these youngsters how you've made it to where you are – how you grew up in the Caribbean, worked night and day to ensure your education, and rose to be one of Britain's most eminent barristers.'

'You're such a flatterer, Marie. Of course I'll come,' said Lincoln generously.

I started inviting in successful people from all walks of life as inspiration for the students while I was Douay. I call it 'planting the golden seed', and I know that if, after a visit, just one child says 'I could do that', it's been worthwhile. At St George's we have a large percentage of children with African and Caribbean backgrounds, so I'm very pleased to have Lincoln here as the first of what we nickname the 'GGs', the Greats and Goods.

I take Lincoln over to the hall to meet the group of about a hundred children who've signed up to come. We've deliberately limited it to the three top years, so that each child has a chance to ask a question and connect in some way with the speaker. Lincoln, who is tall and handsome, with a quick wit and a ready smile, works his magic on them, telling them all about his early life, his feelings when he arrived in Britain as a young man, as well as his life now. Tracey has prepared them for this meeting, and they come up with good questions: 'How did you train?' 'What's the hardest part of your work?' 'What's the best bit?' I feel a glow of pride as

I see the children asking these questions so eagerly, listening atten-tively to the answers, and coping with the formalities of thanking Lincoln and presenting him with a book token. Afterwards, as I walk along the corridor behind them, I hear the buzz in their voices as they discuss him. The girls think he's 'gorgeous', the boys think he's 'cool'. And later when Neil, a bright but pugnacious little character from Year 9 who's frequently in trouble for answer-ing back, tells Ariadne in a studiedly offhand way that perhaps he 'might think about' being a lawyer, I know it's achieved what I wanted.

Nadine is a great organizer, and I decide to ask her to help me set up a programme of visits. One of the first people she approaches is Ray Fearon, the first black actor for many years to play Othello on the London stage. She also rings the Football Association to try to get Kevin Keegan. She's told he doesn't normally do school visits, but it's not an outright no, so we keep our fingers and toes crossed. He's someone who would be hugely popular with the children, and a great boost to their morale.

I'm always on the lookout, and whenever I come across someone I think might be helpful to the children, or to St George's, I'm shameless about approaching them – my husband tells me I'm like a heat-seeking missile. Old friends and colleagues also rally round to help me out in various different ways. One of the biggest problems I'm facing is with the administration, and Tim O'Shea, the Master of Birkbeck College, agrees to send in a colleague to carry out a free survey of our Information Communication Technology. They're able tell us straightaway how many comput-ers we need and which systems we should install.

Thanks to extra funding from Westminster Council we can afford some expert advice, and I persuade Teresa Doyle, the Bursar at Douay, to work at St George's as an occasional consul-tant. Teresa, whose gentle personality hides a laser-like brain, is a financial whizzkid, and the best administrator I've ever met. She starts off by examining our finances, and when she reports back to me at the end of the first day, she confirms my worst fears.

'There's a £5,000 to £10,000 margin of error in the accounts. There's a massive list of orders not put into the system. Sean has found drawers full of invoices. There are no accruals, no expenditure codes, no audit of standard funds, which you know the Government requires. As for all the forms which are supposed to be copied in triplicate . . .'

'And now you're going to give me the bad news,' I joke. Teresa laughs, but we all know the situation is serious. Sean looks drawn. This is an area he'll have to sort out. 'I'm worried about Sean. I've never seen him look so tired,' Nadine says to me when she bumps into him outside my office.

Our School Finance Officer has moved to another post. Westminster LEA recognizes the problems we're having, and they send me Lesley Bairdon, a pleasant young woman with a quick mind and a highly professional attitude, who comes in one day a week to run the petty cash and the day-to-day finances. Together she and Sean compile a list of the shortcomings of the financial system, which runs to 24 important points. These include no record of petty cash, personnel records out of date, no record of sickness absences, lack of salary details for support staff, no control over the use of the school stamp, no agreed budget, no accurate pupil data.

There is an up side to the financial chaos, I have discovered. I can simply get on with ordering whatever I want for the school, within reason and, of course, making sure we keep a careful record of all expenditure. It is a heady feeling.

My PA, Dot, is a lively personality and a great organizer. I tell her that I'm keen to set up a proper print shop in the school, and after discussion, I'm delighted when she agrees to take over the running of it. There's an important job to do there. Teachers simply haven't time to do their own photocopying and I want school materials to look attractive and well-designed. So now, as well as a new Finance Officer, and a good Office Manager who knows about computers, I'm going to need a new PA. Finding one who can deal sensitively with the intense press interest St George's is generating isn't going to be easy.

While all this is going on, we're also frantically preparing for the return of Graham Ranger and his colleague, who will be with us on Monday. I go round the school chivvying all the staff into handing in their lesson plans and reminding them that all children must have exercise books. I can tell that many of them, especially some of the young ones, are as anxious as we are for the Inspection to be a success, and have begun to enter into our efforts with a will.

Sitting in on classes I can see how thoroughly some of these young teachers have planned their lessons, yet how difficult it is for them to deliver them because they haven't yet truly got the co-operation of the children. I feel real concern for them, because they've put in a huge amount of work and there's some wonder-ful material there, but it just isn't getting through.

Today Tracey and I ask one of them who is having trouble with an unruly Year 7 class if she would like to unpick the lesson with us afterwards, and I start by saying quite genuinely how impressed I was with her lesson plan and imaginative approach.

'How much of the lesson do you think you spent trying to talk over the children while they were interrupting and misbehaving?' I ask. Tracey nods.

'Oh, too much I know,' she says.

'You must be exhausted by the end of the week. I don't know how you survive – I couldn't do it,' I say sympathetically. 'Maybe we could think of how you could use quiet as part of the lesson.'

'Quiet? With Year 7?' she says, raising an eyebrow.

'Yes. Children might win lottery tickets for good work and good behaviour, for example. They could enter for a weekly draw at their year assembly. Year 7 would do anything to win a lottery ticket for bags of sweets – or pencil cases,' I say, laughing. 'One approach might be to say something like, "After I've explained this I'm going to give you two minutes of quiet to think about it. Maybe you won't understand it all, so I'm going to see if there's one brave person who will put their hand up and ask to have it explained again. And that person's going to have a lottery ticket for being so sensible."'

She nods thoughtfully. We discuss other tactics for involving the children – perhaps by asking the rest of the class to help when someone is finding something difficult.

'But then they all shout at once,' she says, clearly troubled.

'So then,' I suggest, 'you might say: "No, I'm sorry, but I can't answer people who shout out. If I see hands going up quietly I'll be able to pick someone." Then you choose someone who you know will get a real boost from being able to help. Even if the child doesn't get it quite right, it doesn't matter. You can praise her or him and say "I think what Jenny's explaining to us is . . ." You know, positive reinforcement.'

And the same is true for young teachers, I reflect. Building their confidence is a terribly sensitive process, and I'm glad to see that when she goes off she doesn't look resentful, but clearly relieved that someone will help her improve her teaching.

Sean, with his usual humour and dogged determination, is out in the playground every day, chasing the gamblers with his collecting boxes for CAFOD and Oxfam. If he catches them he insists they hand their money over. 'They know when I'm coming – I hear the alarm going up: "Devlin's here",' he tells me. 'They have their money back in their pockets like lightning, so I'm collecting less and less, but I think the message is getting through. There's definitely less gambling going on.'

Tracey's time, during these first few weeks, seems to be spent mainly in conferences with social workers, and in making sure that staff are aware of children's problems and can respond accordingly. The scale of these problems is hard to comprehend. Fortunately St George's is a small school – less than 600 children, compared to 1,500 at Douay – so it really is possible to get to know each child. With her sensitivity and practical common sense, Tracey is wonderful in these situations which I know are extremely demanding. I worry about the burden on her, but she says that she does manage to put them behind her at the end of the day, knowing that she has done all she possibly can.

On Friday, I insist that we all leave school in reasonable time, and try to forget St George's for the weekend. The Inspectors will be here on Monday, and I don't want them to find an exhausted team. I know this is a vain hope, but I'm making an attempt to pack up on Friday afternoon when Tracey puts her head round my door. She describes a situation we have experienced many times before.

'I'm afraid I've got someone here who says she can't go home. Michelle says she's fallen out with her mother and she's going to stay at her friend's house tonight, but we can't contact the friend's mother.' Behind Tracey stands a Year 8 girl whose expression is a mixture of anxiety and defiance. I can see she's been crying. 'Here we go again,' I say to myself.

'Could you wait out there for a moment please Michelle,' Tracey says, coming into my office and closing the door.

'Have you phoned her mother?' I ask.

'Yes, and she says she's not having her home. She's rude and out of control and worse things than that.'

'Oh, these teenage traumas,' I say. 'The mother really can't do this, you know. Ring her and say if she won't have her home we'll have to phone and tell the duty social worker Michelle hasn't anywhere to go tonight.'

Tracey goes into her office to make the call. Apparently the threat of involving Social Services is enough to turn the situation. After another three-quarters of an hour it's sorted and Michelle and her mother are speaking again – just.

So much for leaving early. There's often some trouble like this that blows up at the end of school, which means of course that we can't leave. But eventually, and thankfully, we get away.

Predictably, over the weekend, none of us is able to forget St George's, and before I've even had my first cup of coffee on

Saturday, Sean is on the phone with a worry about the new computer system. After breakfast I drive to the supermarket, where I purchase an unaccustomed number of instant meals – William has philosophically accepted that I no longer cook much. As I drive home it occurs to me that the reason traffic flows easily (some of the time) is that there is a white line down the middle of the road, and everyone knows they have to drive to the left of it. This, I decide, could be the answer to the congestion problems on the stairways at St George's.

On Sunday William and I go to Mass at St Etheldreda's. I love this beautiful old church, where the parish priest, Father Kit Cunningham, has conducted the marriages of my children and baptized my grandchildren, and has become a family friend. I feel how fortunate I am to have such a spiritual guide and mentor, and as I sit quietly, watching sunlight falling on ancient stone, I feel some of the tensions of the week roll away. I'm aware more than ever how much St George's, faced with such terrible problems, needs a spiritual dimension to its life.

The Ofsted visit passes off as well as we could hope. The Inspectors spend two days with us, and Graham Ranger tells me before they go that he can see we have set a lot of changes in train, but that it will take a little while for the effects to be felt. He says that the school feels better, and seems calmer. He also gives me figures about the numbers of poor lessons, a fifth of the total. Not good. I'm not looking forward to the written report.

The day after the Inspectors leave, I ring another old professional friend, Peter Mortimore, head of the Institute of Education at London University. 'Help!' I say, not for the first time since I arrived at St George's. Peter and his colleague Professor Barbara MacGilchrist, who is in charge of initial teacher education, rally round instantly: they send me a team of lecturers from nearly every subject area to help with lesson planning, assess lessons, and give professional advice and support to the teaching staff.

Not all of the teachers are happy about it: 'I'm a professional, I've been teaching for years. I'm not having anyone sitting in on my lesson,' one of them says. I'm amazed at this response, and we spend a long time persuading him to accept the support, which he eventually does, grudgingly.

Nor is everyone happy with our insistence on detailed lesson plans. 'We know what we're doing. We don't have to write it all down,' is the response, and in some ways I sympathize. Every teacher is an individual, and at one time schools were full of eccentric people who taught in unconventional ways. But there aren't many real geniuses around, and the results could be patchy. Nowadays, quite rightly, schools have to be more accountable, and there has to be some way of measuring what they do. You certainly can't afford the luxury of being idiosyncratic when you've got Ofsted watching your every move as we have.

As I tell the disgruntled members of staff, when we come off Special Measures maybe we'll be able to be a bit more flexible, but at present a strict format and detailed lesson plans are necessary so that we can judge and analyse the aims and outcomes of each lesson. Privately I also feel it's not fair for some teachers to dig their heels in and say they're going to do things their way when the rest of the staff are struggling conscientiously to come up to expectations. Another terrible Ofsted report would mean certain closure. 'I'm the biggest trade unionist of you all,' I say. 'I'm trying to keep your jobs secure.' I have to smile at the glares this produces.

There's a small cause for celebration when the new phone system is installed. I have a secure line into my office, and there's a special number for parents to ring, a hotline to Social Services, and a phone line dedicated to arranging cover for absent teachers. Covering for teachers who report in sick is a major headache: just getting a teacher into a classroom for every lesson is a huge feat at St George's. Sean is in charge of arranging cover and is determined to organize it more efficiently and fairly.

'We'll have to introduce the AKIA form,' I tell him. Sean chuckles. 'They won't like it,' he says. 'Who does?'

The AKIA form was something I set up while I was at Douay. The letters stand for 'Absence Known in Advance', and any member of staff who wants time off for any reason has to fill in the form at least seven days in advance, giving Sean a chance to arrange cover, and giving me control over how much time individuals are taking off. In some schools it is done on a nod and a wink basis – no good for a school like St George's which needs stability. I'm happy to let a member of staff have time off to attend an important family event or vital medical appointment, but I'm also prepared to turn down requests if I think the excuse is flimsy, or if a dental or medical appointment could have been made out of school hours. Appropriate details of staff absences are also displayed on the staff noticeboard. I believe in the open approach.

When I announce the arrival of the AKIA forms at one of our staff briefings, I see the union representatives exchange glances. I can't read their reaction, but I hope they will welcome the system because it will mean we can organize fairer cover for their members.

One afternoon during the third week I go in search of Francisco Martin, the assistant schoolkeeper. Francisco is a great ally. He only works for us part-time, but he has quickly become my mainstay in practical matters, especially since Mick is having trouble with his back after falling off a ladder.

Francisco is Portuguese, a warm and exceptionally willing person with a fresh complexion, bright eyes and a ready smile. He does the work of ten men, and I have already discovered that he is always happy to give evenings, weekends and holidays to the school. He has a heart as big as the outdoors, and is a genuinely good man who cares about the children – worth twenty of the bureaucrats with files whom I keep encountering in education.

'Francisco, I've got a job for you,' I say. 'I'd like you to paint a line down the middle of the stairs with a different colour on either side.' My idea is simple: everyone has to travel on the left, and not cross the line. Looking at the ugly grey concrete stairways, we decide to go all out for colour – yellow and green on either side with a bright red line down the middle.

Francisco is entranced at the idea of brightening up the school. He brings in paint charts, and he and I spend a happy lunch hour poring over them together, with Sean and Tracey joining in. We decide to give the corridors priority, and choose a different colour for each floor – a sunshine yellow, a brilliant red, and a very bright blue. I call them 'McDonald's colours', the sort of colours I know young people like. Ask any teenager what colour he or she wants a bedroom painted and I guarantee the answer won't be 'magnolia'. For the atrium we choose a cheerful yellow for the walls and a lovely bluish pinewood green for the paintwork.

There are probably dozens of official channels to go through, and I should have spent hours debating with various agencies, but we're now so excited we want to start now, so I give Francisco the go-ahead to buy the paint. The Governors have been extremely helpful about releasing money from their funds, for which I'm grateful. But 'Well, it's the children's money anyway,' I think.

I remember that when I started as Head at Douay, fifteen years ago, I wasn't even allowed to buy a pot of paint for a visit by Princess Anne, because I didn't have the authority to order it, and no one who did had the time. Most heads of today can't believe how restricted heads were then. It's true that eventually I said to myself 'Am I me or am I a mouse?' and went ahead and bought the paint. But it was a big decision, and I could have been hauled over the coals for it. However, it set me on the path of keeping faith with what I believed in. Perhaps my reputation for being a maverick started at this point. How times have changed for heads.

I speak to Paul, our technician, about providing us with some noticeboards and he and and I walk around together measuring walls to work out sizes. 'Paul, I want one here – and a big one here – and another one at the end of the corridor.' Paul is always calm, however frantic my instructions. 'Right you are,' he says each time. He orders vast quantities of chipboard and gets on with the job right away. Busy, updated noticeboards are a sign of a thriving school and before long they're filling up nicely with pictures and information about the children and their activities.

I also buy in some electronic signs which are updated hourly – I call them 'silent radios'. We put them at the entrances to the school from the road and from the playground, and we have a large one in the atrium. We use them to display welcomes in different languages, to give birthday greetings, and to announce visitors who are coming to the school. We have fun with them, with notices like 'The first person who reads this and goes to the Deputy Heads' office will get a prize'. The prize is a chocolate bar or something from the McDonald's box. The children love the signs: they think they're buzzy and modern, and there's a regular little queue at the Deputy Heads' office with requests to put up friends' birthdays.

Thinking of my daughter Fiona, I have another simple but revolutionary idea. Fiona has two Labradors, and in order to keep them off the kitchen floor when they're wet and muddy without actually shutting them out, she's had the door between her kitchen and her utility room chopped in half to make a stable door. It seems the perfect solution for the atrium, which, especially when all the doors are shut, has a dead, airless feel which I can't abide. Why not chop the doors in half, I think. It will help the circulation of air and give a feeling of greater openness. Sean, Tracey, I and my PA can keep an eye on the atrium and still get on with our business without people wandering in. Half-doors will also mean that the medical room, which I've had moved to one of the rooms off the atrium, and Dot's print shop will seem less cut off and more accessible.

'I'm such a little housewife at heart you know,' I say to Tracey, when I tell her, with some excitement, about my plan. It's true. I love cleanliness and organization. I think I've inherited it from my grandmother on my father's side. Her house in Glasgow was almost unnaturally spotless – she even used to scrub the piece of lino that the shoe brushes were kept on. The records of her Co-op divi – that all-important payout to regular Co-op customers –

were kept neatly in order on a spike, and as a small child I always wanted a spike like hers to keep paper on. I was her favourite grandchild and we were very close, but she often warned me that if I didn't calm down and become less theatrical I'd end up 'a laughing stock'. I was never quite sure what that was. I now keep a spike on my desk and impale all the messages I don't like on it – usually from those I call 'the bureaucrats' of the Diocese or the LEA.

I also take enormous pleasure in ordering flowers, pot plants and newspapers in several languages for the atrium, as well as some comfortable IKEA chairs. I want anyone who waits there – visitor, parent or pupil – to feel relaxed and welcome. For the children it used to be a place they were only allowed in when they were being sent to the Head for punishment. Now I want it to be a place where they enjoy lingering, reading notices, feeling part of their school.

Right from the beginning we organized a system of Reception Duty for Years 8 and 9. There are always two children now, seated at a table in the atrium, quietly doing work set for them by the teacher and ready to welcome visitors or run errands. We give them a badge and a special training session on how they should greet school visitors, asking who they have come to see, getting them to sign the Reception Book, giving them visitors' badges and offering them a seat. The children absolutely love it. It gives them responsibility and makes them feel part of the running of the school. They take their duties very seriously and are word-perfect.

'Can we ask who you have come to see today?' I hear a serious Year 8 asking a driver who has arrived with a delivery from a local shop.

My own office is also beginning to look a bit more cheerful. My daughters have bought me some delightful French kitchen prints to put on the walls, and at difficult moments I find contemplating *'les légumes'* and *'le chocolat'* extraordinarily calming, especially the latter. The support I'm getting from the three of them is touching and terribly important in keeping me going. In one of my office cupboards I come across a statue of our patron saint, St George, minus his dragon but standing proudly with his shield in his hand. He's brightly painted, about two feet tall, and as statues go he's rather good. I dust him down and put him hopefully on a shelf next to the Action Plan.

All these improvements to our surroundings are part of telling the pupils, and the staff, that they are valued and important, and deserve the best. They are also great fun. I realize that I am beginning to enjoy St George's.

I often think of Philip Lawrence. I'm very much aware of his presence in the school. There are photographs connected with him in the atrium, including a lovely picture of his son Lucien with the Duchess of Kent and Cardinal Hume. In the library there is a commemoration clock. I am concerned that some of these items need to be looked after properly, so I take them down and store them carefully. By rights, they should go to his family. I promise myself that I will arrange this when the school is settled.

I feel Philip would be terribly pleased to see how the children are responding day by day. I feel he would also understand that we must move on. Soon there will be no children here who knew him, and the school has to create a new image for itself. I feel Philip's best memorial will be a successful school, where we pray for him regularly and remember with pride all he did for the community. I shall really feel we've achieved something when I see a newspaper article about St George's that celebrates the school without dwelling on its tragic past.

When Sean and Tracey walk into my office after the end of lessons one day they find me holding a lovely old brass hand bell with a wooden handle. I've discovered we have a set of them put away in a cupboard and I decide we're going to start using them.

'That bell system we've got is so unsatisfactory,' I insist. 'You can't really hear it out in the playground – that's partly why they're all so late dawdling in after lunch. And it's such an irritating sound. Anyway, I think there's something very satisfying about these old-fashioned bells.'

Sean and Tracey tend to humour me over my more eccentric ideas, but clearly they think this one is very odd-ball. The children love it, though. At first it causes a lot of amusement when a teacher stands in the playground swinging the bell energetically, but soon it just becomes a reassuring feature of the school day.

Although it would make life easier, I refuse to use the Tannoy system to call children to the office or the medical room. I know that it was used before our arrival to call pupils for punishment, making the whole school aware of who was in trouble. I think this association runs too deep: whenever anyone needs to see a child, I insist they send a messenger to find them, even if it takes longer.

Now, with all the doors open at lunchtimes and breaks, I use the Tannoy system for music. There's nothing like a bit of Bob Marley to lift the spirits – I play 'Don't worry, every little t'ing's gonna be all right' just before the Ofsted Inspectors are due to arrive, discreetly changing to something classical when I spot them approaching! If I feel the school is getting too lively I put on a CD by Enya. It's what I call 'beauty shop music', it has a soothing effect which is sometimes very useful. I suspect Graham Ranger doesn't approve of my music idea, but he is always too polite to comment, unless it is too loud, when he grimaces. We buy CDs of music from all over the world, and of all different types: classical, choral, instrumental, ethnic. We play one type for a week, with notices on the central noticeboard explaining this week's theme.

'Can we have Garage one week?' one of the older boys asks me.

'Of course,' I say, 'But you must provide the music and write the description to put on the noticeboards. We want to know all about the history of the music, not just the names of your favourite artists.'

He does his research extremely well, and the school suddenly resounds to Garage one day at lunchtime. It sounds a dreadful cacophony to me, but then, as I tell the children, I'm really old-fashioned.

On the last day of March I celebrate the end of our first month at St George's by cutting a swathe through all the red tape and restocking the school. Textbooks are in shamefully short supply, children who lose exercise books are not given replacements, children are not allowed to take any books home in case they lose them or don't look after them properly.

'We have to trust the children, or they have no chance to show they can be trusted,' I tell the staff, and there are a few cynical looks.

However, when I say: 'Give me a list of everything you need – books, stationery, videos, audio-visual equipment. You can't do a job without the tools', they are like children in a sweet shop. Some of them go out and buy what they need themselves, and members of the support staff go out for others. We keep a close check on what they spend, and now we begin to operate a proper ordering system. I feel it is a good note on which to end the month.

On Friday I manage to get home earlier than usual, at about seven pm. My husband, who is about to fish yet another ready meal out of the freezer, is delighted to see me. Fiona phones and comes round, bringing a celebratory bottle of champagne. Momentarily, though I'm more tired than I think I've ever been in my life, I feel optimistic and on a high.

Walking into St George's on Monday morning is certainly cheering. Francisco has been hard at work over the weekend painting the corridor walls, and the depressing magnolia has disappeared under coats of cheerful yellow, red and blue. The effect on everyone's spirits seems almost instant. 'You're a miracle-worker,' I tell him, but he just shrugs his shoulders and smiles.

The staircases have been painted too – Francisco must have been working round the clock. They are now clearly divided into green and yellow tracks with a bright red line down the middle. I explain the concept in assembly, and it seems to appeal to the children – 'Wicked, Miss!' is one small boy's verdict afterwards. It also gives me the opportunity to talk to them about why we need rules and discipline. There's a staircase we all have to climb in order to become grown-up individuals, I explain, starting with the lowest step of basic physical respect for other people and going right up to how we support and include one another, and even how we relate to God.

'We believe here that each one of you springs directly from the hand of God, whatever your religion,' I say. 'Each one of you is unique, and we respect your uniqueness. In the same way you must respect the uniqueness of the other people in the school. And that's why we have rules.'

They listen with surprising attentiveness. I believe children like an ordered environment, even if they aren't conscious of doing so. On some of the faces I can even see what I call a 'Eureka!' look.

Of course the new system doesn't eliminate every scuffle and logjam, but it enormously reduces the number. Members of staff whose classrooms are close to the staircases stand outside supervising the stairs at times of lesson changeovers and I hear the call, over and over, '*Remember to keep to the Left!*' Altogether the atmosphere is less frenetic, even when the children pour in from the playground like wild creatures, as they inevitably do.

In most schools there are a few children who have a lot of trouble controlling their emotions, and St George's is no exception. One person who hasn't calmed down is my friend Debbie, who is in deep trouble. In the middle of a lesson she loses her temper, picks up a chair and throws it across the room, narrowly missing a classmate. She's sent out of the lesson, and Tracey is all set to deal with her, but I decide it's time I confronted her myself. For the past three weeks she's been getting away with swearing silently under her breath when she sees me, which I've decided to ignore.

She is red-faced and unrepentant. 'Just because you're LADY Stubbs, you think you know everything. You can f— off man,' she almost shouts at me when I find her with Tracey in the atrium.

'It's because I'm Lady Stubbs that it doesn't make sense to call me "man",' I say calmly. 'If you don't want to call me Lady

Stubbs, that's fine. Call me Headmistress. But don't call me "man". We women should be proud to be strong. And we don't need to swear to express our feelings.'

We both know very well that 'man' is used for either sex, but she plays along with me and my remark seems to amuse her. I ask her to follow me into my office. Once there, I use one of Tracey's favourite ploys: I make an excuse to go outside and fetch something. Leaving someone on their own is a very good way of calming them down – it's hard to be angry if there's nobody there to be angry with. Of course, it's a matter of judgement: some youngsters are so out of control that they would try to damage things. But I can sense the beginning of a dialogue with Debbie. I can imagine her mooching around my office, looking at the prints, taking everything in.

When I return I sit down beside her to talk to her. It puts us on the same level and is a lot less confrontational than standing. Besides, Debbie is several inches taller and broader than me, and she certainly isn't intimidated by me physically. I look at her clear skin and tangled hair and somehow I want to smile. There's something Pre-Raphaelite about her looks, though she hasn't got the necessary soulful expression.

'We haven't got off to a very good start, have we Debbie,' I say. 'First of all, I'm extremely fussy about good manners, so can you talk to me without swearing and without calling me "man".' Now, tell me why you were so upset today. Whatever it was, behaving like that is totally unacceptable.'

She shrugs and says, 'I just blew my stack.'

'Why? What made you blow your stack?'

She gets animated and angry again. 'That f—ing cow called me names . . .'

'We don't describe people in those terms,' I say finally. 'Start again.' So she does.

'But there has to be a better way of dealing with her, don't you think?' I suggest after hearing her out. 'After all, right now she's the one having the laugh – she knows you're in trouble. Let's think about other ways you could deal with it when someone calls you names.'

By this time she is calm, and we start to talk about her problems at school, and finally her problems at home. Her mum, she tells me, is a single parent, and Debbie was born when she was only seventeen. There have been a succession of live-in boyfriends, and Debbie has a younger half-brother and sister. Debbie sometimes stays home to look after them and this means she misses school. When she's not doing that, she often plays truant, hanging out around the High Road with her boyfriend, who is at another school. 'Can't really see the point of school, anyway,' she says with a shrug. She is behind with all her schoolwork, although she is obviously bright, and because she's so often away from school, she hasn't got any close friends among the other girls. She feels they make fun of her, and being very sensitive to criticism she overreacts.

I make her promise that the next time she feels she is going to 'blow her stack', she will come and find Miss O'Leary and talk it all through with her. And if she can't find Tracey or another member of staff she feels comfortable with, she should come to me. Then I ask her to go and fetch her Personal Learning Plan. In a year's time she is going to be sitting GCSEs, and we discuss how she can set about catching up with her work.

'If you work hard this year Debbie,' I say, 'I think you could get an A–C grade in four or five of these subjects.' I can tell from her face that I've surprised her. I don't think anyone has ever convinced Debbie before that she might be capable of succeeding at anything.

'You'll have to start doing a lot more homework, and you'll have to be here paying attention during lessons,' I warn her, 'So that means no more staying away from school, no more being sent out of class for bad behaviour. It will be worth it, though, won't it? You could go on then to Sixth Form College.'

'Yeah man . . .' I arch my eyebrow. 'Sorry Miss . . . er . . . 'eadmistress.'

Finally, we talk about school uniform. As usual, Debbie is

dressed in a very random version of it, and I've seen her when she's barely wearing an item of school uniform at all. Her outfit usually includes enormous hoop earrings and far too much makeup.

'I'm very proud to be Headmistress of St George's, and I think you should be proud to be a pupil. Wearing uniform is a way of expressing that – it tells everybody outside the school who you are, and it means everyone in school looks smart. At weekends I wear jeans, but I wouldn't dream of coming to school in them.'

I've used this line before with pupils, and it always makes them giggle. Obviously, the idea of their geriatric headmistress in jeans is highly amusing. I show Debbie some of the photos we had taken when Lincoln Crawford visited, and she agrees it looks really good that all the children are smart.

The written Ofsted report arrives on 5 April. The first page is dispiriting: it says that 'the school has made limited progress since the last monitoring inspection and limited progress overall since being subject to Special Measures.' But the report acknowledges that the inspection took place less than two weeks after we started work at the school, and there are some encouraging comments:

> In the time available the senior management team have worked hard to welcome and reintegrate pupils after an extended half-term break, and have begun to consult widely with pupils about their needs and expectations . . . There has been considerable activity in a short time. The effects of the changes have, in the main, yet to be felt. However, one immediate gain is the more positive attitudes from most pupils.

Having said these few kind words, the report goes on to highlight all the problems we already know we have, and are doing our best to deal with, such as poor attendance and late-arriving pupils interrupting lessons. In one-third of classes the children are not seen to be making satisfactory progress, and in only one in four is their attainment in line with that expected for their age group. Of the 26 lessons the inspectors monitored, they found only one where pupils were 'responding well'. Although there was some good teaching in English, Maths and Science, there was also unsatisfactory teaching in these three core areas. The provision for children with special educational needs is also deemed to be unsatisfactory, as is the school's strategy to promote literacy.

After I have read the report I pass it to Sean and Tracey. 'We're dooo-med, dooo-med,' I say, imitating Private Frazer in *Dad's Army*. Laughter seems the only possible response, not because we don't take the report seriously, but because it was written so soon after we arrived. Even in the short time since the Inspection there have been changes. It just makes clearer what an enormous mountain we still have to climb.

Life is made more stressful by my difficulty in finding a replacement for Dot, who is now making a great job of running the print shop. I'm at the mercy of a string of temps. One or two, like quiet fairhaired Frances, do their best for us, but many of them fail to turn up at all, or if they do, fail to do anything productive. One even has a minor breakdown and screams and throws paper round my office.

I've little time to write much in my diary these days, but on 7 April I scribble: 'No G and Ts offered up this year. Sorry God!' Normally I give up alcohol for Lent. Helps the soul and figure.

'There was such a noise from the dinner queue I could hardly hear myself teach,' Tracey says, as we discuss one of the many problems highlighted by Ofsted: the way lunch is organized.

Lunch is served in the school hall in two shifts, with half the school having lunch while the other half is in lessons, and then vice versa. The change-round is very disruptive and it means that the school is using two hours of contract catering time instead of one. The dinner queues are rowdy, and fights and scuffles are always breaking out. There's an unpleasant atmosphere in the hall. Nobody wants to do dinner duty – only three teachers volunteered at the beginning, though we've already managed to double that.

'What usually sparks off these fights?' I ask Sean. 'Is it just because they get bored waiting?'

'A lot of the scraps are over dinner tokens,' Sean tells me. 'I think there's a bit of a black market. It's the usual problem. The kitchen staff can't keep checking on who's really entitled to them, and they get fed up with trying to get money out of children who say they've had their tokens stolen.'

This worries me a great deal. A large proportion of our youngsters are entitled to free school meals, and it's very often the only proper meal they get during the day. 'It's got to be possible to organize lunch in one sitting,' I say. 'This school is only a third the size of Douay, so I can't see why it's taking twice as long to serve lunch.'

We decide to streamline it into one sitting with a cafeteria system, with an orderly, strictly supervised queue. The catering staff are great, a group of warm, lively women, who genuinely seem to care about the children. Barbara, the boss, is keen to help us in every way possible. She's one of my favourite people, a kindred spirit with a lively interest in hair colours and clothes. She's also one of Sophie's favourites. Barbara spoils her dreadfully when she comes into school, and always has an iced lolly for her. 'Grandma, can I go and see Barbara' is the first thing Sophie says. I've noticed, too, that Barbara has a soft spot for Sean: he always seems to get an extra-large portion of chips.

Barbara's chips are excellent and so, I'm happy to find, is the general quality of food at St George's. We consult the children about what they would like, and they ask for a choice of sandwiches and cold drinks. Some children bring their own packed lunches and I love to see them now, sitting out in the tables in the spring sunshine, chatting to their friends.

Sean, Tracey and I do playground duty every single day, and when I'm not snatching something at my desk I always try to eat with the children. It's a great time for chatting and making informal contact about school or homework, complimenting someone on a new hairstyle, or getting through the message about table manners. The very idea of a meal as a time to socialize is new to some children, for whom the norm is a lonely snack in front of the telly.

'Why are you eating with your fingers Darren?' I ask a small bespectacled boy who is holding a sausage with one hand and surreptitiously wiping the other on his shirt.

'These plastic forks ain't clean Miss,' he says lugubriously, shaking his head.

'Oh, well let's go and sort that out with Barbara,' I say, doing my best not to smile. 'Because you wouldn't want anyone to think you didn't know how to use one.'

If we are telling teachers what to do, we have to be seen to be doing it ourselves. Sean and Tracey take on some of the more difficult classes. I have one-to-one sessions with pupils in my office during the lunch hour and occasionally at other times – children who need a boost because they're new to the school, or are having other problems – and I cover certain lessons when teachers are away.

One of Tracey's English groups are about to take their GCSEs. They've had no regular teacher for months, and though they've been set work, it hasn't been marked as yet. 'They're not noisy or difficult or badly behaved,' Tracey says. 'They're sort of passive and apathetic. It's as if they've given up.'

Sean, on the other hand, describes his first Maths lesson as his idea of the lesson from hell. 'Students were throwing sweets around the class and shouting across the room at one another when I came in. People were getting up and wandering around. They seem to feel this is quite normal and they were surprised when I interrupted and made it clear that we were going to do Maths.'

We know that we're all being very closely watched. The Head of English frequently drops in on Tracey's lessons. It is, of course, his job to monitor the teaching in his department, but I think he's now satisfied that Tracey has no difficulties and is in fact a brilliant teacher.

Classroom discipline is a recurring problem. One teacher sends three fifteen-year-old boys to Tracey simply saying he doesn't want them in his classroom 'until they've been dealt with.' Tracey gets the boys' version of what happened: 'We wasn't doing nuffin'. 'e just told us to get out.' 'I tried to go back in and say sumfin',' says one of them with righteous indignation, 'an, 'e just said: You're invisible. I can't see you or hear you. 'e just ignored me.' As usual, we are inclined to believe only part of what the children tell us, and we check out the teacher's point of view. It is quite common for teachers to provide names of pupils they claim they cannot deal with in the classroom, and this teacher has already provided us with a list that includes the names of these particular boys.

Tracey talks to Ariadne, who knows the boys. They're a bright bunch, but they've all got difficult backgrounds to contend with and the one who tried to talk to the teacher has spent his life in and out of care and a procession of different foster homes. You can't tell a boy like that that he's invisible – life has done that to him already. It's the school's job to make him feel he counts. There are always going to be difficult and disruptive children in any school, especially one like St George's is at present. I feel I have to be frank with the teacher. 'It's your job as a teacher to develop strategies for dealing with these children, and it's my job to help you to do so,' I say. 'Some of them are difficult I know, but it means you just have to work harder with them.' He doesn't argue with me, but his sullen silence tells me how he feels.

Rory, a thin, pale-faced, miserable-looking boy, is like many we've met before; he finds it hard to come to school, and has already been excluded from another school because of this problem. When he finally ambles in one breaktime to see his form teacher, summoned by a phone call from the school office, he seems barely aware that there is a new regime. As they talk a row blows up. Rory tells the teacher to 'f— off' and the teacher, exasperated, tells him to leave the premises. Rory refuses to go – now he's here he want to see his friends – and makes off down the stairs with the teacher after him. I come out of my office to find them confronting one another in the atrium. It's quite clear who's got the upper hand in this situation.

As the teacher and I stand talking, Rory, who is hunched inside an old grey coat and wears a baseball cap, scrawls a few obscene – and misspelt – words on one of the newspapers I always keep in the atrium for pupils, just to show us what he thinks of us. I remove it and throw it into the bin – to show him what I think of that. I tell him that we don't put up with that kind of language in school. The realization seems to be gradually dawning on him that something's changed and he gazes around at the plants and noticeboards, rather as if he's in a foreign country. I tell him I'm looking forward to seeing him tomorrow in assembly and rather surprisingly he says he'll come. As he and the teacher leave the atrium he looks sheepishly back at me from behind his coat-collar and says 'Sorry Miss, for what I wrote.'

As I'm walking along the first floor corridor after break I hear an alarming roar coming from one of the classrooms. Opening the door I'm met by a scene of total chaos. Most of the class seem to be on their feet, a group of boys are throwing paper pellets at one another, and the teacher, who is red in the face with frustration, is simply shouting ineffectually above the noise. I stand motionless in the doorway, and as Year 10 see me the noise gradually subsides and people begin to shuffle half-heartedly back to their places. I know that the last thing I must do is to undermine the flustered teacher, so I walk to the front and say politely, smiling at her as if I've seen nothing untoward, 'Excuse me. I have something I'd like to share with the class. May I have your permission to speak to them for two minutes?'

She can only nod mutely.

'I'm putting together our Distinguished Visitors list for next term,' I tell the children, 'and one of the people I'm inviting is an actor from the Royal Shakespeare Company called Ray Fearon.

He's very keen for people to come to his talk who are genuinely interested in acting, or who might be interested in going on to drama school.'

By this time the teacher, who has recovered her composure somewhat, is looking at me in astonishment. What on earth is she on about, I can see her thinking. But the class is interested, and I go on to tell them a little more about the Distinguished Visitors I have in mind for next term.

When I've finished I say: 'Maybe my glasses need cleaning, and I don't know whether Miss would agree with me, but when I came into the room just now I certainly had the feeling that some of the people in here were in Year 7 rather than Year 10. Now what do you think I mean by that?'

''cos we were flinging paper around Miss,' someone pipes up.

'You said it,' I tell him. 'But I'm sure this isn't going to continue, because I couldn't possibly let anyone into these talks who was going to behave badly – or who was going to stare out of the window, or wear a baseball cap for that matter.'

I turn to the teacher. 'I'm terribly sorry to have interrupted the lesson,' I say politely. She murmurs something, still looking at me strangely. As I leave the room, you could hear a pin drop, and there is no more noise as I walk slowly down the corridor. When I creep back later and peep through the window, the paper pellets are being picked up and the teacher looks cheerful.

Tracey produces a leaflet as a back-up for staff about ways of defusing conflict. It suggests rewards and sanctions for staff to use, along with a reminder that the carrot is usually more effective than the stick. The rewards include a ticket for the school lottery; a voucher to allow children to go to the front of the dinner queue (extremely popular); an 'own clothes' day; a congratulatory visit to the Head; a letter from the Governors; a free school trip; and a special celebration with parents, who will be invited to school to see good work.

It's a real pleasure when children gradually start arriving in my office to show me how their work is improving. Sometimes they're sent because their behaviour has improved. 'I'm really really *really* trying hard this week,' one little girl tells me. I'm particularly touched by the amazement in the eyes of a small Angolan boy when he shows me his lottery ticket. He's only just arrived in school and speaks very little English, but he always opens doors for teachers with a smile. His ticket is for politeness.

I think Father George's presence has been an extraordinary catalyst in changing the school atmosphere, and I'm so thankful that he agreed to come. I often laugh and tell him he's high-maintenance. He needs lots of personal attention, and I have to create a kind of carapace of tender loving care around him. But that's my job, and he's worth all the effort because of what he brings to the children and the staff. He's a terrible tease and he and Khadija are always laughing together. I joke that I'm so glad that at least there's one teacher who's older than I am, even if he and Khadija do giggle like teenagers.

On Fridays, now, I'm delighted that he's started saying Mass in the atrium before school. It's a wonderful, peaceful start to the day, and he does it so beautifully, creating an atmosphere with special carpet and candles. The chapel, too, has been transformed from the somewhat sterile place it was, and the children obviously enjoy simply being there among Father George's plants and paintings and chalices and wonderful vestments.

We have a huge cross-section of staff. A few of them are very devout Catholics, but most of them are not Catholic, and the children come from everywhere in the world of course. But Father George includes everybody – Muslims, Christians, Buddhists, children who've been brought up with no religion at all. He appeals to the spiritual in everyone. 'Now we are going to pray in our way,' he'll say, 'which is a Catholic way, and you may wish to pray in your way.' No one feels excluded, and heads are soon bowed, and faces peaceful.

Today he gives us one of the readings for the second week of Lent: 'Jesus said to his disciples: Be merciful, just as your Father is merciful. Don't be a judge of others, and you will not be judged;

do not condemn and you will not be condemned; forgive and you will be forgiven.'

As I stand among these children, the reading seems to have a special meaning. A surprising number of them come to Father George's Masses, and the atmosphere is quiet and thoughtful.

A mother who has asked to see me arrives during the Mass and peeps into the Chapel. Her eyes are moist talking to me about it afterwards, she's so touched to see this happening at St George's.

There are more difficulties with Debbie. She's in Tracey's office, cooling off. I think we really must find her some help to deal with this simmering anger of hers. She got into a fight in the dinner queue with a couple of boys in her class, and it looks as if she's given the smaller one a black eye. He's in the medical room with Wendy, our Welfare Assistant, pressing an ice pack on the swelling.

'Oh dear, what was it all about?' I ask Tracey.

'Can't quite find out. Something about these two throwing her coat over the wall on the way home yesterday. Really one is as bad as the other, as usual.'

'What's she doing now?'

'I've left her playing with the Zen garden, eating her lunch. I'll go back and talk to her in a minute or two.'

'I must put this into the Incident Book,' I say. We are, of course, required to record any such incidents by the LEA. It's comforting to see that our Book has a diminishing number of entries.

Sean teases Tracey about her Zen garden, but it does seem to have a magically soothing effect. It's a miniature garden, with sand and plants and boulders, and a tiny rake. Children love it. They move the stones around and rake the sand. And remarkably, whatever kind of tantrums are thrown in Tracey's office, it never gets tipped over or broken. Even Sean and I find ourselves ruminatively raking it over when a problem seems particularly intractable.

*

Excitement is gradually beginning to build over the May Ball, which is scheduled to take place on Friday 26 May, the last full day in school for the Year 11s before they go off on GCSE study leave. I'm determined that it's going to be a stylish event – no half-measures – and the pupils have elected a committee: three boys, three girls and two staff, Sean and Ariadne. I want the children to be involved in the whole process – researching venues, examining costs, choosing the music, designing the invitations, working out the menu.

What to wear is clearly going to be the main preoccupation for everyone, not just the committee. Many of these youngsters have a wonderful carriage and natural style and when they're dressed up I know they'll look stunning. I feel almost as excited about it as they do. I'm afraid, though, that some of the staff clearly think this is an absurd, extravagant, time-wasting idea and not appropriate for a school like St George's.

I'm asked if I will attend the second of the May Ball meetings as the children want to lobby me about something. I know what it is because Sean has warned me. They want to ask if they can invite guests. Sean is against the idea, and I agree with him. As he says, we've got enough worries with our own students without having strangers there whose behaviour we can't control.

'This is a special event for St George's School,' I say, when they ask me. 'It's for you, to mark the end of an important phase of your lives, when you were part of the family of St George's. So I feel we should keep it in the family.'

I can see they're disappointed, but they accept the decision without arguing.

'I've never dressed up like this before Miss, and I want my boyfriend to see,' one of them tells me afterwards.

'We'll take lots of photographs,' I promise. 'And maybe you can get your boyfriend to take you somewhere nice so you can wear your dress again.'

*

I've decided that with the staff it's a case of 'Those who are not for us are against us.' We really do need an exceptional degree of commitment and enthusiasm if we're going to educate the children properly and get St George's off Special Measures. Sean, the economist, sees the situation in terms of 'opportunity costs', which means that the time we will have to spend nurturing and overseeing some of the staff just will not be worth it, with so many other calls on our time. I'm very much aware that for some of them my style is not to their taste and understandably they will want to find jobs elsewhere. It's my responsibility to do what I can to help them. You can't profess to have Catholic ideals if you ride roughshod over other people, and every day I question myself about whether I'm right in what I'm doing. I want to make things as easy as possible for all staff, but I'm under such pressure to sort out the children's education in a brief rushed year that sometimes I may seem abrupt and demanding. I am! And one thing I won't negotiate on is the outcomes for the children.

Teachers who are going to leave are required to give the school early notice, so I brace myself for a flurry of resignations before Easter. I receive some, including one from the long-serving Head of Music, though not as many as I expect. But we are getting some very interesting applications. Sean has interviewed the professional singer Katerina Mina, who has applied to be our choirmistress. This is encouraging as to me singing is food for the soul, and I want to set up choirs for all age groups at St George's. I don't think you need to have a wonderful voice to enjoy singing. I was in the Glasgow Children's Choir, and I loved it, though it was my sister who had the voice. To have someone of Katerina's talent on the staff, I feel, would be thrilling.

'I'm not quite sure how long she'd last though,' Sean says cautiously. 'She says she mustn't raise her voice to the children because she has to protect it.' Nevertheless, we decide to take Katerina on. When Sean introduces her to me I find her fascinating. She's slender, with a wonderful carriage and a truly classical head, and she glides rather than walks into my office. The impression is certainly one of fragility, but I can see determination in her enormous dark-fringed eyes. I think music is going to flourish in the school in new ways.

Just days after we recruit her we have another stroke of luck. A young South African supply teacher, Gillian Rabie, comes to fill in for one of the staff who is off sick. She teaches English and Drama, and we love her talent and her enthusiasm. She gets the children involved straightaway. Tracey, Sean and I spend a lot of time watching the supply teachers who come, and if they're good we dedicate ourselves to wooing them into staying. Gillian is one we all agree has to stay, and we manage to persuade her.

An event is being planned for the end of term which I've decided not to attend, though I'm very keen on extra-curricular activities. It's an evening's entertainment for parents called the 'Spring Showcase', involving the choir, the school's six-piece rock and roll band and various dance groups. It was arranged some time before we arrived and a few of the staff have been helping the children rehearse.

'It won't do your blood pressure any good, Marie,' Tracey says after she's watched a rehearsal. 'You'll be getting up on stage and taking over. The children are so excited they're all over the place. It's a bit like a youth club show – not much of the formality or presentation we like.'

Hearing about it makes me more determined than ever to encourage proper dance, music and drama clubs. I speak to Gillian and she announces that a dance club will now meet once a week in the gym in the lunch hour. The response is astonishing. The children love the idea and queue up to join – to the surprise, I think, of some of the old hands on the staff, who predicted that 'these kids' would never participate.

A lot of teachers, however, are keen to get involved. We start a lunchtime video club and I send Dot out to choose a selection of suitable videos. On one occasion I pop my head round the door and am met by the sight of something that I can see definitely has an Adult rating. 'What on earth are you watching?' I say, going over to the set and switching it off.

There's a silence, and a few sheepish giggles and snorts. 'I thought you were watching *Toy Story*', I say. 'Come on, put it back on please.'

'Aw, we've seen it. It's stupid,' they whinge. But when I check later they seem to be engrossed and actually enjoying it. After that I'm on the lookout for smuggled videos, and my rule is 'If in doubt, confiscate.' As I'm approaching I always call 'Look out, Grandma's coming' and this makes them laugh.

We've now acquired computers for the library and we start a successful computer club, though one day the teacher in charge suspects, from some of the children's guilty expressions, that they are using our free Internet access to try to get into a soft porn website, and we have to make sure they can't do this. I'm appalled when I think what some of the children are probably exposed to out of school, both as regards the videos watched at home and via the Internet.

There's also an after-school cookery club which specializes, naturally enough, in international cuisine, and I sometimes discover Sean making towards the enticing smells drifting from the Food Technology room.

We set aside a classroom for each year group where they can spend free time, and where they can play their own choice of music on cassette and CD-players which they collect from the office. We draw the line at some of the lyrics, and Sean soon collects a drawerful of Eminem.

The whole building seems to have come alive now during the lunch hours, and I love to walk around it, hearing the sounds of dance music drifting out of the gym and catching glimpses of groups absorbed in various other activities. I'm always keen to know what the children themselves want, and I put suggestion boxes at strategic points around the school asking for their ideas about how St George's can be improved.

They are a bit suspicious of them at first, and some of the staff pooh-pooh the idea, but after a week or so suggestions begin to come in. Some are just flippant – 'Burn the place down.' 'Get rid of Mr or Miss So and So', 'More sex education', 'Abolish school except for children under ten' – but there are heartfelt messages too: 'Get more black teachers', 'I'd like bigger dinners', 'Buy us a playing field' and, over and over, 'Can we have football teams'. Touchingly, some of the messages are thank-you messages. 'I don't have any suggestions, but if I did I know you would listen,' one child wrote.

Following on from the suggestion boxes, we decide to set up year group committees, with elected representatives from every class. They come up with more ideas. The younger groups ask for lockers to keep their things in, more varied lunch menus, and for girls to be allowed to wear trousers. The older ones say they'd like more responsibility, more close monitoring of their work, more computers, and a counsellor in school to help with behaviour problems. And every year wants football teams and games with other schools.

Most of the committees' suggestions are eminently sensible. We discuss them all, and when we don't feel we can agree to them, we explain why. We refuse to allow children out of school at lunchtime. We explain that we feel this is an interruption to the school day, but secretly we suspect a lot of them wouldn't come back. I also turn down the older ones' request for a pool table, which I feel would only increase the youth club atmosphere I am trying to stamp out.

'Well, if there's one message coming through loud and clear, it's that they want more sport and more teams,' I tell the staff at one of our briefings. 'It's too much for the PE department to handle, so I'd be very grateful for any volunteers.' A number come forward and I hope that in September, when we have a new intake of staff, there will be more.

The head of PE is off sick with a long-term problem, which has put the department under considerable stress. However Eve Churchward, the young acting head, is tremendously enthusiastic, and she approaches the situation with a will, setting up soccer teams and exploring the possibility of basketball and football fixtures with other London schools.

Up to this point the children have been wearing a ragbag of different bits of sports clothing for games and PE and now the committees come out very strongly in favour of having a sports kit – who says children don't like uniform? Together we decide on black shorts, black tracksuit bottoms and yellow sweatshirts and T-shirts. We sell them in school, or provide them out of private funds if children can't afford them.

The word has got out! Kevin Keegan is going to visit St George's. Nadine followed up her phone call to the Football Association with a letter suggesting that, with the Euro 2000 tournament coming up, it would be wonderful if he could visit a school named after England's patron saint. To her amazement Kevin Keegan's personal assistant rang and put the great man himself on the phone to discuss dates.

As I walk down the corridors children keep coming up to me: 'When's Kevin Keegan coming Miss?', 'Can I meet Kevin Keegan Miss?' Normally with distinguished visitors we put up a list for those who want to come to sign, but there's clearly no point with Kevin Keegan – all the boys and at least half of the girls would be on it, not to mention most of the staff. Maggie's in a high state of excitement and already thinking about what's she'll wear in case she gets to meet him.

Nadine's done wonders with setting up a programme of visitors for us. Almost all the people she's approached have said yes. We've already had a visit from the top florist Paula Pryke, who arranges flowers at some of London most distinguished addresses, including 10 Downing Street. Paula is a charming person who was once a teacher, and she totally involves both boys and girls, talking to them about the magic and mystery of flowers and allowing them to try their hands at their own floral arrangements. She's very practical too, advising them on how to make the most of flowers when you're on a tight budget. I'm thrilled when she comments afterwards on how nice the children are.

Professor Nadey Hakim, the distinguished transplant surgeon from St Mary's Hospital, who's well-known for conducting the world's first hand transplant in France, is also going to visit us. And Fiona's husband Mark is coming. Mark is a handsome and lively young doctor, but he's also a keen amateur pilot and he's going to talk to the children about one of his passions in life – flying, and the physics and maths it involves. The Lord Mayor of Westminster and the Lady Mayoress have promised to come and take part in a workshop on *A Midsummer Night's Dream* that Tracey has organized as part of a Westminster Schools Shakespeare Fortnight. Their visit will also give us a chance to explain a little about the way the community outside the school gates works.

Tracey makes a point, with these visits, of asking the more problematic and disruptive children to play host to the visitors. It works, and our visitors behave with perfect understanding when greeted by a youngster whose school uniform looks somewhat oddly put together, or who is struggling hard to communicate.

'We want people who come to St George's to feel comfortable,' Tracey tells the children before a visit. 'If we yawn, or slump in our chairs, or gaze around the room, it will make them feel uncomfortable, because they will feel you are not interested in what they are telling you. So we all have to look as though we are listening and interested, don't we?' I can think of a number of conferences when the adults present could have used that advice.

Rory, who was sent home for telling his form teacher to 'f— off', did turn up for assembly next day. But now he is only turning up sporadically again, and he seems incapable of getting to school on time. Time-keeping in general has greatly improved, but there's still a hard core of children like Rory who just can't or won't get up in the mornings and arrive late and half-asleep. I'm pretty certain these problems have nothing to do with drug-taking – to my relief, this doesn't seem to be an issue at St George's. I do know that some of the younger ones have to get themselves off to school because their parents do shift work, or simply aren't there to help them.

Tracey and I ask the worst offenders to come to my office one breaktime. Rory comes, still wearing the old grey coat with an enormous collar that he rarely seems to take off. It's like a security blanket, and he tends to keep the collar up, so that it is hard to see his face. He has it up now.

'Please put your collar down, Rory, I'd like to see your face.' He hunches the coat round his face more closely, so that there is only a slit at the front. He knows why he's here. 'I don't want to listen to you,' he says, in his oddly mechanical voice. Rory really does have difficulties. His statement of educational needs says he has communication problems, and he has a very strange, stilted way of speaking. When he thinks I'm not looking he lowers his collar and peeps out to see what's going on.

I ask the children to sit down. We talk about their lateness. 'I often don't feel like getting up in the mornings,' I say. 'But shall I show you what I do? May I borrow your coat Rory?' He's sufficiently intrigued to let me have it. I take an old-fashioned alarm-clock out of my desk drawer, set it, and lie down on two chairs with Rory's coat draped over me. As soon as the alarm goes, I throw it off and leap to my feet immediately.

This makes them all laugh, including Rory. Tracey, who has seen it all before, smiles and participates by cluck-clucking at the appropriate moments.

'I've bought you each an alarm clock,' I say, 'and I want you to promise me that you'll do what I do, and leap out of bed as soon as it goes off – and of course you'll have to remember to set it.' I get them all to set their clocks for 7.30 am, which is the time most of them say they *ought* to get up to be in time for school.

'You're mad you know Miss,' one of the girls says to me as they leave, in a friendly, matter-of-fact way.

'Ah,' I say. 'There is a pleasure, sure, in being mad, which none but madmen know.' That was the quotation they wrote after my name in the yearbook when I was training to be a teacher. Why change the habits of a lifetime?

My little demonstration seems to make an impact, for a while at least, even with Rory. We run a tremendous timekeeping campaign, rewarding children who manage to get in on time and setting up a league table for the classes with the best attendance, with the results put up prominently on the noticeboards and flashed across the electronic signs. Sean does the statistics. The winning class each week gets a big bag of sweets, and a Headmistress's certificate, which is ceremoniously handed out at assembly. I also go into the classrooms to hand out book tokens and certificates to individuals who have done especially well. The children have got the hang, now, of how to behave when the Headmistress enters the room, and rise to their feet quite smartly.

Some children, it's true, are up against genuine problems in getting to school. After one boy is caught jumping the tube barrier, Tracey discovers that he lives outside the borough and the family haven't managed to get him his free pass, which Tracey helps them to do. Another little Bangladeshi boy works on a market stall before school because his mother hasn't sorted out her benefits.

Those who have no really credible excuse for being persistently late have to write letters, in which they spell out the problems they have with getting in on time and how they are going to improve: 'I promise to go to sleep earlier at 10 pm', 'I will get my stuff ready for the next day, and spend less time going into shops', 'I will take less time doing my hair and makeup' – this from a Jerry Hall lookalike in Year 10 who arrives each day very late, but looking glamorous enough for a modelling assignment.

The children sign their promises, so do their form teachers, and then I sign them as well, and hand them back. Like most children, they need help to understand how to improve.

It's the 13th of April. Tomorrow is the last day of our first term, but today is *the* day. Kevin Keegan really is coming. Eve is organizing year teams from the youngest up, and he's going to launch the Year 7 team. Everyone seems to be in school on time, and attendance reaches an all-time high.

Thanks to a generous donation from David and Elaine Potter, the founders of the Psion computer firm, we've been able to purchase a lot of sports equipment, including some goalposts. I've bought an enormous roll of red ribbon and I hand it to Eve Churchward and Tonya Frost who is in charge of Art. 'Can you run out and put a ribbon right round those posts,' I say, as we all wait rather nervously for the hero's arrival, which is scheduled for eleven.

Fiona arrives and briefs me as Nadine is abroad: 'Now, he's said he'll do one picture for the press Mum and we've agreed to that, so don't expect any more.'

The children who have been selected to form the greeting committee wait anxiously in the atrium, whispering as if they're in church. When Keegan walks in an awed silence falls. Then Maggie rushes up and says 'Welcome Kevin' in a reverent tone which makes everybody laugh. He's charming and relaxed, immaculately dressed in a sharp Italian suit, with lively eyes and an engaging smile.

We conduct him to the playground, where he cuts the red ribbons in front of an admiring group of children. The *Evening Standard* has arrived, as well as the local press, and the cameras are popping. I know this is supposed to be the only photocall, but I just can't help it: 'Could you just have a bit of a kick around with the boys,' I plead. He immediately slips off his beautiful jacket, says 'Come on then lads' and joins in with the Year 7 football team who are lined up to meet him, despite the fact that it's drizzling and he's wearing expensive-looking Italian brogues. He genuinely looks as if he's enjoying himself and when he picks out a girl from the crowd to head the ball with him, a spontaneous cheer goes up. He's so unassuming, I can see why he's idolized.

Each year group has its turn to meet him in the hall, where he's going to hand out some sports cups to individual children on teachers' recommendations. The children look so overawed when we walk in that it's almost painful. When he speaks you could hear a pin drop. He talks about the importance of team spirit, and of determination: '*Anything* is possible, if you really want to do it and you're prepared to work for it,' he says.

A sea of hands shoots up at the end, and there are questions galore, though I must admit I can't understand most of them, knowing nothing about sweepers, the offside trap and the four four two. There's a lot of animated chat about which London teams the children support. As he signs autographs afterwards Kevin Keegan tells me it's been like facing a tough press conference of the most experienced football reporters. We have some wonderful photos and when I see them I laugh at how bemused I look while Sean looks so animated.

I don't suppose he realizes quite how much his visit has done for our image. At the tube station next morning the newspaper-seller is all smiles – he wants to talk about Kevin Keegan. When our pupils go into local shops where they're usually treated with suspicion, the assistants want to know if they've spoken to Kevin. It feels like a turning point for St George's in the local community. I think people decide the school can't be such a bad place if Kevin Keegan wants to visit, and that does wonders for the children's self-esteem, for which I'll be eternally grateful to him.

Their written comments afterwards bear this out. A lot of the boys, of course, talk about the soccer tips he's given them, but quite a few have taken in a broader message. 'I learnt from Kevin Keegan to co-operate with others. If everyone co-operated the world would be better.' 'Kevin Keegan said start young and keep going for your goals. I think he's right.'

Of course, you can't satisfy everyone: 'It was nice he came, but I wish he had brought David Beckham,' one girl wrote.

Today is also the day of the Spring Showcase. We decide that Tracey will go to the performance and report back while Sean and I will patrol outside – last time apparently some children from another school got in and rampaged through the building. It's not exactly all right on the night. Tracey feels the presentation doesn't match the children's talents, perhaps because of all the previous disruption, and at the end three girls who have been told they can't perform their dance simply take over the stage and do it anyway, egged on by the boys who are in charge of the lights and the music. 'They hijacked the show,' Tracey tells us afterwards, outraged that they could dare do such a thing.

But what was really encouraging was the number of parents who came, obviously keen to support their children. The hall was packed.

Friday 14 April. The last day of the spring term. We've been at St George's now for six weeks, though to me it feels like a lifetime. There's the kind of cheerful 'school's out' feeling that you get in any normal school on the last day of term. I can feel it in assembly and in the corridors, and in the little snatches of excited chatter I overhear.

We've decided to send out a regular newsletter to families and I'm pleased at the look of our first attempt. The fast-track graduate whom I've managed to get seconded to the office by the DFEE has helped us put it together. As well as keeping them in touch with news, I want to communicate to the families my genuine feelings of optimism. 'In a few weeks the new Deputy Heads and I have taken the children of St George's School to our hearts. We find your sons and daughters open and delightful young people who are full of ideas about their learning and their futures. We intend, with the staff, to do all in our power to give them the best education possible,' I write, and I really mean it.

Term ends with a reflective service conducted by Father George, which includes everyone and draws us all together. As the children leave, Sean, Tracey and I stand at the gates handing out a mini Easter egg to each of them and taking the opportunity to remind them all of the date they're due back. As they saunter off in groups down Lanark Road some of them wave cheerfully to me, and I wave too. Then, as the last one disappears, I turn and go back into the empty school.

3

Easter

Though at least my alarm doesn't go off at 5.30, I'm still awake scarcely later on the first day of the Easter holidays, my mind racing like an engine out of gear as I lie watching the day gradually brighten behind the curtains. Finally I get up, put on the coffee and for once William and I are able to linger a little longer over breakfast. He knows that all this is for a limited period, and he's good at compartmentalizing things, but from time to time I catch a look of exasperation on his face as I arrive home with a briefcase full of paperwork, or when I say I'm really too tired to join him for some function he has to attend.

The family, too, are getting restive. 'You won't be working over the Easter weekend will you?' Nadine phones rather pressingly to ask. 'The children have hardly seen you lately, and they keep asking whether you'll be here for the Easter egg hunt.'

Sean, Tracey and I have decided that we'll have to go into school over the holidays to tackle the mounds of accumulated paperwork, but we've resolved not to go in till mid-morning, and to leave by five. Before leaving the flat on Monday I have an edgy conversation with Nord Anglia, the business consultants who were involved in recruiting me for St George's and negotiating Sean's and Tracey's release from Douay, for which I was very grateful. After we've been at St George's for half a term, the two of them still have no contracts. My relations with Nord Anglia, whose brief is to monitor the school on behalf of the LEA, are somewhat tense. I have no anxieties about being monitored, but as I pointed out to their consultant when she raised the topic of an exchange between a teacher and a pupil, it is better that I deal with such matters. We have a professional structure for dealing with these situations, and that is up to my staff and me. I suppose we're all of us so anxious to do our best for the school that these tensions are understandable.

How I begin to long for the kind of understanding I got from good Inspectors and LEA officers during my early days at Douay. I have a nostalgic vision of my first LEA Advisor, Judith Wade – tall, humorous and friendly, perched on the edge of a table, nursing a mug of coffee as she listened patiently to my worries. How I could do with her now. And with Denis Felsenstein, a brilliant Inspector in the ILEA who understood children and teachers – he made a huge impact on my thinking.

Walking into St George's lifts my spirits – it feels so alive and cheerful, quite unlike the ghost school we first saw six weeks ago. I run into a number of Year 11s in the corridors who are in for GCSE revision classes organized by the staff. There's the sound of hammering coming from upstairs, where contractors are ripping up the disgusting sticky carpets from the corridors and fitting lovely thick green vinyl flooring, and everywhere there's an invigorating smell of fresh paint.

I find my office transformed. Over the weekend Mick and Francisco have painted the walls a pale sunshine yellow, and now they're at work on the school office. After much discussion the office staff have chosen pinky purple for the walls, which we're going to set off with a purple carpet and – I hope – plenty of plants. I'm a great believer in the beneficial effect of plants, and by the time I left Douay there was one on every staff desk.

Putting my head round the door of the French room, where a revision class is in progress, I'm struck by how lively and business-like it feels. The sun streams in on to the big new whiteboard the teacher is using and the walls are busy with attractive French posters, lists of French phrases and information about everyday life in France.

I've been delighted, too, these past few weeks, to see how well the children are treating the playground. Interestingly, vandalism is not a problem at St George's, but when we first came there was often litter left lying in the playground after breaks. Since we put in the plants and tables and basketball nets, though, the children have begun to think of it as 'their' space.

On the whole, as I take a break in my freshly decorated office, I feel optimistic. We now have some key members of staff in place, in particular Father George, David Hearn, a really dedicated and cheerful geographer I spotted quite early on who has become our curriculum development manager, and of course Ariadne.

Ariadne has been invaluable to us in the process of getting to know St George's, but I'm not unaware of the difficulty of her position. As teacher governor she's caught somewhere between the Task Force and the staff, some of whom, I suspect, give her a hard time for supporting us. She's a model colleague, never afraid to speak her mind, but always sensitive and tactful. Among her many talents she's a computer whizz and she's stayed late night after night with Sean, helping him sort out the attendance figures. But I do worry about her. There's something quite fragile, even ethereal about Araidne and I sometimes catch a very strained look on her face.

In fact I think trouble comes only from a small group of teachers, who, for one reason or another, resent the new regime – they're the ones who don't meet my eye and turn and walk the other way when they see me coming. I like and admire most of the staff – a bonus for any head – and, after some initial uncertainty, I think most of them like me. There's a good atmosphere at our early morning briefings. We have a weekly newsletter, which forms the basis of the briefing, and we talk about the themes we're going to concentrate on each week, exchange news, and congratulate people who've been doing something interesting. This week we even had a laugh when all the Art Department turned up wearing pink and I told them not to sit next to David Hearn, who was wearing a bright yellow shirt.

Teaching is a subtle process, and you have to be relaxed and confident to do it. It's about understanding what is unique in each child and enabling that child to discover it. All my meetings with the staff, whether we discuss problems with discipline or new crockery for the staff room, are aimed at making them feel confident and cared for so that they can inspire and care for the children.

No, it's not the staff I'm worried about. It's the people who are officially supposed to support me – the Governors, the Diocese and the LEA. If I had five years instead of five terms, perhaps I might have time to be more tactful, but my experiences during these first few weeks have made me anxious as to whether some of the Governors are people I can take with me on this desperate mission to turn St George's round. A company that has failed completely needs a new board, and the same applies to a school.

Towards the end of March I phoned to ask for help from Bishop Vincent Nichols, then Chairman of the Education Board for Westminster Diocese. Sean, Tracey and I felt we needed a new governing body to complement the Task Force and its new vision of the future for St George's School. The Bishop is an exceptionally able, good and charming man, but like many Churchmen I suspect finds it hard to deal with strong and determined women, and I think he sometimes finds me a trial. But since he suggested me for my present position I was hopeful that on this occasion he would respond to my cri de coeur. His response, however, was that it would 'surely be unwise' to 'undermine' the Diocesan Education Officer. What on earth did that mean? Bishops are supposed to give wise counsel, I grumbled aloud to myself.

'It's like the Mad Hatter's Tea Party,' I said to William as I put the phone down, fuming. 'I need help, but I can't make the people who count understand me. If there's some other agenda, why don't they tell me, like adults?'

I worry away at the situation over the Easter weekend. Did I misunderstand? Why does it have to be so difficult to make these changes? We go through the lovely familiar rituals – church on

Maundy Thursday and Good Friday, Mass on Easter Day in a church fragrant with spring flowers, Easter family lunch and an egg hunt in Nadine's garden. We have a beautiful walk in the country and a visit to a bird sanctuary.

I look at my grandchildren, so loved and happy, with so much interest in their lives, and I think of some of my St George's children – Rachel alone in her bed and breakfast room, Debbie looking after her brother and sister, Rory hiding behind his collar for fear of what he might see. School really is the one chance they've got, and I know we must get it right. We owe it to them.

4

Having a Ball

Summer Term, 2 May to 21 July

' 'Allo Meeze!' I'm struggling up the stairs, clutching my heavy briefcase in one hand and trying to hold down my skirt with the other in the teeth of the wind that funnels endlessly through Maida Vale Tube station, when I hear a cheerful voice. A little brown hand pats my arm, and I'm greeted by a toothy smile.

'See Meeze, no bad hat.' It's Ali, a diminutive thirteen-year-old from Eritrea, who has been in trouble for refusing to take off his battered grey and black baseball cap in school. Over the holidays he has obviously decided to toe the school line, a momentous decision he urgently wants to share with me.

'Ali good boy. No bad t'ings now.'

'That's good Ali. Well done. You look much smarter,' I say with an encouraging smile as I continue to battle with my unruly skirt.

We carry on up the iron stairs together. At the top I catch the eye of the newspaper-seller who is also battling with the wind.

'This is Ali, he's a good boy,' I say emphatically, and the news-vendor nods his head in a not unfriendly fashion – an indication, I think, that St George's stock has gone up in these parts.

'Me nice, me good,' Ali continues with a sideways glance at the display of sweets and chewing gum. Before he gets any ideas I walk him briskly out of the station, calling cheerfully 'See you this evening' to our shivering friend behind the stall. I always feel guilty because I buy the international newspapers we have available in the atrium from one of the larger suppliers, although Sean and I buy our *Evening Standard*s from him each night.

'Did you enjoy your holiday Ali?' I ask as he lopes along beside me, looking up at me now and again with bright enquiring eyes. He doesn't answer.

'Nice holiday Ali?' I ask again, aware of his fragile grasp of English.

'No Meeze, no good. Ali him nuttin' do.'

'Never mind, we've got lots of interesting things for you in school this term,' I say. I'm about to list them, but Ali spots some friends and is off down Lanark Road.

I walk on, thinking about Ali's Easter holiday, remembering the look in his eyes when he saw the sweet stall, and wondering whether he's had any breakfast. It occurs to me that taking up Tracey's idea of providing breakfast in the cafeteria before school might be very helpful for children like him. Quite a few pupils arrive early now to kick a football around in the playground, or to meet friends, and all these things encourage them to arrive on time for school. I decide to speak to my ally Barbara.

As I pass the tower blocks that overlook the playground, I keep a wary eye out for falling missiles. I was narrowly missed by a bag of ice cubes dropped by some kind resident one morning last term, and one young teacher arrived back in school after the lunch break covered in an orange powder that had been thrown down on him from above. I was concerned about what it might be, but it turned out to be only a sticky powdered drink. Urban myths abound about freezers and televisions being hefted out of the windows in this road.

Sean is in the atrium, pinning up some notices. Before Easter I felt concerned about Sean because he never spares himself and he looked worn out, but a few days of the golf he loves so much have clearly restored his usual boundless optimism, which is one of the things that most endears him to me. He tells me he and Dorothy have been doing some shopping for their wedding, which is fixed for July, and he beams as he mentions their plans.

Tracey also arrives looking refreshed and relaxed after a break in the sun with some of her many friends, and we adjourn to their office to talk. We've had eight staff resignations now, several of them expected, and Sean is concerned about recruiting staff for a school that he feels won't be top of anyone's list, though I try to seem more hopeful to keep our spirits up.

What I'm most worried about is attendance. It's improved slightly from the dire 70 per cent it was when we first arrived, but many of the children are still getting to school late, and even when pupils are here for registration it's no guarantee they'll remain in school. 'Education, Education, Education' was Tony Blair's election mantra, and 'Attendance, Attendance, Attendance' is mine. You can be offering the best education in the world, but it's meaningless if you can't get the pupils into school.

Over the holiday I've spent some time putting together a leaflet for staff on how to encourage good attendance, summarizing some of the recent research on truancy and absenteeism. One of the things that emerges is that it needs only a single factor – dislike of a particular teacher, failure to do a piece of homework, anxiety about a particular aspect of school life such as showering after PE – to make a child truant, but this doesn't mean that that child dislikes school in general. I emphasize the importance of welcoming children back into school after an absence, whatever their attendance record, and *never* greeting them with sarcastic remarks such as 'Well, well, look what the wind's blown in.'

'Do you remember Anna?' I ask Sean and Tracey as the three of us chew over the problem.

Anna was a sensitive eleven-year-old at The Douay Martyrs who had developed a phobia about school. She had a history of non-attendance stretching right back to her early primary school years. My instinctive solution was to ask Anna's mother to bring her in one day to meet me. When they arrived I showed Anna the library, and asked her to help me with cataloguing some books while her mother and I talked. She enjoyed this, while keeping her ear tuned to what we were saying I could see, since she was used to being the main topic of conversation at home. I kept my remarks deliberately bland as her mother and I had sorted out her programme on the telephone that morning.

Half an hour later, she was completely engrossed and very unwilling to leave. I told her she must go home now, but that she could come back for an hour later in the week to give me some more help. She came, and again she wanted to stay longer, but I refused. Gradually, hour by hour, we increased the amount of time she was in school, and I slowly introduced her to her form group and her classroom. In the end, she was begging me to allow her to stay all day, and in the end, graciously, I capitulated. Would that all absenteeism could be as satisfactorily solved as Anna's. It is proving to be a challenge.

An angry voice interrupts our conversation: 'You've gotta give me my mobile back Miss. You took it off me before the holidays and my dad's mad.' Stephan, a boy the teachers find troublesome, is glaring over the stable door. 'He says you don't have no business keeping it. He says if I don't get it back he's coming down here to sort you out. He's big, my dad,' he continues threateningly, his voice rising. 'An' he knows my rights, too . . .'

We all give Stephan a cool look. We have met so many Stephans before. Tracey swings round in her chair and says pleasantly: 'I know it's frustrating not to have your phone Stephan, but this isn't the way to deal with it. Go away and think about what you want to say, and come back when you've calmed down. I think that's best, don't you?'

'I think that's a very good idea,' I add, supporting Tracey. 'And when you come back I'd like to hear you say sorry, too. You know we don't put up with rudeness – and we're all rather busy so you've got exactly three minutes.'

There's a pause while Stephan gazes sulkily at his fingers. Yeah – OK,' he says finally, and slouches off, every inch of his six feet expressing frustration and resentment.

Mobile phones are a big bone of contention. Using them in school was banned before our time, but no one seems to have taken much notice and when we first arrived phones were ringing in lessons, and children were standing in the corridors making calls and coming into class late. I sympathize with parents who want their children to have mobiles for safety reasons, but I insist they're turned off in school, and if they're not I confiscate. We have a safe full of phones – and a cupboard full of baseball caps, which were almost part of the uniform when I arrived. I don't like the kind of New York subway culture they represent, but when I banned them the boys grumbled and said their heads were cold and they'd get pneumonia, so I offered them the option of wearing neat woollen hats in dark colours. A few of them do, but I can see that the sartorial impact isn't the same, and they haven't really caught on. Nor has anyone developed pneumonia.

We're getting down to the figures again when there are more raised voices outside the door: 'You fat cow, my mum's not a slag . . .' Flushed and furious, Lucy and Jolene from Year 8 are confronting one another in the atrium. Jolene is trying to hit Lucy with her school bag while Lucy is ducking and shouting. As I step out to intervene I catch a superior look from one of the more experienced members of staff who glides past. 'Let's see what you're going to do about this, then,' I can almost hear him saying.

The girls stop when they see me. Somewhat wearily I rehearse my standard talk about manners, they manage to apologize to each other and to me with a bit of huffing and puffing, and go off to report to their form tutor. I return to my office and my PA, Suzie, a tall, calm, efficient red-haired graduate whose arrival has transformed my life, puts her head round the door to tell me the LEA is already on the line because we haven't yet faxed in our attendance figures. But we have. Another paperchase for me.

'Oh, *really* . . .' I say, exasperated. Suzie, whose calm response to trying situations is a perfect foil for mine, offers me a cup of coffee with a smile.

The summer term at St George's has begun.

At the first staff meeting the main topic of conversation is the Action Plan and how we will accomplish this term's tasks. Tracey talks about the pupils' learning and how to encourage good behaviour in class. Sean discusses the ways in which teachers will be challenged and supported and I outline the events of the coming half-term and how important they will be for the children. All staff are exhorted to help. We conclude with prayers for our success led by Father George, after our usual anguishing about attendance.

We're developing a many-pronged approach. Sean and Ariadne have now cracked the dreaded Bromcom system, and by 9.30 every morning we know precisely who is and who isn't in school. Wendy Kemal, our Welfare Assistant, who is the soul of tact, then calls the absentees' homes to discover whether there is a good reason for their absence – sometimes the parents don't even know about it – and if a child is away without a good reason for a second day Year Heads and Form Tutors will phone and talk to the pupil, and if necessary to the parents.

For more hardened cases Sean has composed one of his masterly letters – friendly and polite, but pulling no punches:

Dear Parent

It is with concern that I have to inform you that . . . . . was absent from class during Period . . . . . today without permission or an authorized pass. Your child has been told several times that the school's demand and your expectation is that students arrive promptly to lessons and focus upon their studies throughout the lesson.

Your child's casual approach to learning and attending lessons will not assist in achieving educational qualification and success. If your child is not in lessons then valuable learning opportunities are being wasted.

Please discuss this matter with your child and visit the school tomorrow with this letter to see a member of the Senior Management Team. This letter is placed in your child's file for future reference.

I do look forward to your support in this matter.

Mr S. Devlin, Deputy Headmaster

We're also in the process of appointing an Attendance Officer – the heavy gang – who will visit in cases where we don't manage to make an impact. But usually the threat of a letter home is enough – nobody wants to have their family called into school.

I make another suggestion for monitoring attendance and making sure children stay in the building. I propose that we should have a table in each corridor where a member of staff will always be sitting, marking or preparing work during free teaching periods. I know it's yet another demand for the staff to take on board, so I'm delighted when they agree.

It's not only the children's attendance I have to worry about. Several of the teaching staff are away sick after the holidays. 'Generalized anxiety' seems to be a popular reason, according to their doctors' certificates. I'm not sure what that is – surely it's the human condition? We take illness seriously, so if any of my staff are very run-down or exhausted or stressed, I'm the first person to encourage them to stay at home. But these absences cause huge administrative and financial problems. In one term alone the cost of arranging cover for absent staff at St George's ran into many thousands of pounds, and Sean spends hours on the phone arranging for supply teachers. So I pray that the anxiety might soon take a more specific form and be treatable, or even better, disappear altogether.

Despite the system of AKIA forms there are still some unexplained and unauthorized absences. Sean and I arrange to see the teachers concerned, inviting them to bring their union representative if they wish. These are sometimes fraught meetings, at which I stress the need to follow the correct procedures for absences. I express disappointment that they don't appear to be responding to the spirit of the discussion, and the reply is that they feel it is 'demeaning' or 'childish' to have to respond. I think it is simply professional.

These teachers tend to be the same staff who smile wryly at the 'refreshers' I work into the staff bulletin. We are having a big drive on literacy throughout the school, not just in English lessons, and it is useful to teachers of other subjects to be reminded of some of the basic rules. I don't think any less of a science teacher who has forgotten all about similes: we can all be forgetful about what we don't teach every day.

'I never did know when to use an apostrophe,' one young teacher tells me cheerfully, and I thank him for being so honest. It's a case of Tracey to the rescue.

I also include basic maths principles in the bulletins. 'We all need to refresh and revise things we learnt when we were at school – which in my case was a very long time ago,' I tell the staff. 'Literacy and numeracy are so vital, we should all be tackling them with the children at every opportunity.'

We all of us learn a great deal from Frances Hodge, a gifted young teacher who has come to us as Head of English as an Additional Language, a department that covers 60 per cent of our pupils. Tracey, who is taking a second set in English, asks Frances why a Slovak girl called Maia, who speaks no English at all, should be in her set: wouldn't she be better in Special Needs, learning to read English slowly? What can she possibly get out of listening to the class discussing a poem by Tennyson? Frances explains that Maia is bright, and will assimilate language from the rhythms of speech and the words on the page, combined with the extra teaching that Frances is giving her. It is wrong to treat her as a slow learner. At St George's everyone is on a steep learning curve including Sean, Tracey and myself.

'Stop, stop, I order you to stop.'

Mounting the stairs in search of Sean one morning, I'm astonished to see a teacher standing rigid in the middle of the first floor corridor holding up her hand like a traffic policeman, while a large angry boy continues to advance towards her until they are almost nose to nose.

'If you touch me it will be an assault!' the teacher almost screams at him. It's almost as if she is trying to provoke an incident.

'What is all this about?' I ask, going up to the young teacher.

Her explanation is one that is very familiar to Sean, Tracey and myself – she is anxious about doing a good job and frustrated that she can't.

'I asked him to write a report and I've been asking for weeks and weeks. He's got problems with his writing and I'm just fed up,' she tells me, her voice rising hysterically.

'Why didn't you ask him to tape the report?' I ask. I'm irritated at the approach she's adopted. I think it was that great headmaster Thring who said that the teacher's task is to shape himself to be 'the ward of the key that unlocks the child's mind', and here is a child with a whole universe of experience that he's being prevented from expressing because the teacher is not using what I call common sense.

Sean appears from the other direction, and I beckon him to the end of the corridor, bringing the boy with me and asking him to stand several feet away. 'Can you take this person away and explain to her that if someone can't write, there's an arrow in the pedagogic quiver that says "tape",' I say to him. 'Using it is called good teaching.' Sean can see I'm about to explode – he understands the shorthand.

When they've gone I speak to the boy. His lip is quivering. 'She told me my writing's a disgrace,' he tells me. 'I was so mad I ran out the classroom and slammed the door, and when I went back in to get my things she came out after me and started shouting.'

'Well, let's talk about other ways to deal with your frustration,' I say. I feel sympathy, too, for the teacher, who is also obviously frustrated as well as tired. I've read many staff memos about this boy's 'nuisance' activities. Looking at his records later Sean discovers he is dyslexic – a fact that the teacher must surely have known. It's a worrying episode that tells me there's still a huge job to be done in changing the attitudes of some of the staff. 'Never humiliate a student' is one of the first rules of good teaching, and 'Avoid confrontation' is another – messages we're trying to get across via leaflets and training days.

The incident also highlights the importance of providing teachers with accurate information about their classes. Knowing who is in your class sounds simple common sense, but it's extremely important, and it has been a problem at St George's because the data haven't been available. Without knowing about each child's particular needs – who should sit near the front because they wear glasses, who is dyslexic, who has behavioural difficulties, or speaks English as a second language – a teacher can't plan a different approach or learning material to suit each individual child.

Now Sean, Ariadne and our lively young science teacher Harvi have sorted out our data systems we shall be able to provide all this information. Teachers will have it in their mark books, and this will mean that they can plan lessons by analysing the learning aims and outcomes they want for each child, and working out the best ways of achieving them. Soon after we arrived Sean, Tracey and I went round writing on all the whiteboards: 'At the end of this lesson I shall know ... understand ... be able to ...', and these words are on the boards in every classroom as permanent reminders. At the end of each lesson teachers and children have a five-minute session in which they discuss whether these aims have been achieved. It may sound prescriptive, but for the present it is the only way of raising our standards. We must walk before we can run.

Most St George's parents, I've found, are extremely supportive of what we are trying to do, perhaps because many of them have arrived here from parts of the world where education is held in great respect, and they are anxious for their children to make a good start in a new country. But there's always the exception that proves the rule.

I've heard a lot about 'Jason's Mum', and on the third day of the summer term I meet this legendary figure, whose unseen presence I've been made aware of almost from the day I first arrived.

Jason himself isn't often in school, but when he is he makes himself felt. He's a handsome boy, tall and muscular, with black hair shaved in patterns and a truculent expression. If there's trouble in the playground, Jason's usually somewhere around with his gang. He has a bad record and has been temporarily excluded several times. He's extremely bright, but he's also manipulative and he can be very abusive. If he's ever in trouble, he rings his mum on his mobile and she's round like a shot. It was almost part of her weekly activities until we arrived.

I hear her now, before I see her. Bypassing the two children on reception, she's making for the school office, demanding in strong language to see one of the young teachers who has dared to tick Jason off. She's small and tanned, with short bleached hair and a lot of gold jewellery. Seeing her, I know that I must intervene. As Headmistress, it's my job to deal with the really difficult cases, and show the staff that I am there to support them.

'Why don't you come into my office and tell me what the problem is,' I say, steering her away from the two rather alarmed-looking Year 8s who are on reception duty.

'Yeah, it's about f—ing time we got a few f—ing things straight round here,' she flings back at me.

I give her a glare. 'Please do not use that language in my school,' I admonish.

Then, 'Would you like a cup of tea or coffee?' I ask, conscious that I'm sounding like Lady Bracknell. 'Suzie, would you mind making a cup of coffee for Mrs—'.

She looks at the proffered cup of coffee, her forehead wrinkling. I can almost hear her thinking 'What's all this, then?'

'What seems to be the problem about Jason?' I ask when we're sitting down.

She begins what can only be described as a rant about St George's staff and pupils and I know I have to interrupt. 'Mrs—, let us be clear,' I say. 'You did choose this school for Jason. Am I to assume from what you've said that it has failed in so many ways that you would like him to be transferred elsewhere? If so, I'm sure Miss O'Leary will be pleased to arrange it.'

I turn to Tracey, who is sitting in on the meeting. 'I believe we could have someone waiting for a place who would be delighted to have Jason's. Is that correct?' I say. Tracey nods vigorously. We both know it's a little like gamesmanship, but we also feel it would be a great pity to lose Jason, who has a lot of potential, and we believe is very much in need of our help. We want to keep him, so a bit of theatricality with his Mum is worth it.

'Na,' his mother says quickly. 'Na, I didn't mean that.'

'Then I think we should be very clear about the nature of St George's, of which we're very proud,' I continue. 'It is an inner city school and we have people of all nationalities. Everyone's equal here, and Jason has to accept the rules like everyone else. If he doesn't, then he's in trouble.'

'Yeah, but it's not fair because he f—ing gets picked on, don't he? Some of them others, them that's got no right to be in this f—ing country anyway, get away with anything. Don't suppose you'd f—ing dare to punish them. But my Jason, he can be in trouble for anything you f—ing choose.'

'I'm sorry, but if you continue to use that kind of language, I'm going to end this conversation,' I say evenly. She pauses for a moment, but I think she's hardly aware of the words she's using. No wonder Jason's so abusive.

'Jason was late for a lesson and when the teacher asked him the reason, he swore at her and she felt the language he used was racist,' I press on. 'We don't tolerate racism. As you know, it's against the law.'

She's completely unembarrassed. 'Well, everyfink's against the law now, innit? But 'e ain't a bad boy Jason,' she says suddenly, 'and 'e misses 'is Dad. Can't say I do – 'e deserves to be doing a stretch for what 'e done. I wish 'is step-dad could have taken to Jason, though. It's a real pity. They 'ate each uvver like poison.'

I get a little insight into Jason's world, and I feel sympathetically towards him. The complexities of our society mean that there are many children like him, trying to live with loss and with their parents' new relationships, struggling for attention by behaving in difficult and sometimes anti-social ways. But it won't help them if we tolerate their bad behaviour. And thank goodness they don't all have mums like Jason's, however much one might warm to her feisty approach. I've met many people like her before, and they usually end up being amenable.

Later in the day I have a conversation with Wayne, our community policeman. We agree that, though it may not be the case with Jason, children sometimes have no idea how offensively racist some of the words they use can sound, nor indeed that racist remarks are actually against the law. Wayne agrees to come in and talk to the school about it, and knowing him, I'm sure he'll do it in an extremely sensitive and effective way.

Great news! The Governors have agreed to contribute £3,500 for the May Ball from the Governors' Fund. Tickets are to be £10, which is quite a lot for some of the children, so we're going to quietly subsidize anyone who really can't afford it. I want the May Ball to be a lovely send-off for Year 11 before their exams, and I see it as a kind of thank-you to them for the warm and open way they've responded to the Task Force. They've genuinely tried to listen and to hear, and to adopt a completely new way of working. We want them to know that without their example the school would not have improved. And it has.

There's a wave of excitement building up about it. The Ball Committee has been meeting regularly after school, and everybody knows what's going on – in fact it's been a useful model for the younger children who are now very much into the idea of Year Committees and keen to be involved. It's also been useful in the campaign for good behaviour. 'I'm not sure if I can trust you to behave at the May Ball if you're going to be as silly as this . . .' is a line I've heard from both Ariadne and Sean.

The Ball is going to be held at the Hilton Metropole just down Edgware Road. The name has such a ring to it, and it's just the kind of large, rather glitzy modern hotel the children will enjoy. Sean and Ariadne have been to see the management, and they've been helpful. Sean and Ariadne inspire confidence when talking about the children, and I think they've also given the hotel the feeling that by hosting this they'll also be doing their bit for society.

'Would it be nice to have the starter served and then have a buffet?' I ask Year 11.

'Oh no Miss, the boys'll eat it all.'

So we've arranged that all four courses will be served, and they'll be seated at tables with their friends, with a teacher at every table. I've told them what the budget is, and they know we've got to work within it. The hotel has come up with a menu, and now the committee is discussing the music. I've suggested hopefully that we might at least have something nice and classical while we're dining.

The dress code we've decided on is dresses below the knee for the girls, and suits, shirts and ties for the boys, tuxedos if possible. We're going to have formal toasts – we've already discussed what's going to happen so there'll be no giggling. I want these children to know how to behave if they're faced with occasions like this when they go out into the world. I refuse to assume that this isn't going to be part of their experience. The world is their oyster too.

Talking of behaviour, I came out of my office the other day and saw a handsome young black man whom I took to be a friend of one of the pupils, standing casually in the atrium looking at the noticeboards. He was tall and rangy, casually dressed in a leather jacket and a baseball cap, and chewing gum.

It was on the tip of my tongue to tell him to take his cap off and throw away the gum when Nadine suddenly appeared from the staff room. 'Mum,' she said, 'this is Ray Fearon.'

'I'm delighted to meet you,' I said, laughing. 'I'm afraid I was just about to tell you to take off your cap and get rid of your gum.'

Ray grinned easily as he shook my hand. 'Don't worry,' he said, 'It wouldn't be the first time I've been ticked off in school!'

Ray, who is currently playing Othello at the Barbican to rave reviews, was wonderful with the group of stage-struck youngsters who'd signed up to meet him. He spoke a language they understood, and they could identify with him when he told them that he'd found school hard, and could easily have got caught up in a rough culture and a completely different way of life if it hadn't been for his passion for acting. He communicated the sheer thrill of acting Shakespeare and of working in a company like the RSC, but he also talked about the tough realities of being an actor, of having to find the courage, when you've been turned down for a part, to pick yourself up and carry on.

'If you're going to succeed you have to be very, very determined,' he told the children, 'and I hope you'll remember that, whatever you decide to do.'

'Well,' said Tracey afterwards. 'He was a real find, wasn't he? I think he's done more for Shakespeare in one day than I've done in a whole term.'

'Come now Miss O'Leary, you're being unnecessarily modest,' I tease her.

Nadine is working hard for the Distinguished Visitors Programme. She pins up displays in the atrium, announcing and describing new visitors, and she's getting a train of extremely interesting people into school. Richard Pearce, a London podiatrist, fascinates the children by showing them why athletes have to learn to walk properly in order to run faster, and gets them all practising. Khadija even decides she's going to consult him professionally – though perhaps not now, I suggest, and we both laugh.

His visit chimes well with our expanding sports programme. It's such an important part of the curriculum, especially in a school where we have a lot of big, athletic children with lots of energy to burn off. Up until now we've been more or less confined to our small playground with occasional visits to the Paddington Recreation Ground, but now, thanks to Eve and Sean, we're beginning to make more use of the Ground. Eve is thrilled at the idea that next year we might have a proper sports day, with high jump, track events and relay races, and Sean, who's interested in sport, as always is keen to help. For literary Tracey however, the thought of running round a sports ground with a tape measure is clearly very unappealing.

This term I've asked Lords Cricket Ground, which is just up the road in St John's Wood, if they will help us with some tickets. The ground is within walking distance of the school, but for our children, I realize, it's a world away. It's just part of my campaign to get the children connecting with the local community and taking advantage of what's going on around. So on a sunny May afternoon twenty excited children and two teachers set off to see England play Zimbabwe. Afterwards I receive a letter from eleven-year-old Leonard:

> Dear Headmistress, I was so excited because I have never been anywhere as big as Lords cricket ground before. Miss Churchward made us look after our own tickets and I took a lot of care of mine because I did not want to lose it. We took pictures and the trip was really good. Thank you headmistress for making it possible for us.

Perhaps even more thrilling, Kevin Keegan arranges for five of our youngsters to spend a day with the England Team at their training ground at Bisham Abbey. They arrive back tired and flushed with excitement, their shirts and trainers covered in autographs. Eve rushes into my office to tell me about it – 'Just brilliant. We met all the top players, and they were just great with the boys, Marie. I took lots of photographs and I was so pleased with the way the boys behaved.' Eve looks so endearingly young I could hug her.

I glow when I hear this kind of thing. In fact I'm beginning to collect quite a file of complimentary letters about our pupils. One group has made a short animated film as part of their art studies, and they and their teacher Tonya Frost are invited to a screening at the Odeon Leicester Square, along with pupils from four other Westminster Schools. A few days later a letter arrives from Ronnie Raymond-Cox, a former Lord Mayor, who was also at the screening. 'I travelled on the same train as your boys and girls and was favourably impressed with their behaviour en route, both in the underground and walking to the cinema,' he tells me. I shall read this letter out at Assembly and copy it all round the school.

I feel St George's isolation is gradually breaking down, and the school is beginning to be accepted back into the community. One really helpful element in this has been our local police. The two local constables Wayne and Laura often drop into the playground and chat to the children in a casual but encouraging way, telling them how pleased they are that behaviour is improving, or giving them a pep talk if something has gone wrong. Simon, another young constable based at Paddington Green, has also become something of a role model for the youngsters. In fact they're giving us the kind of support I still hope I'll get from the Governors and the Diocese.

'You're late again Rory,' Sean says, as Rory, hands thrust in pockets and face, as usual, hidden inside his collar, appears at the school gates half-an-hour after lessons have started. Rory's attendance is getting better but he hasn't quite mastered arriving on time, in spite of the new alarm clock.

'What's your excuse today?' Sean asks, pleasantly but firmly.

Rory mumbles something unintelligible and Sean notices a thin wisp of smoke emerging from inside his collar.

'What's happening Rory? You seem to be on fire,' he says.

A nicotine-stained hand emerges from Rory's pocket and plucks a smoking stub from inside his collar.

'It's my cigarette, sir,' he says with some embarrassment.

Sean struggles to keep a straight face. 'You know smoking's not allowed in school, so get rid of that please,' he says. 'And if you must do it outside school, do it outside your collar or you'll go up in flames one day. It would be much better for your health if you decided to give it up you know. There's a lot of useful information in the Welfare Room.' Rory grunts, but we can both see he's glazing over at the prospect of yet another anti-smoking talk.

I find myself thinking about Rory. These are his last two weeks at school – he won't be coming back to take GCSE's after half-term because, like quite a few Year 11s, he wasn't entered for any when the forms were filled in last year. Tracey tells me he lives with an elder sister and her boyfriend, but they've got problems of their own, and he's going out into the world like a lost soul, without a qualification to his name, as she puts it.

Knowing that he's interested in cars, Sean has approached the manager of a garage in Kilburn, and he's agreed to take Rory on for a fortnight's work experience, doing basic jobs like cleaning the forecourt and unloading supplies. There's just a possibility they might keep him on, but will he be able to get up in the morning? Perhaps working with cars will be enough of an incentive.

'Is Rory going to have proper supervision?' I ask Sean. 'I do want him to have the best chance. It could be a breakthrough for him.'

'There's a really sympathetic supervisor,' Sean tells me. 'I've been up to see him and so has Ariadne, and we both feel he's genuinely keen to do something for Rory. I must say, people's response to our work experience enquiries has been very encouraging. They really do seem to want to help.'

I know it's vitally important to help children like Rory early. This is one reason we're planning a Learning Support unit where children like him and Debbie can be taught for a while in small groups and helped with their learning skills and behavioural problems, then gradually reintegrated back into school. At least we've got a site for it – a rather indifferent-looking collection of school huts, now known as The Sanctuary, on the opposite side of Lanark Road. I'm not sure what went on there before we came but I gather it was where so-called 'troublesome children' were dealt with. Why it's called The Sanctuary I don't know either, but it sounds to me like a Health Spa, and we're renaming it St George's House. Francisco's been decorating there at weekends, we're applying to put in some toilets, and we've recruited Maeliosa, an enthusiastic teacher with an appealing Celtic lilt to her voice, to take charge.

Starting next month we'll also have the services of a counsellor called Ryan Lowe, who's being supplied by the Catholic Children's Society. She's from the Tavistock Clinic, and she'll be with us all day every Friday. I felt confident as soon as I met Ryan. She has a lovely open manner, and much experience of working with refugees and adolescents, and knows her way round all the relevant agencies and social services departments. We're having some leaflets printed for the children with Ryan's picture and information about how to make an appointment, making sure they understand that anything they tell her will be completely confidential.

With limited time available, she'll have to give priority to children who have really serious problems and may need long-term help, but we've also discussed setting up a group for girls who have difficulties managing their behaviour and getting on with other children.

'What's that child doing out in the playground?' I say to Sean one warm but streaming wet breaktime as I stand looking out of my open office window.

'She won't come in,' says Sean. 'I've tried to persuade her, but she says it's her own business if she wants to get soaked.'

'That's Alexa,' Tracey tells me. 'I know her. She's in another world – the only thing she seems to be interested in is an astrology book she carries round all the time.'

Tracey puts on her coat and goes out to where Alexa is standing, not far from my office window. Alexa is shivering, and she looks like a small soaked animal.

'Why are you standing out here Alexa?' I hear Tracey ask.

''s my business,' she says sullenly, the rain running down her face. 'You don't care anyway.'

'I do,' Tracey says. 'I don't want you to catch cold, and I have to think about health and safety. I can't leave you out here without a teacher to supervise you. The Head had her hair done yesterday – did you notice?'

'Yeah' – grudgingly.

'I don't think she'll be very pleased if I ask her to come and stand out here in the pouring rain. Now it wouldn't matter with Mr Devlin, would it, because he doesn't worry about getting his hair done.'

This makes Alexa burst out laughing in spite of herself, and eventually she agrees to come inside.

I read Tracey's face and I go out into the corridor. 'Alexa's come inside because she didn't want you to have to stand out in the rain with your nice new hairdo,' Tracey tells me as, apparently casually, we approach one another.

'Oh, that's very thoughtful of you Alexa,' I say. The ghost of a smile passes across Alexa's face. What we're both trying to do, of course, is to give her a sense that she is worthwhile. A little humour goes a long way in these situations, and so does praise.

When I spot Alexa a few days later with her head down on the desk during a French lesson, I remove her and take her to my office. She tells me she hates French and would rather learn Chinese – so I surprise her by showing her the few words of Chinese I know. This seems to engage her interest. After this we greet one another in Chinese when we pass in the corridor, and we agree with her teacher that she will come to my office during French periods and we'll explore ways of helping her to concentrate.

I ask her to do me a report on the revision guides we've compiled for the Year 11s. Her comments are intelligent and I thank her. Gradually we begin to build up some kind of a relationship – an experience I'm not sure Alexa has ever had – and Tracey tells me her concentration and her co-operation in class are improving. She even agrees to take an essay back and check it, whereas normally her work and her approach are careless and chaotic.

But Alexa has big problems at home and is very vulnerable. This kind of personal mentoring, which I do with a number of the children, can only begin to touch on her problems. She really needs the kind of professional help that I hope Ryan will be able to give.

*

'Miss! Look Miss! I've brought my dress in to show ya.' Carla, a gorgeous, leggy, Naomi Campbell lookalike from Year 11 is holding up what appears to be a red chiffon handkerchief for me to admire.

'T'riffic or no?' she says, pressing it against herself to give me the effect.

I can see now that the length isn't too bad, but the top . . . to say it's low-cut is an understatement – it's barely there and it has no visible means of support. 'That's a really beautiful colour,' I say cautiously. 'But you might be a bit cold. What about a pashmina or something to go over it?'

I'm aware that I'm sounding like a granny, but fortunately I'm saved by Tracey.

'I tell you what would look lovely with that – one of those embroidered Chinese-y shawls,' she says tactfully. 'It would just set it off. Do you know the kind? I think I bought one in Warehouse. I might lend it to you.'

Preparations for the Ball have reached fever pitch. A few of the girls have made their own outfits, but most have been off on weekend shopping expeditions with their friends. The Year 11 common room has begun to look like a beauty salon during lunch hours. They're all in there experimenting, taking it in turns to sit with mirrors propped up in front of them while their friends apply makeup or put their hair up in elegant chignons and twists. Sometimes I hardly recognize the schoolgirls I know, they suddenly look so much older and more sophisticated.

The boys are also sorting out what they'll wear in a slightly less excitable way. Some of them are borrowing smart suits from elder brothers, some are buying them, some are hiring dinner jackets. One boy tells me his mother has given him the money to buy a new suit, but it's his next birthday and Christmas present rolled into one.

To keep their eye on another kind of ball – the GCSEs they're about to take – we've issued all Year 11s with a revision guide. Every subject head has contributed, outlining what revision is needed and suggesting revision techniques. There are hints from Sean on coping with exam stress and a lot of common sense advice from me about getting a good night's sleep before the exam, not eating too much junk food, revising systematically, ignoring friends who tell you there is no need to revise, and reading the questions properly.

We've called the guide *Countdown to Exam Success*, 'and *Success* is what I'm expecting,' I say to them confidently as I hand it out, though secretly I fear for them.

Tracey confided to me today that her cheeks ache with smiling, and she's exhausted with the effort of being relentlessly positive. I know what she means. I spend so much time complimenting the children on their hairstyles I think they must think I'm a frustrated stylist. Our natural approach is to reinforce good behaviour rather than criticize bad, but it's sometimes hard work at St George's.

In general, though, staff are catching on to the idea, and some of them are coming forward with very positive ideas. This week, for example, at the suggestion of Uvian Walters who teaches Maths, we've joined in with Westminster LEA's Black History Week. Uvian took on the organization of it all, and it really has been a most joyful experience. We've had presentations by the children about notable black people such as Martin Luther King and the Victorian nurse Mary Seacole, classroom displays, and some good singing and dancing. Afro-Caribbean food has been served in the staff room and the canteen to highlight the celebrations. I think it's been wonderful for our children of so many different nationalities to see everyone in the school celebrating something very precious and important to the black community. You could almost feel the self-esteem in the hall rising as you watched. Everyone gained from the experience.

Friday 26 May, the day of the May Ball and the last day before the half-term holiday, dawns clear and warm. The trees along Lanark

Road are a haze of new green leaves and as I walk to school, thinking about the evening, pictures float through my mind of other May Balls, the kind they have at Oxford and Cambridge colleges – champagne, long floating dresses, privileged under-graduates with all the opportunities in the world. I want my St George's children to taste at least a bit of that. I'm aware that a few of the staff think I'm snobbish, and giving 'these kids' ideas above their station, but I can live with that. What on earth is one's station anyway?

I'm in the middle of taking assembly when Sean appears in the doorway. 'Help!' he mouths at me.

The children start singing a hymn, and Sean comes to stand beside me.

'What is it?' I whisper.

'I've just heard Ariadne's left the building,' Sean hisses, 'and she says she's not coming back.'

'Why? I don't understand,' I whisper urgently. I can feel my pulse beginning to race. My first thought is that Ariadne must be ill. How on earth are we going to manage without her tonight . . .

As soon as assembly is over I walk unhurriedly back to my office, determined not to show my anxiety to anyone who may be watching. I find Sean waiting for me – Tracey is on leave from school today, attending a close friend's wedding.

'What's happened?' I ask.

'When Ariadne came in this morning, she couldn't find any of the files and papers she keeps in the staff room,' says Sean. 'Francisco had bagged them all up in a black plastic bin-liner because he's going to be decorating in there over half-term. Not being able to find her files seems to have been the last straw. I suppose she could have gone off to look for them. I don't know.'

Sean and I sit down together to consider the situation.

'Ariadne's been working terribly long hours,' I say, 'and being a teacher governor must have put her under a lot of pressure, having to act as an interpreter between us and the staff. I'm worried that there are signals I haven't been picking up.'

Having a Ball

All morning I keep ringing her but there's no reply. As the day goes on I become more and more anxious. I phone her mother, but there is no reply from her either. Eventually Wendy, who is a good friend of Ariadne's, does manage to get hold of her, and spends a long time talking to her in an attempt to find out what is behind it all. At least we know that she's all right, but we still don't know whether she'll ever come back, let alone attend the ball. At lunchtime I send her a large bouquet of flowers with an affectionate message, urging her to come.

I get the feeling that a few of the staff are watching to see how I'm going to react to all this, but I refuse to let them see that I'm ruffled. 'What a pity Ariadne isn't feeling well, let's hope she's all right for tonight,' is all I say when the subject comes up at breaktime. I never give a clue, even by the movement of an eyebrow, that I suspect some staff may have been putting pressure on her, or that I'm concerned. It's another of those situations Tracey and I were talking about, when you know you've just got to smile, smile, smile, though inwardly I feel upset at the sheer unpleasantness of it all.

Things get even worse. At the last check yesterday thirteen members of staff, plus Sean and myself, had signed up to come to the May Ball, but when Sean does a final after-lunch check, it seems that he and I and David Edwards, the third Deputy Head, are now the only ones able to make it. Everyone else suddenly can't come. Maybe there has been some discussion with the union representatives. In the end three more agree to come. So now we have six staff to supervise more than fifty over-excited youngsters, which is simply not enough. It's beginning to look as if we may have to cancel the ball.

At five o'clock, desperate at the thought of the disappointment this is going to cause, I suddenly feel I am back at The Douay Martyrs battling with staff to try to make them see that the children's interests are not being served by their actions. Sean goes to the staff room and struggles to change the minds of the teachers who have refused to come to the ball. He returns to my office half an hour later, unsuccessful.

'OK, I've been here before,' I think. I stride into the staff room and ask those who are coming to the ball to leave. They do so, apart from one of the union reps, looking bemused. I start off reasonably, but it's clear that this approach is not working. Soon I'm in a fury. I feel the children could be used as pawns, and tell the teachers in no uncertain terms what I believe our obligations are as Catholics, and what it means to be a Catholic teacher. They repeat that they have no intention of going to the ball. 'You can't force us to go', one of them says, and of course he's right.

We then progress to further home truths. It's clear that the Task Force is not liked by some of the staff, who I believe are trying to build a like-minded nucleus around them. Nothing I say has any effect, but I return to my office feeling better for having got a few things off my chest. However, I'm no nearer to having enough staff for the ball. By now it's getting on for six, Year 11 are at home in a flurry of excitement getting changed, the ball starts at 6.30, and I haven't even thought about getting ready.

Then I have a brainwave: Nadine and Fiona are both qualified teachers. That would make eight, which I'll check would cover us legally. My voice is hoarse with anxiety when I get through to Fiona: 'Can you stick on something glamorous and get down to the Metropole Hilton. *Now!* We've got a staffing crisis, so I need your help. I'll explain later.' As usual they both respond brilliantly, Nadine saying she's sure she can get a friend to babysit, and she'll be along right away. Meantime I'll contact the Chairman of Governors.

Fortunately Sean has his dinner jacket in school, so he changes and goes straight off to the hotel. I hail a cab in Maida Vale and dash home, fuming at the heavy traffic, where I grab the first outfit that comes to hand – no time to shower or do my make-up – while William is out in the street trying to flag down a taxi in the rain.

As I flop back in it, panting, my heart going like a hammer, I catch sight of my reflection in the window. I see a weary-looking woman with a lined face, her hair slightly awry, dressed in a dreary pink suit that does absolutely nothing for her. I couldn't feel less glamorous, but who cares? Nobody's going to be looking at me. It's the children's big night. I close my eyes, take deep breaths, and try unsuccessfully to put the traumatic day behind me.

I walk into the ballroom at the Metropole and I know the agony of the past few hours has been worthwhile. It's an impressively large room, and tables with starched white cloths have been set out round the edge, charmingly laid and decorated with candles and posies of flowers. Lights reflect in polished glass and glistening silver, and waiters are circulating with trays of soft drinks, offering them with impeccable formality to the slightly awed groups of children standing politely around.

As for the children themselves, the girls look like exotic birds, with plumage ranging through all the colours of the rainbow. Some are street smart, and some are in traditional full-length evening dresses, but they all look stunning. Some of the boys are in dinner jackets, some in lounge suits, and there are some interesting variations, including a polo neck under an elegant white jacket. They certainly know how to wear clothes, these boys, and everyone's made an effort. Even the 'too-cool-for-school' youngsters are walking around beaming. I go from group to group, complimenting them. 'It's just like in a film isn't it Miss?' one of the girls says to me, looking round.

We sit down to a delicious dinner, with a main course of marinated leg of lamb, followed by a mouth-watering pudding of raspberry mousse with a strawberry coulis. Everyone behaves beautifully – I catch Fiona's eye as she chats to Carla of the red chiffon dress, and Carla gives me a smile and a thumbs-up. She hasn't taken Tracey's hint, I note, but who cares – everything's wonderful and exhaustion is beginning to make me feel a bit lightheaded.

When we reach the coffee and petit-fours Sean, who is a natural with the gavel, rises to propose the toasts. We have a loyal toast to the Queen, and a toast to the school, and one to the pupils' future

– Sean mentions them all individually. I'm suddenly aware of how much we're missing Ariadne who knows every child so well, and would have given Sean something very special to say about each of them.

Then it's time for the head boy and I to take the floor for the first dance. I admire the panache with which he deals with the situation, and we get round the floor to an old-fashioned waltz without mishap. The children have agreed that, since this is a formal occasion, some of the dances will be traditional, but before long things loosen up, and they're bopping away to their favourite Garage while Sean and I take a welcome breather. A photographer we used to use at Douay has agreed to do the photographs for very little, and he circulates, taking pictures.

'Do you come here all the time Lady Stubbs?' one boy asks me politely.

'No, I don't think I've ever been in this hotel before,' I reply.

'Oh, I thought it was the kind of place lords and ladies would come to every day,' he says, and I think how disarmingly honest and open these children are.

There are no problems, apart from a little bit of over-enthusiastic travelling up and down in the glass lifts, but Nadine cleverly puts an end to it. 'Come on guys, be careful,' she says. 'There's someone important staying here tonight, and there are plain clothes policemen everywhere. We don't want any of you arrested for suspicious behaviour.' She says later, with a twinkle in her eye: 'I just assumed there would be Mum.'

The Deputy Manager is charmed by the children and tells Sean that he simply can't believe these are pupils from the 'dreadful' school he has read so much about. At the end of the evening the teenagers all crowd round us as we stand outside in the drizzle that has begun to fall again, thanking us in such a warm and genuine way that I feel I'm going to cry. But I keep smiling, and hope they'll never know what went on behind the scenes, or how nearly this evening didn't happen. Seeing them disappear, talking and laughing in their twos and threes, I know that the trauma of the past twelve hours has all been worth it. I'm beyond being tired when I finally collapse into bed.

Over half-term I'm utterly drained, barely able to drag myself around. I feel feverish and predictably I develop a terrible cold. William looks at me and shakes his head. He's sympathetic up to a point, but I can tell his look is saying: 'Well Marie, you've got yourself into this, and I'm sure you can get yourself out of it.'

Steve does my hair, and he cheers me up with his mixture of humour, sympathy and common sense. I've found that some of the support I appreciate most comes from warm, human people like Steve, and Francisco, and John, the car park attendant at the flat, who are genuinely interested in what I'm trying to do to help the children. Simon, Wayne and Laura, our young local police constables, also give me terrific support and so, though they probably don't realize it, do the smiling Iranian ladies at Persis, the little beauty salon round the corner from the school.

I spotted Persis on my way out of Maida Vale station during my first week at St George's, and I sometimes drop in there before an evening meeting to try to repair the ravages of the day. Sean, Tracey and I all have our own brand of therapy. Tracey tends to lose herself in a book, Sean goes for a walk, and I go to Persis. It's cosy rather than smart, and after a day at school, I find it a pleasure to sit back in the feminine atmosphere and let the charming, graceful Iranian ladies, with their long dark hair and manicured nails, smooth my problems away for a while. They don't speak English very well, but they instinctively seem to understand what I need. It's a little oasis and I always come out feeling ready to face whatever's in front of me, whether it's a business appointment, a Governors' meeting, or a parents' evening. I feel very strongly that a Headmistress should always look fresh rather than dropping from exhaustion, so my occasional visits to Persis are important. 'Well, I must go and prepare myself for the Harem,' I sometimes joke to Sean and Tracey as I set off.

'Have you got an Action Plan for that too?' Sean asks with a grin.

On the Tuesday of half-term I feel somewhat recovered, and go into school. Sean and Tracey are there already. Sean tells me he's spoken to Ariadne.

'How is she?' I ask anxiously. 'Is she coming back next week?'

'I don't know, and I honestly don't think she does either,' says Sean. 'I'm not sure she even realizes how exhausted she is. She makes such huge demands on herself.'

'I do have a sense that something's been going on,' I say, 'that she's been under some kind of pressure.'

'She still is,' says Sean. 'I'm not the only person who's been in touch with her you know. I can't believe that any of our colleagues would sink to such depths . . .'

Nor can I. All change is difficult, and the goodwill of the dispirited, bewildered staff at St George's, who have had constant struggles and a poor press, must be exhausted. Sean, Tracey and I were certainly prepared to be unpopular, but I don't think any of us were expecting this. And on top of it all, we've got a full monitoring inspection from Ofsted coming up in less than two weeks. We're well on target with the Action Plan, but I'm not looking forward to having to present a cheerful and united front to Graham Ranger.

I sigh heavily as I sit down to my paperwork. On my office noticeboard I have a copy of a prayer written for Father George by a girl called Sara in Year 9. He and I liked it so much that I had it printed as a poster.

Teach me Lord
Teach me things I should know
The things that are good for my life
To develop my talents and gifts
The gifts that you gave me for good use in your world

Help me when things are difficult
When I'm tired and confused
When I don't understand or when I'm in trouble. Amen.

Sara's simple and moving prayer expresses my feelings at this moment.

At least there's one bit of cheerful news the following Monday.

'Ariadne's back,' Tracey tells me.

I go to find her and bring her back to my office. She wants to apologize, but I won't hear of it. She looks thin and drawn, but quietly determined.

I don't want to make things even more difficult for her, but we talk a little and agree that she mustn't give in to this harassment. At least it's out in the open now. 'We all need you Ariadne,' I tell her, suppressing an impulse to give her a hug. 'You're a wonderful colleague and a wonderful teacher. We couldn't keep going without you.'

It's time for the staff briefing, and Sean, Tracey, Ariadne and I go in together, making a very clear point. You could cut the atmosphere in the hall with a knife. Father George has clearly given some thought to today's reflection, which is based on the Apostle Nicodemus's question to Jesus: 'How can there be rebirth for a grown man?' and Jesus's answer, giving the Apostles a dynamic force to replace cowardice and self-recrimination.

I too have given this encounter some thought. 'It's good to see all of you back,' I say warmly, 'and I hope you've had a very enjoyable break.' After the usual notices, Action Plan briefing and Ofsted update I add, 'I'm sure you'll be pleased to hear that the May Ball was a tremendous success. The children had a wonderful time. They looked stunning and they all behaved beautifully – in fact we had numerous compliments from the hotel staff, who told me they were a real credit to us and St George's. I'd like to thank those of you who came to help, and I'd also like to say to those of you who didn't that I'm sure you felt you had good reasons for not doing so. Only you will know what these are. In the final reckoning we are all accountable for what we do to a higher authority even than Ofsted.'

I know I'm sailing a bit close to the wind, but I'm determined to prick their consciences and remind them of how badly they let the children down. Some of them have the grace to look abashed, and some can't meet my eye. One or two sit with their arms resolutely crossed, staring at the ceiling.

The briefing is quickly over, but the topic of the May Ball runs and runs. The Year 11s are in and out of school to sit their exams and they buttonhole Sean whenever they see him.

'Sir, have you got the photos yet sir?'

'Sir, when are the pictures coming?'

When the photographs do arrive later in the week we waste no time in putting them up in the atrium, and there's always a group in front of them, laughing and teasing one another like any happy, normal group of teenagers. It's not just the Year 11s who crowd round either. The event has fascinated the whole school. The pictures of Sean and me tell the true story. Both of us look ten years older.

'STAFF QUIT AS HIT SQUAD FAILS TO TAME LAWRENCE SCHOOL.'

It's Sunday 11 June, the day before the Ofsted inspection. When I heard Sean's voice on the phone just after nine am I knew it meant trouble. We had an inkling that the *Sunday Times* was going to print something about St George's because they'd phoned Sean to ask about the number of staff who were officially resigning on Friday. But when I see the papers, it's even worse than I feared.

'St George's Roman Catholic School, whose head teacher Philip Lawrence was fatally stabbed in 1995, is embroiled in a new crisis,' I read. 'Nearly half the staff have quit or are on the verge of walking out amid bitter recriminations over a new hit squad aimed at improving the troubled comprehensive.'

An unnamed teacher is quoted as saying that the school is almost out of control, the children as rowdy as ever, and morale appalling. He (or she) claims that 15 out of the 35 teaching staff 'have said they won't be there next term and the fear is they'll eventually have to shut the school down.' Two teachers, the report claims, have independently confirmed the size of the staff exodus.

There is one paragraph aimed directly at me: 'Teachers at St George's have been particularly angered at the management tactics used by Stubbs. They say their workloads are almost unbearable and that in one meeting Stubbs warned them, when reflecting on their performance, to think about the final judgement at "the Pearly Gates".' I smile wryly at the last sentence. This could, I presume, be an allusion to our recent staff briefing and my comments about a 'higher authority'.

I suppose nothing should surprise me after what happened over the May Ball, but I'm astonished by the personalized nature of the attack. Who or what precisely is behind it, I wonder. It couldn't be professional jealousy? I can't believe that any of my staff would behave in such a way. Could the success of the May ball have upset some people? They can't want the school to close!

I suspect the intention of whoever has talked to the *Sunday Times* is to destabilize us – it can't be a coincidence that it's happened just before an Ofsted inspection. Perhaps I'm slightly naive, but I'm truly amazed. I'm prepared to acknowledge that I can be demanding and possibly eccentric, but surely it's obvious that we're trying to do the best possible job for the children. And isn't that what teaching is supposed to be about? After all, no teacher is a volunteer. We're all paid for by the taxpayer, and we're all accountable.

Looking for the friendly support that a Head expects from the Chairman of Governors I telephone Peter Clare, and am confused by his response. 'It was nothing to do with the Governors,' he says immediately. The thought has never crossed my mind, so I wonder what's happening. I have a sudden sense of blurred boundaries and tangled connections. Perhaps the arrival of the Task Force has caused reverberations at more levels than I've realized

141

because I've been so preoccupied with the children. I make a mental note to talk further with my Governors.

I refuse to let a newspaper story entirely ruin my weekend. The family rallies round: my daughters all phone, and William takes me out for a specially nice lunch, which cheers me. 'I'm just not going to let these people beat me,' I say through gritted teeth. He understands. We're both eldest children, and not easily bullied.

Next day when I get to school the first thing I notice is a big television van parked outside the playground. 'It's Newsroom South-East,' Sean tells me. 'They know Ofsted's coming today. They're here to film all the terrible goings-on in the playground they've read about in the *Sunday Times*.'

Despite the stress of the situation, we both manage to laugh.

The atmosphere in the hall at staff briefing is predictably tense, but I go in radiating confidence and enthusiasm. In fact I feel sorry for the majority of the staff, good people caught up in a territorial battle for the soul of St George's. After a few words about the inspection I say, quite casually, 'By the way, if anyone hasn't seen the *Sunday Times* article, I've asked Sean to put a copy up in the staff room. More of that anon.'

I can see they are watching me closely, and some of them are clearly astonished by my cheery manner. I think they probably wonder if I've taken leave of my senses. What's actually running through my head is something we used to say in Glasgow when I was a child: 'Wha daur meddle wi' me.'

*

When the two Inspectors, Graham Ranger and Margaret Williamson, arrive they are, as ever, pleasant and professional, saying little but clearly noting everything. I'm sure they must have read the *Sunday Times* article, but they don't mention it. They have, however, read the pre-inspection report I wrote last week.

'Whilst sympathetic to all the turmoil the teachers have experienced over this academic year, I am clear that my shift of emphasis from so-called disruptive pupils and "St George's problems" to a clear professional accountability scenario is not acceptable to a number of staff who are, in Anglo-Saxon terms, lazy and sloppy,' I wrote. 'I am convinced that to have a fresh start with a good number of new, committed staff allied to the teachers who will remain in September is a good thing.' Under the circumstances I feel vindicated.

We've received only the eight resignations. Some are for practical reasons, others are from staff who don't care for the new dispensation and might prefer to work in another kind of school. So who, I wonder, are the remaining seven mentioned by the *Sunday Times*? I wonder whether there is a campaign to get as many staff as possible to resign. After all, heads have seen teachers operate in that way before. 'If we get a lot of people to resign, it will be evidence of poor management.' What is cheering, however, is that we've received 80 applications for the posts we've advertised, an astonishing number at a time when most London schools are desperately struggling to recruit staff.

I've informed the Inspectors that a number of staff are absent. I've picked up on the grapevine that there is a protest against what they see as over-inspection. We've done our best to fill the teaching gaps, but this situation is yet another problem, and I'm on tenterhooks. I can barely sit still in my office. I keep checking, as unobtrusively as I can, on where the Inspectors are and how things are going.

Mrs Williamson strikes us all as a sensitive and reflective Inspector who is particularly interested in the Catholic life of the school. As it happens, the famous statue of Our Lady of Fatima is currently touring Britain and Father George has managed to arrange a visit to the school. The statue's arrival, accompanied by a uniformed guard of honour, is impressive, the story of Fatima is explained to the children, and there is a service in the chapel which Mrs Williamson attends. It all feels very natural, and I feel so glad that Catholicism is now an accepted part of life at St George's.

At the end of the second day we sit down with the two Inspectors. Perhaps I am only now really beginning to feel the effects of the past fortnight for I am unusually tense. I watch Graham Ranger, trying to anticipate what he's going to say as he arranges his papers unhurriedly on the table. When he does speak it's music to my ears. His report is extremely positive and entirely supportive of the approach we are taking.

I feel a surge of gratitude to the staff who've stuck by me and can't wait to get to the staff room to share the news. When I do there's an audible sigh of pleasure and relief, and Maeliosa rushes straight over and hugs me. I'm so moved by this warmth after all the hostility I've encountered that my eyes fill with tears. I've never been hugged so enthusiastically by a member of staff in all my 32 years as a teacher. Next day an enormous bouquet of spring flowers arrives. It's from the staff. 'Thank you for making St George's a success,' says the card. 'And thank you,' I think, 'for restoring my faith in human nature.' It confirms what I already knew – that it was only a few awkward people who must have inspired the *Sunday Times* article and that the majority of the staff are behind me.

I decide that it's time to go on the offensive. Since the day I came to St George's, requests from the media for interviews have been flooding in. Normally I feel I have more important things to do, but now seems a tactical moment to take up a long-standing invitation from Margarette Driscoll of the *Sunday Times*.

Before the interview appears, however, we have an unannounced visit from another journalist. As I'm seeing the children out of school one afternoon I spot her outside the gates, talking to the children and parents. She tells me she is Rebecca Fowler of the *Daily Mail*, and she has obviously been brought here by Sunday's tales of doom and gloom. We have a brief conversation and I explain to her that eight resignations is not a significant number, especially as one teacher is leaving to get married, another to move closer to her parents, and two for promotion. As she says goodbye, I can tell that she's thinking hard.

When her piece appears the following Saturday it's both fair and friendly. She lists the criticisms that have been levelled at me, but in reply quotes the Chairman of Education for Westminster, Tim Joiner, for whose support I've already had reason to be grateful: 'When you're leading this sort of school, you have to lead from the front and be very visionary. You're the person on whom everyone relies. You want teachers on board who are fighting all the way with you. It separates those who want to be with you and those who don't very quickly.'

Altogether the picture she paints of St George's is warm and encouraging. One interview, however, with Mr and Mrs Ganlath, who decided last term to move their thirteen-year-old son Patrick to another school in September, makes me sad.

'It was very hard for us watching Patrick lose the opportunity of an education every day, before Lady Stubbs came,' Mrs Ganlath told Rebecca Fowler. 'They have only one chance, don't they? But at least it looks like the children who stay here are going to get the chance now. You can feel the difference, the change, the life coming back to the place.'

Yes, they have only one chance . . . it's that knowledge that drives me on.

Next day Margarette Driscoll's equally comforting piece appears in the *Sunday Times* under the upbeat headline 'FAILURE IS NOT AN OPTION'. She prints some lines I quoted that express another of my guiding principles:

> If thou of fortune be bereft
> And of thine earthly store be left
> Two loaves,
> Sell one, and with the dole
> Buy hyacinths to feed the soul.

What we're doing at St George's isn't just about getting off Special Measures or achieving a given set of Government targets. It's about richness and inspiration, about providing a true education in other words – not just loaves, which are essential of course, but hyacinths as well. I think today we're often in danger of confusing the two.

As I sit in church on Sunday morning, I tell myself that it's really not Christian to crow. But I can't deny the satisfaction with which I take in the weekend's cuttings to pin up on the staff noticeboard on Monday morning.

'Here's Marie, tottering in,' says Sean. He's referring to Rebecca Fowler's description of me.

'I'm sure she really wrote "teetering" – you know, the way Joan Collins might,' I say, laughing.

'As she totters outside on her high heels dressed in a smart red suit and full make-up,' ran Rebecca Fowler's piece, 'she brings unexpected glamour to her role and looks younger than her 60 years.'

I don't know about the unexpected glamour, but I certainly feel younger this morning than I did last week. It's as if all the recent ructions have cleared the air and shown us exactly where we stand. Certain staff are still absent on sick leave, which is draining our budget, and I wonder whether we're ever going to see them again. But the atmosphere among the rest of the staff has lightened, and so has the staff room itself, which has been redecorated over half-term. There's now a staff room committee chaired by Tonya, Maggie makes teas and coffees for the staff and Barbara provides hot snacks for them at lunchtime, her bacon rolls being particularly popular. Altogether I sense that people feel things are looking up.

We have a staff-training day planned for 20 June and I've decided that instead of having it in school, we'll take up an invitation from the manager of the Commonwealth Club, Julian Malone-Lee, to hold it in the more relaxed surroundings of the Royal Commonwealth Society in Whitehall. Julian is the brother of Kevin Malone-Lee, a gifted teacher and Tracey's predecessor as Head of English at Douay, who died suddenly and unexpectedly not long after she came to the school. It is very poignant to see Julian again and I'm touched by his generosity in providing us not only with such a luxurious meeting-place, but also with a splendid free lunch.

The emphasis of the day is on challenging and exciting teaching, and being cosseted like this, away from the pressures of St George's, everyone can relax and share ideas. We have a laugh when I come up with one of my favourite metaphors for what we do as teachers – polderization – that extraordinary process perfected in the Netherlands whereby the wild sea is driven back and seedlings planted and nurtured in the mud to create more land. That is certainly how I see my work as Head.

I weave in a few more of my favourite quotes, including Keats' famous lines:

> Then felt I like some watcher of the skies
> When a new planet swims into his ken;
> Or like stout Cortez when with eagle eyes
> He star'd at the Pacific – and all his men
> Looked at each other with a wild surmise –
> Silent, upon a peak in Darien.

That, I tell the staff, is the excitement that the children should feel for at least some of each lesson. I call it the 'Eureka factor'.

I end with some words of Pope John Paul II: 'The educational capacity of every scholastic institution largely depends on the quality of the people who are part of it and, in particular, on the competence and dedication of its teachers.'

I hate educational jargon, and being an English teacher, I tend to talk to the staff in what I feel is a more lively and meaningful way. From their indulgent expressions, I can see that some of them think I'm slightly mad. But at these meetings I believe it is my function to provide the larger picture, to try to communicate the wonder and privilege we have as teachers of educating children, which I still feel after 32 years.

*

Peta is peering over my door again. I go on with the notes I'm making for the next Governors' meeting.

'I want to *speak* to you,' she says loudly.

'What is it Peta?' I say. 'Don't shout.'

I'm used to Peta's unannounced appearances, usually to deliver a lecture on some aspect of the school she finds unsatisfactory.

'The trouble with you is that you're too busy to pay attention to what I want to tell you,' Peta continues in her shrill, unconnected way.

'Why aren't you in class?'

'Because our teacher is supposed to be *ill* today, and I don't think the person who's coming to teach us is a proper teacher. I thought you were here to sort things out. I don't call this sorting things out.'

'Thank you for that,' I say. 'Now go back to your class Peta. I'm certain your teacher today will be fine. You can decide what you think after you've seen him.' Tracey appears out of her office, and under protest Peta returns to class.

Peta's anxiety level is always high, and she finds it hard to settle to anything. She's been diagnosed as hyperactive and prescribed Ritalin, but her mother doesn't want her to take it because of the possible side-effects. I understand why – it's a controversial drug and the jury is still out on it. But children like Peta are a real problem – quite unable to concentrate, disturbing to the rest of the class, and a great strain on our Special Needs resources. Peta is extremely bright but she's unable to get much out of school. I'd hate to see Ritalin routinely prescribed for behaviour problems, but I do seriously wonder if she wouldn't be better off taking it. It's a difficult choice for everyone concerned with her welfare.

'Excuse me. What do you think you're doing?'

As I round the corner of the corridor just after the start of lessons I almost collide with two girls. One of them, a large girl from Year 9 called Sherry, has Tina, another girl in the class, by her blazer lapels.

'Nothing Miss, just fooling around,' Sherry says, quickly letting go. I can see she's holding something in her other hand.

'Is that true?' I ask Tina, who nods mutely.

'Give me what you've got in your hand, please,' I say to Sherry. Reluctantly she opens her palm and hands over three pound coins.

'Are these yours?' I ask Tina, and again she nods, but she looks petrified.

I know about Sherry. Sean and I had her in a couple of weeks ago over another bullying incident, and I'm not going to let this pass. She and her little gang seem to have got the rest of their class where they want them. They're a bit like the Mafia – if you don't toe their line, life's not worth living – and their class teacher is concerned about the best way to deal with it.

Sherry's only fourteen, but even in school uniform she could pass for eighteen. She's a tall, well-developed girl, with cascades of fair hair and a raucous voice that carries across the playground, and she always has plenty of boys around her. She looks at me now from under her thickly mascaraed lashes with an expression that says 'OK, I dare you.' Tina I can see is easy prey – physically young for her age, with greasy hair drawn back in two slides, a quiet, conscientious girl who's only too anxious to please.

'Tina,' I say, handing her back the money, 'Go into class now, but I'd like to talk to you later. Sherry, come with me.'

Once in my office Sherry starts telling me some unconvincing story about Tina owing her money, but it quickly falls apart. When I ask her to imagine what it feels like to be bullied by someone bigger and to be frightened to come to school, she says nothing, but gazes sullenly back at me, winding a strand of hair round and round her finger.

I suspect that Sherry, like a lot of bullies, is really more frightened than frightening and as much in need of help as her victims, but meantime I have to do something to break her hold on the rest of the class. Tracey suggests adopting a strategy we sometimes successfully used at Douay – asking the offender's parent or carer to come and spend a day with them in school. Often the mere threat of such an embarrassment is enough.

Sherry's mother, I know, died when Sherry was at primary school, and she lives with her mother's sister, who has two small children of her own. I glimpsed the aunt one day when she was waiting in the parents' room – a thin, uneasy-looking young woman who was clearly cowed by being in school. Many parents, I think, have bad memories of their schooldays, and I try to make school as welcoming for them as possible. I've set aside a small room for them near my office, we've painted it and put in some nice chairs and a table and telephone and I always make sure there are things on the walls to interest them. When they come into school for an appointment, it's a place where they can wait in comfort and feel they have some control of the situation.

'Miss O'Leary and I have decided, Sherry,' I say evenly when she's summoned to my office again, 'to invite your aunt to come and spend a day in school with you. I'm sure she'd like to see how you behave in the classroom.'

Sherry, as usual, is fiddling with her hair, but she stops and regards me with some alarm.

'Whadda ya mean?' she says, looking straight at me for the first time.

'Speak politely please,' I say. 'Well, 'I think your aunt would want to know what you're getting up to in school. So this afternoon I'm going to phone her and suggest a day for her to come in. She can have lunch with you here too – there'll be no going out to McDonald's or Pizza Express. You can take her to the canteen.'

Sherry's face by now is a picture of dismay. 'Na,' she says quickly. 'She ain't got no time. And she ain't interested. And anyway – triumphantly – she ain't 'ome this afternoon.'

'Isn't,' I say automatically. 'I know she's very concerned about you, and I'm sure she'd be interested to spend the day going to lessons with you. I know she's very busy, so maybe we'll leave it this time. But Sherry, if I have any more reports about your behaviour, I'm going to phone her. Do you understand what I'm saying?'

Sherry regards me with obvious relief. 'Yeah,' she says finally, 'All right then.' But she tosses her hair defiantly as she leaves the room.

Our little encounter doesn't solve everything, but Sherry does seem to lose some of her power to petrify after this, and we have fewer complaints about her. I think word about my threat has got round and Sherry feels her street cred has been dented. She's also put on a special mentoring programme with Tracey, and starts catching up on school work. 'More Shakespeare, less mascara,' I tell her, and she has the good grace to smile.

A fortnight after the Inspection the written Ofsted report arrives. It confirms everything we have already been told, but it's great to have it in writing. The judgement is carefully weighed: 'The school has made reasonable progress since the last monitoring inspection, with good improvements in the ethos of the school and reasonable progress overall since being the subject of Special Measures.' What it means is that, for the first time in two years, St George's is moving in the right direction.

There is praise in the report for improvements in teaching standards, pupil behaviour, extra-curricular activities, the school environment, and in opportunities for staff development. I'm pleased, too, after the *Sunday Times* attack, that I'm seen to 'lead the school with a firm hand and a sense of urgency', and to be 'keenly supported by the senior management team'.

But one sentence in particular makes me glow: 'Most pupils are delightful and are willing to engage in polite discussion with adults,' says the report. Can these be the same 'kids' who were said to spit on Inspectors from the stairways?

I want the children, as well as the staff, to feel proud of their achievement, and I explain the report to each year group at a separate assembly. When I finish by saying; 'Well done all of you. Now we really are moving forward together, so let's keep at it', huge smiles of pride break out around the hall.

I also have large notices printed and put up around the school:

CONGRATULATIONS TO ALL PUPILS OF ST GEORGE'S
FOR AN EXCELLENT OFSTED REPORT. WELL DONE!
WE ARE MOVING FORWARD TOGETHER IN 2000

The Headmistress and teachers and support staff

The children aren't the only ones to get written congratulations. Knowing how keen I am on certificates of achievement for pupils, the staff have one made for me. It's a 'Certificate for Dedication to St George's' and all the staff who are in school sign it. It really is the icing on the cake, and I hang it on my office wall.

The BBC picks up on the Ofsted story and their education correspondent Mike Baker is seen touring the school in a glowing report on the nine o'clock news. He follows this up with a piece in the *Times Educational Supplement* in which he contrasts my 'old-fashioned' approach with that of Lenny Henry's laid-back headmaster in the series *Hope and Glory*. I'm rather bemused to be compared, later on in the piece, to Lady Thatcher whose 'extraordinary air of authority' I apparently share. 'If this quality could be bottled,' Mike Baker writes, 'the National College for School Leadership should prescribe it to all aspiring heads.' He's absolutely right, though, to say that I reject the 'superhead' label. I couldn't have achieved any of this without Sean and Tracey and all the other members of staff who have thrown themselves behind me. No Head is an island, and if I have a secret it is being able to recognize the special qualities in others and put them to good use. My staff have the skills I lack.

We also get coverage in the local and Diocesan press. The *Westminster Record* reports on the Inspection enthusiastically, though I read the last paragraph several times:

As Anthony Mackersie, Director of Schools Administration in the Westminster Diocese, writes: 'Notwithstanding the improvements that are clearly evident, if we are to justify the retention of the school as an essential part of Diocesan provision in Central London, we must be able to demonstrate support from the Catholic Community.

In other words, the school must start to recruit pupils from our Catholic primary schools.

There is something about the tone of these remarks that disturbs me. They feel like a Sword of Damocles hanging over us, and I hope, again, that the will to keep St George's open really is there among those who matter. Combined with some recent spats I have had with the Governors, and with one in particular over his general attitude, it leaves an unpleasant taste in my mouth. It seems to me that pomposity and a total lack of understanding of the bigger picture are poor qualifications for helping a school in crisis.

Of course Tony Mackersie is entirely right about the need to get the message about St George's through to the local community, and we have already set about it with a will, visiting primary schools, arranging an open day for prospective parents, and an induction day for next September's Year 7s during the second week in July. The school council is involved in the planning, and children from Year 9 take parents and children round the school in a polite and friendly way that makes me really proud of them. Afterwards I receive a letter from one of the parents whose daughter has attended the induction, ending: 'My daughter had feelings which I am pleased to say were emotionally and physically positive. She found your pupils friendly, helpful and full of positive information about your school. Having the experience of meeting the teachers, parents and some school pupils, this has left me feeling confident for my daughter to become a pupil of St George's RC School.'

*

'What on earth is that huge queue outside the hall?' I say to Ariadne one day after school. 'They're making such a noise it's giving me a headache.'

'Gillian's auditioning,' Ariadne replies.

Of course. No wonder the corridor looks like a scene from *Fame*. 'What kind of thing is it?' I said to Tracey when Gillian Rabie asked if she could put on a production of *Sister Act*.

'I can sort of remember the film,' said Tracey. 'Whoopie Goldberg's a cabaret singer from Reno or somewhere who hides out in a convent to get away from her gangster boyfriend. There's lots of singing and dancing.'

'Do you think it's suitable?'

'I'm not sure, but I know Gillian's done something like it before in South Africa. I'll ask if I can see the video.'

'It's fine, great,' Tracey reported back later. 'And Gillian's so terrific, if anyone can put on a high-standard production, she can.'

Gillian has really got dance going at St George's, and to a lot of the children it's as natural as breathing. Gillian has professional dancers coming into school to work with them, and the boys are as keen as the girls. We're getting quite used to seeing muscular-looking men in the atrium with ballet shoes strung rather incongruously around their necks.

Another glamorous figure who appears in the atrium this term is the actor Ralph Fiennes. There's been huge interest ever since we heard that he had agreed to visit, and by the time he arrives excitement among some of the female staff is on the Kevin Keegan scale, though they're suppressing it to appear cool.

'Did you see him in *The English Patient?*' one young teacher asks me. 'Wow!'

Ralph has been appearing in two Shakespeare plays at the Almeida Theatre in Islington, and as part of our Millennium Shakespeare celebrations I've asked him to come and share his thoughts about the relevance these plays can have for an inner city multi-ethnic group of twentieth-century teenagers like ours. I'm touched that he's come. He doesn't normally do school visits, his personal assistant tells me, but he's decided to make an exception for St George's.

He talks with wonderful conviction about his passion for Shakespeare, and the way he is constantly discovering new meanings in Shakespeare's words which have direct relevance to life today. I find him intelligent and diffident. Tracey tells me how struck she is by a girl called Lina, who sits absolutely still in the front row during the talk, entranced, leaning forward with her mouth slightly open, her eyes never leaving Ralph's face. We've found it hard to get Lina to settle to her work. She seems restless and anxious, owing perhaps to the fact that her mother is intending to split up the family and take Lina's younger siblings with her, leaving her more or less to fend for herself with a series of relatives. 'She's too aggressive,' she said to Tracey.

Never one to miss a positive press opportunity for the school to balance up the more negative stories, I've arranged for a photographer from the *Independent* to come along, and when we break for a cup of tea Ralph agrees to have a picture taken with some of the children. It appears next day and it's delightful. Nadine phones, and during the conversation she tells me to remind the children to buy a copy of the paper.

'Did you get the *Independent*?' I ask a group of them several days later. Some say they have, but some don't answer and one turns quickly away. 'I think they probably can't afford it,' says Wendy, who witnesses the exchange and who knows all the children well. 'Would you like one of these spare papers?' Tracey asks them tactfully, 'I bought some for our files and the Headmistress did the same, so now we've got too many.'

It's mid-July and the term is gradually winding down with outings and quizzes, and thoughts of the long summer ahead. I promised the children that before the end of term every one of them will have been on a school trip of some sort, and now we're making good the promise. Some of the older ones take the Eurostar to Calais, where they practise their French on a visit to a theme park and a hypermarket – both of which prove wildly popular. Some younger ones have a day out at the Millennium Dome, there's a trip to the Globe Theatre, and another to Chessington World of Adventures, from which they return babbling with excitement about the hair-raising Samurai ride. As for me, I feel a bit like Gregory Peck struggling through the desert in *The Purple Plain*. If I can just hold out a little longer I'll make it to the holidays.

When we come back it will be autumn and things will be different. For one thing, Sean will be a married man – he and Dorothy are getting married the week after we break up, and Tracey and I are looking forward to the wedding.

I'm hoping both Tracey and Ariadne will be under less pressure from September. We've filled practically all our vacancies, and there'll be a group of new young staff. It will be good to have a full staff room at last – teachers who are here because they really want to be. I haven't seen some of the staff who are leaving since they went off sick earlier in the term. I'm somewhat surprised when it becomes clear that they want to return to school for the last few days, which I feel would be pointless and disruptive for the children, and after some thought I write to them saying that I feel returning might be 'injurious to their fragile health', though they are welcome to collect any possessions out of school hours. The children have largely forgotten them and I can't see what they'd contribute to school when they're off somewhere else in September. Perhaps I'm unnecessarily suspicious, but their desire to return doesn't ring true to me.

I think of something George Bernard Shaw said: 'This is the true joy in life, the being used for a purpose recognized by yourself as a mighty one, the being a force of nature instead of a feverish little clod of ailments and grievances complaining that the world will not devote itself to making you happy.' Most of the staff seem to have decided that St George's is their 'mighty purpose'. We can do without the others!

*

'Miss, Miss, I'm gonna help with the play. Miss Rabie says I can,' an obviously excited Debbie informs me loudly as we come out of the last assembly.

'That's *great*,' I say. 'What are you going to help with?'

'Not sure yet, but Miss Rabie says there's ever such a lot to do – costumes and scenery and makeup and that. She says it's just as important as acting.'

Tracey found Debbie looking disconsolate one day because she'd missed the last audition, so had a quiet word with Gillian. It's probably just what Debbie needs, something co-operative where she has to work alongside other people and learn to keep quiet when necessary.

A school production, more outings, more exciting visitors – that's how I feel the school year should be, like a necklace hung with interesting events. These visitors of ours 'plant the golden seed' in children's imaginations, make them feel 'Maybe I can do that too' and I can't see why some people consider the idea snobbish. It's a dull school where there's nothing to look forward to. And even though I'm utterly exhausted – unheeled shoes, tired skin, lines under my eyes, hair crying out for Steve's magic touch, broken fingernails that I haven't had time to file – I realize, as I close my office door, that I am actually looking forward to next term.

5

Summer

A summer quiet has fallen on the city. The tube is almost empty, many of the big, wisteria-clad houses in Maida Vale have their shutters up, and the streets feel deserted on Monday as I walk from the station.

Sean is getting married at the end of this week, but he and Tracey are both in school. We spend the first few days wrestling with next term's timetable, and Sean does some frantic last-minute interviewing for the few posts we haven't yet filled. As I sit chewing over the pros and cons of starting school half-an-hour later next term, I keep thinking guiltily of Dorothy, managing all the last-minute preparations for the wedding on her own. She's the most capable person imaginable, with an astonishing ability to absorb and accept whatever comes along, but over these last few months she's seen sadly little of Sean, and when they have snatched time together, he's often been on the phone to me, discussing school.

'Shouldn't you be helping Dorothy?' I keep asking him, but he just laughs and keeps on with what he's doing.

By Thursday I decide to take a firm line. 'You are *not* coming in tomorrow,' I tell him. Go and get your hair cut, polish your shoes, do whatever you've got to do. But don't come into school.'

At the wedding on Saturday I can't help smiling when I see him at the front of the church surrounded by his brothers, so obviously happy as he waits for Dorothy to arrive. The organ swells and there is a small but unmistakable intake of breath as Dorothy, tall, beautiful and statuesque, appears at the back of the church and moves down the aisle. She is wearing a gorgeous satin dress and striking jewellery that sets off her dark skin and aristocratic bearing. Beside her and her Ugandan guests, resplendent in their national costume, the rest of us look somehow washed-out and insignificant.

I'm so happy to be here to see Sean and Dorothy take their vows. I think of all the small ways, as well as the big ones, in which Sean has supported me over the past two gruelling terms, and know that I shall never really be able to repay him. The whole St George's experience is intensely demanding and emotional because there is so much at stake – for the staff, for the three of us, for the parents, and above all for the children. It's their lives, their futures that are on the line, and what we're trying to do is about much more than just getting through an Inspection. When my contract ends next summer I want to leave someone in charge who can keep up the momentum we've started. Five terms isn't enough to bring about really deep change. That takes about five years – as long as it takes a child to go right through the school. Sean, to me, is the obvious choice. I know he's thinking about applying for the Headship, and how I hope he gets it. If he does I know Tracey will be happy to stay on, and for the school that would be invaluable. I glance at her tranquil profile, and think how immeasurably much I owe her too.

The reception at a nearby hotel is exhilarating. Guests have flown in not just from Uganda, but from Ireland and Taiwan, and there are several of our former colleagues from Douay, who are keen to hear about St George's. But this is Sean and Dorothy's day, so we answer as lightly as we can and steer the conversation away. After the reception a delighted Sean and Dorothy leave to fly to Mexico where, Sean tells me, they plan to lie on a beach and completely forget about St George's. 'Mind you do,' I laugh.

Some of Tracey's good friends are getting married this summer, so she's decided not to go away. As for me, I take off on 1 August for a fortnight in the Dordogne where we've rented a house, and where we're joined by the rest of the family. We try to do this every year. It's a chance for us all to get together and talk and get a bit fitter too. We share the cooking, and the children splash about in the pool. It's wonderfully comforting and relaxing. At St George's I can never relax, what with the press always on the alert and other not-so-friendly people watching my every move. I'm constantly tensed, waiting for the balloon to go up. But here, among the family, I can let down my guard completely for the first time in months. And now I've let go I feel as if I've been run over by a juggernaut and will never get up again.

Pick myself up I do, however. Term may be over but there's a lot going on at St George's over the summer and I pop in and out to keep an eye on things. All through the long warm days the sounds of banging and hammering ring across the school, accompanied by cheerful whistling and the blare of Radio 2. We've already done a lot of decorating, but Francisco is still hard at it with his paintbrush, and there's some other major work going on.

At Tracey's suggestion the Individual Learning and English as an Additional Language suites, where we give one-to-one help to children with special needs, are being moved from a Portakabin out in the playground to rooms off the atrium. We have so many of these children that it makes sense for the experts to be where the rest of the staff can easily reach them. It feels a much more friendly, buzzy environment now, with posters on the sunny yellow walls and plants, all chosen by Frances, and a widescreen TV.

The Art Department, which was on two floors, is being combined and completely transformed. We've knocked down a wall to make one huge bright studio, put in a special sink unit for silk screen printing, and other new equipment. It feels like an artistic wonderland. We've been advised here by two top class people, Charles Salter, an art inspector from Greenwich, and Dr Norman Binch, a former chief inspector. Norman is a friend from my Centre days, and I'll always be grateful to him for finding me a wonderful art teacher, Patience, who worked miracles with those challenging girls. Meantime the old art room is being turned into a computer suite, where youngsters can use the Internet during lessons and at lunchtime and really feel they are part of the twenty-first century.

The Technology Department is having a badly needed facelift. Unhappily our Head of Technology became ill before I arrived, and inevitably the department has suffered, though Hannah Sakyi has shown enormous commitment in keeping things going. But the facilities weren't good, and Technology had become a dreary area where children with nothing better to do would hang out and get into fights during breaks and lunchtimes. In September we'll have new staff for the department, and far better facilities. I'm excited that one of them – by coincidence called John McDonald, like the Canon – is also very keen to help us introduce rugby into the sports curriculum, which is something I've always wanted to do.

I'm particularly glad that Hannah Sakyi, who is in charge of Food Technology, will have well-motivated new colleagues to work with in the autumn. I noticed Hannah immediately I walked into our first staff meeting – a striking-looking black woman who sat quietly, looking focused and serene. Since then I've come to like and admire her greatly. She's a first-class teacher and she always looks enviably well-groomed and presented. 'Mrs Sakyi,' I sometimes say to her, 'would you kindly stop looking so centred and glamorous. You're making the rest of us feel inferior,' and this makes her laugh. She reminds me of Margaret Larkin at The Centre, one of the best food technology teachers I've ever met.

Sean is a particular fan of Hannah's – and her cooking. 'You do seem to be doing a lot of visiting in Mrs Sakyi's department,' I teased him the other day. Sean looked at me mischievously. 'She really does make great pizza,' he said.

I realize again, as I walk round watching things take shape, chatting to the contractors and to a cheery Francisco, how much I'm looking forward to working with a united staff and to welcoming the new teachers. Some of our best supply teachers are coming on to the permanent staff, and we have some very high quality new teachers, including some from Australia, New Zealand and the African continent.

Francisco has redecorated the school house in Lanark Road. It's really intended for the schoolkeeper and his family, but Mick prefers to live in his own home, and when I came the Governors were renting it to a part-time member of the office staff. She has left now and vacated the house though she's returned to the Governing body, so I've been able to take it over for a new member of staff who is moving to London.

The occupancy of the school house seems, unhappily, to be another bone of contention between me and some of the long-standing Governors. Ours has certainly been an uneasy relationship at times. Though most of the Governors are well-meaning people, I'm not convinced that they fully understand their own role. I find that some of them want to get involved on the telephone in the day-to-day minutiae of running the school, whereas their job is to look at the larger picture, the overall strategy. After all, this school has been in its death throes, with very little being done about it. I feel a number of them must have a limited perception of what a governing body in the twenty-first century is about. I worry about how distant they are from the children and the parents.

I also find some of their attitudes hard to take – one of them even questioned the mention of 'Gospel values' in the Mission Statement of this Catholic school. The Chairman of Finance was certainly helpful about releasing money from the Governors' Fund before the rest of our LEA funding came through, but that was as it should be. This money does, after all, belong to the school, and I feel I shouldn't have to beg for it.

However, I'm delighted that Canon John McDonald, who joined the Board last term, is now taking over as Chairman since Peter Clare is retiring on grounds of ill health. Canon John and I see eye to eye over most big issues. He's very much the kind of 'critical friend' that every head needs, and having been a social worker, he cares deeply about the children. He will be supported by Father

Leo, a local priest and a helpful Governor. We also have two new Governors who will be invaluable on the finance side: Peter Brown, a sympathetic, astute man with a great sense of humour who has been recommended by Father Kit at St Etheldreda's, and Sister Margaret Walshe, a splendid, thoughtful woman who is Bursar for her order, the Sacred Heart. We have excellent teacher governors too – Ariadne of course, and David Hearn. All these appointments should make a tremendous difference to the school and to my morale.

The twenty-fourth of August, the day of the GCSE results, dawns. I and a number of other staff are in early to share them with Year 11 who came in today. Predictably, they are not good. In fact by most standards they'd be regarded as appalling – only 12 per cent with five or more A*–C grades, when the national average is 50 per cent. By no means all pupils were entered for five or more subjects anyway, and a third of them aren't yet able to speak, read or write English fluently. And a surprising number of them haven't been in the school for the full two years before GCSE. Considering what these children have been up against it's remarkable that they've done as well as they have.

I see Ariadne with her arm round someone who is obviously crying, and feel a sudden surge of anger that this group have been so badly let down in the past. Ariadne herself always gets exceptionally good results from her classes, but I wish we'd been able to help Year 11 earlier on.

A few of the results are really cheering. Despite her language problem and all her other difficulties, little Somalian Rachel has five good grades and will be going on to sixth form college. So will Maia from Slovakia, who has decided to take A level Economics, Political History and Maths. And Miodrag from Kosovo, who also has five good GCSEs, will be able to take up a bursary to do A Levels at an independent school.

There's one more bit of good news. An analysis of attendance figures over the time we've been here shows that attendance is up to 80 per cent – a ten per cent increase from March. I share it with

Francisco, who feels genuinely involved in St George's struggle to improve.

'The children, now they like it here. You make school good place. That's why they come,' he says simply, wiping the sweat from his forehead with a paint-covered arm.

It's the greatest compliment anyone could have paid me.

6

Getting Our Act Together

Autumn Term, 4 September to 20 December

I always enjoy the start of a new school year. There's such a feeling of anticipation in the air, the crisp hint of autumn that takes me back to my childhood in Glasgow. This year I really can't wait to get back to school, and neither can Sean and Tracey. We all feel we've reached that crucial turning-point where the ship has swung away from the rocks and is beginning to move with the tide. All three of us have had a good break over the summer, especially Sean.

Walking into the first staff meeting of term and remembering my reception of two terms ago, I feel as if I've suddenly emerged from fog into bright sunshine. All around the hall I see cheerful, welcoming faces. Candida, our new young Science teacher with the freckles and masses of red-gold hair, gives me a mischievous look that reminds me irresistibly of *The Naughtiest Girl in the School*. Charles, the new teacher who has arrived from overseas to join the Science team, smiles at me warmly, Kyle Dawson, our new young Australian, a welcome addition to the ITC staff, looks bright-eyed and bushy-tailed, and I'm delighted to see Mark Bland, a friendly northerner who I can tell already is a gifted Maths teacher, and Teresa Chibogu, who is looking forward this term to helping Father George with religious activities.

Towering head and shoulders above the rest of us is the tall, stylish figure of Eddie Gaynor, who has rejoined St George's this term as a Deputy Head. Eddie, who is also Acting Head of

165

English, has been under secondment to another school, and it's all too easy to see why this sensitive, erudite man was not at home last year at St George's. But I'm delighted to welcome him back now, and I know immediately that we're going to benefit greatly from his calm and reflective approach.

It's cheering too to see the familiar faces, looking rested and refreshed after the holidays – David Hearn, Ariadne, Gillian, Eve, Tonya, Hannah, Khadija, Harvi and all the others. And last but not least of course there's Father George, as always the picture of ecclesiastical elegance and looking ten years younger, who leads us in a prayer for the new term.

In many ways it's going to be a difficult one, I warn the staff after my initial welcome. We have a crucial Ofsted Inspection at the end of November, and our every move is being monitored. Far from feeling threatened and resentful however, everyone, I can see, takes this as a challenge. There's a real buzz in the room, a feeling that we can win through and that we're all in this together. Looking at my wonderful team I feel thrilled and inspired.

The children, too, come bouncing back, happy to be in school and keen as mustard. The first thing that greets them as they come through the door is a big poster saying '*Welcome Back! We've missed you! This is the year we get off Special Measures!*'. The second is a notice about the new school Breakfast Club. Barbara has agreed to open the canteen at 8.15 every morning from now on, and breakfast orders are to be placed the day before.

We've decided to start school half-an-hour later this term and finish at 3.30 instead of 3 pm. Starting at 8.30 seemed an impossibly early target for some of the children, and this will give the more energetic ones time to get to school, have breakfast if they want it and do some sports practice. It's more civilized for the teachers too. With staff briefing at 8.15 three times a week they had to be in school very early to get material photocopied.

On our third day back Eddie and I walk round the school together. I want to get to know him and to hear how St George's strikes him after his time away. He is, I can see, genuinely astonished by the changes that have taken place. 'I can't believe it,' he keeps saying. 'It's so calm and it all feels so purposeful. I can't believe it's the same school.' He's impressed by the system of staff desks on each corridor. Far from finding the new rota a chore, staff tell me they enjoy their periods on corridor duty. It gives them a peaceful time to get on with their marking and preparing, and it's also an opportunity to catch children they want to see, or just to have quiet one-to-one chats.

I'm aware that Eddie's memories of the playground are harrowing. During his time here he witnessed some terrible fights and has memories of police arriving and of children being taken to hospital. At breaktime we walk out into the playground together and as usual when they see me the children rush over and cluster round. I can see that just for a split second Eddie is taken aback, but the children's interest is so obviously friendly that he responds immediately and soon we're all relaxed and chatting. As so often Debbie is at the forefront of the group, loud, enthusiastic and desperate for attention. 'Got any new ones?' she demands, taking hold of my wrist quite roughly and peering at my charm bracelet.

'Ouch!' I say involuntarily as she presses the spiky bracelet into my skin. 'No, not yet. I'm waiting for the champagne bottle when we come off Special Measures.'

When the children lose interest and begin to drift away I take Debbie aside. 'I know you don't mean to be rude, but it's not good manners to grab hold of people,' I remind her. 'It's important for us all to respect one another's personal space.'

'I know,' she says philosophically, 'like Miss O'Leary said. Sorry.'

When we first arrived Tracey's long hair came in for a lot of attention. As she says, a lot of the children are more like five- or six-year-olds, still at the stage of needing constant physical contact. She explained to them that they mustn't seize our hands or touch our hair or tuck their arms in ours. They seemed puzzled, but since they're anxious to please, this behaviour has gradually stopped.

*

The Breakfast Club catches on immediately, and every morning now there's a delicious smell of toast and frying bacon wafting from the canteen as we come into school. Quite a few of the staff start using it too – Sean's especially keen on his full English breakfast, though he rushes about so much he never puts on weight, which makes me envious – and it's a quiet moment in the school day when people can sit down and talk informally together.

'I think I need a cup of coffee before I take on Year 8 this morning. Do you mind if I sit down with you for a minute?' I hear Tracey asking a new young teacher who has come to us from abroad. I suspect I know what's going on. We've both noticed that he's been looking a bit disheartened.

'I think he's having a problem with one of his Year 8 classes. There are a lot of children in it with learning difficulties, and I've noticed that he spends a lot of time shouting and yelling at the class and telling them to get back to their seats. I think he needs the confidence to relax a bit and stop looking so grim,' Tracey told me when we saw him walking along the corridor with his head down.

I thought how difficult it must be for a young teacher like this, far from home and family, trying to get settled and sorted out in London and coming into a school in a state of flux. 'He's got the makings of a really good teacher. Can you take him under your wing?' I suggested.

'I think it would help if he got to know the children outside school,' says Tracey. 'I know he's keen on chess. How about getting him to start a chess club?' This seems an excellent idea.

I'm only too aware that Tracey has a hundred and one things to do and this kind of situation takes time and great sensitivity, but there's no one who can deal with it better. I'm sure she's opened up an informal conversation over coffee about the difficulties of living in London which will give her an opportunity to ask how our young teacher is finding his classes at St George's, and will lead them on to a professional sharing of ideas. And as it turns out, he's delighted at the thought of starting a chess club.

The Breakfast Club provides a good setting for these informal contacts and I enjoy the homely feeling of it. I like to see the children out in the playground, too, practising their football moves and generally letting off steam before they come into school.

Football fever has really struck St George's and quite recently I made an important new contact which I hope is really going to push our sports programme forward. Looking through past correspondence I came across an interesting letter from a man named Jacques Delacave offering his help to the school. When I telephoned him he told me that he had indeed been in touch with St George's before my time, but somehow the contact had come to nothing, so, never one to miss an opportunity, I suggested we should meet.

Jacques is a businessman with many interests, a charming, debonair philanthropist with an old-fashioned elegance in both his dress and speech. He told me that he had been a friend of the late Basil Hume and had promised the Cardinal Archbishop that he would do all he could to help the cause of Catholic education. He was touched when I told him what one of the children had said to me: 'Please Miss, what's the point of having football teams when we haven't got anywhere to play?'

It turns out that Jacques has a useful connection with Harrow, and we agreed that he would contact a governor, asking if St George's might use some of the Harrow School playing fields for cricket and rugby when they're not otherwise in use. Rugby is a game that channels children's energy and aggression in a really positive way – just the kind of thing we need at St George's, and I'm very keen to introduce it.

After this meeting things begin to happen fast. First of all Jacques visits the school, and is clearly very interested and impressed by what he sees. He meets Sean and Ariadne and offers to use his contacts for our work experience programme, as well as lending us a secretary to help to pull it all together. Ariadne is already doing brilliant work on careers and work experience, but she's got so much to do already this extra input is just what we need.

Soon afterwards we have a friendly letter from Barnaby Lenon, the Headmaster of Harrow, who also comes to visit. He's charming and relaxed, and readily agrees to our using the Harrow playing fields when they are free. It's encouraging to see an independent school head so interested in the challenges of a school like St George's. Barnaby Lenon is as aware as anyone, I'm sure, of the vested interest all of us have in providing a good state education. After all, the vast majority of British children are in state schools, and it's largely they who will be working to pay the tax which will pay for our pensions and for the services we shall all, in one way or another, need. They are the lawyers and doctors and nurses and scientists and engineers of the future, the people who will serve us in banks and shops, so all of us should be concerned about the kind of education they receive.

I've certainly never had any reservations about gleaning ideas from the private sector. I think the Independent Girls' Schools Heads Association thought I was a bit dotty when I applied to join as Head of Douay – a state mixed comprehensive school. But they made me an associate member, and I learned a lot from their experiences. They were a friendly support group of women whose wisdom I valued. I just wanted my children to have the very best of what their children were getting, and they supported this.

Barnaby Lenon's visit leads on to yet another. 'That's not . . . no surely it *can't* be . . .!' Our Governor Peter Brown almost drops the sheaf of finance papers he is carrying as he sees the tall figure of Roger Uttley, Harrow rugby coach and one-time England international rugby star, entering the atrium while male members of staff lurk about outside my office, hoping to be introduced. Roger, a six-foot-six colossus, has come to talk about rugby to the children, and we're all taken by his warm and engaging manner.

Roger not only explains the joys of rugby to the children, but suggests to us that he should coach a group of Year 7 boys on Saturdays at a rugby ground in Brent. I'm delighted. Having help from someone of Roger's calibre is more than I'd ever dreamed of. Our technology teacher, John MacDonald, is very keen too, and has volunteered to run our rugby training and to take our teams to Harrow when the fields are free.

Now all we need is a minibus to transport the teams to and fro. So it's over to Jacques again, who throws himself into fundraising for it with infectious enthusiasm.

'Wicked! Har, har. Wicked!'

It's an exclamation I've heard daily since I've been at St George's, but it's never been followed by such a deep rich chuckle. An enormous hand covers mine, and a beaming face looks down on me.

It's 6.35 pm on Speech Night, 14 September, and much to my delight – and relief – Frank Bruno has arrived to present the prizes. He's been stuck in traffic and has only just made it in time. In the hall 250 parents, pupils and guests are waiting to see him with barely-suppressed excitement. Tickets for the event have gone like hot-cakes and we've only just managed to pack everyone in.

No one can remember St George's ever having a Speech Night – 'Please Miss, what do you have to say to get a prize?' one bewildered twelve-year-old asks me – but I see it as another important landmark in the journey of our recovery. I want to get the children excited about success and set the school year off in a positive way, and if Frank Bruno's presence (for which we have to thank Lincoln Crawford) gives us some publicity too, all well and good. We've got 87 new pupils this term – a lot better than the 29 who originally applied and enough to keep a four form entry, which is vital for our survival – but anything positive that brings us to the notice of the local press and parents can only be helpful.

Everyone has rallied round to make the evening a success. Litter patrols have combed the playground where the parents will park their cars, Wendy is overseeing the catering in her calm, unfussed way and parents have contributed food as excitingly varied as the countries from which they come. The cleaning team has made sure that the hall is cleaned and shining, and Suzie has seen to it that there are glowing arrangements of sharp-smelling autumn flowers decorating the atrium and the hall. Prizewinners have been rehearsed, the head boy and head girl are ready with their speeches, and the Year 7 choir and our small chamber group, the St George's Ensemble, have been conscientiously practising César Franck's *Panis angelicus* and a setting of some verses of Isaiah, which they will perform before the presentation.

We're awarding prizes for everything we can think of: Subject prizes, Form prizes, Year prizes, prizes for Best Attendance, Work Experience, Choir, Citizenship, Special Achievement, Reception . . . the list goes on. There's one that gives me particular pleasure – the Biology Prize, which we have named after Professor Hakim, who is here to present it. He has been such a good and loyal friend to us, supporting the school and arranging work experience visits to St Mary's Hospital for our children. In his usual kind and unassuming way, he was all ready to step in and present the rest of the prizes if Frank Bruno wasn't able to make it.

As with the May Ball, we're doing things with proper formality. After Canon John's welcome as Chairman of the Governors, and an opening prayer from Father George, the choir and ensemble perform with great self-possession and Makeeba from Year 8 reads a light-hearted poem – Hilaire Belloc's 'The Microbe', which we've chosen as a compliment to Professor Hakim's profession.

My own speech is upbeat and fairly brief. So is Frank Bruno's, and it hits the mark perfectly. *From Zero to Hero* is the title of his autobiography, which we've displayed prominently in the atrium, and although I'm sure he is personally too modest to describe himself as a hero, his message for the children is 'If you work at developing your gifts you can make it, even if you start from nothing.' What really seems to delight them most, however, is the growl of 'Wicked!' and the brilliant smile he gives each of the prizewinners as he takes their hand in his enormous muscular one.

The head boy, Wendy's son Tariq, and the head girl, Suzi Mirenberg, give charming speeches which make me very proud of them. These two are a real credit to the school. Tariq is a cheerful boy and an exceptionally hard worker – just like his mother. Suzi I've got to know during our mentoring sessions. She's a delightful girl, very keen to succeed, and interested in going into medicine, so she's looking forward to talking to Professor Hakim again. Thanks to his efforts, she's already enjoyed doing work experience at St Mary's.

Looking at the sea of cheerful, open faces I remember the closed, suspicious looks we met when we first came to St George's, and am thrilled at the change. I'm touched too to see the three Year 11s from last year who have come back to receive their prizes – Rachel, Maia and Miodrag – all three of them refugees who arrived here with little English and managed to achieve good grades despite a host of problems. Maia's father is here, absolutely glowing with pride, and I'm pleased to hear from Tracey that Rachel is settled in good accommodation now, where she seems to be very happy.

I might have known, however, that it wouldn't be St George's if everything went entirely smoothly. As I'm shepherding Frank Bruno and Professor Hakim into the Individual Learning Unit to meet the parents over refreshments, Sean appears at my elbow making anxious signs. I hand over to Canon John for a moment and follow Sean to my office.

'You won't believe this,' Sean tells me, grey-faced. 'One of the cars in the playground has been broken into, and it would have to be Professor Hakim's. The side window's smashed and the door's wide open.'

We gaze at one another for a desperate moment. 'I'd better go and tell him,' says Sean.

I join the others again while Sean and Professor Hakim go out to inspect the damage. Delighted parents clutching exotic snacks and glasses of wine are mobbing Frank Bruno, who is rising to the occasion wonderfully, chatting and joking, signing autographs and handing out Lord Snowdon's picture of him looking impressively suave and handsome.

When Professor Hakim returns Sean tells me he is distraught. Whoever has broken into the car has taken his laptop and briefcase containing the only copy of a book he is working on. It represents hundreds of hours of work, which he will find virtually impossible to repeat. I know Sean will deal with even this dire situation in his usual resourceful way, so I continue to smile and radiate normalcy.

But how terrible, I think, if this hits the papers. I can see the headline now: PROFESSOR ROBBED AT MURDERED HEAD'S FAILING SCHOOL. Simon, one of our favourite policemen who has recently been made a sergeant, is here tonight as a guest and Sean goes over to talk to him. He sizes the situation up quickly and, with a reassuring 'Leave this with me,' goes off – where to, Sean doesn't know.

Under the circumstances it's hard to smile and carry on as if nothing has happened, and poor Professor Hakim looks stricken. Within a fairly short time, however, Simon is back carrying – unbelievably – the briefcase and laptop. He tells us he's been to the youth club across the road, where he knows the youngsters. We thank him profusely but don't enquire further – just give thanks that it was nothing to do with St George's. Professor Hakim is so relieved to have his work returned he brushes the inconvenience of a broken window aside.

Able to breathe at last, I snatch a drink and launch into the crowd again, where things are going with a real swing. Frank is still there, and Fiona asks him if he felt afraid when he climbed into the ring with Mike Tyson. 'Not half as afraid as I was of meeting your Mum,' he replies with a grin, at which everyone bursts out laughing.

The evening is scheduled to end at eight pm, but it's well after nine when the last of the parents leave. 'This is what real schools do,' says one of them, as he shakes my hand.

I take it as a compliment. In fact Speech Night does seem to have been a huge success, and it was good to see people like John Harris, the Director of Westminster LEA, and John Deakin, the Westminster LEA personnel officer who has taken such an interest in our recruiting for St George's. But I reflect on the fact that, apart from Canon John, not one of the Governors managed to attend. Even if busy diaries prevented some from joining us, it was a disappointment that, with the exception of the Chairman, the Governors were not represented at all. What a pity to miss such a wonderful opportunity to feel such pride in their school, and of course to meet the children and their parents.

On 20 September we have another starry visit, this time from Lenny Henry. Gusts of laughter drift from the library as he talks about his work for Comic Relief and his early days as a comedian. He's just like the headteacher he plays in his TV series *Hope and Glory*, very informal and one-of-the lads with his off-the-wall jokes, and he goes down well with the children.

Three or four days after his visit Tracey beckons me to the window of my office at lunchtime. 'Look!' she says, pointing. Two girls are standing together by one of the tables. One of them is showing the other something. It looks like such an unexceptional scene, two little girls talking in the playground, but we know it's not, because one of them is Morwenna, and we've never seen her talking to anyone in the playground before.

Morwenna is thirteen and a child who concerns us. Tracey and I are lucky that we have had the chance to develop the skills to help children with acute problems like hers. Some days she doesn't speak at all, just sits in class rocking and making strange noises. Sometimes she rushes round and round the playground or paces in circles like a caged animal. It's as if she's continually in flight, and it's not surprising, in view of the violence she's witnessed at home. When she's not withdrawn she can be violent herself, reacting to quite harmless remarks from other children by ripping up exercise books or throwing people's possessions around, and as a result she's very isolated.

Tracey is one of the few people Morwenna trusts, and I quite often find her in Tracey's office, playing with the Zen garden while Tracey gets on with something else. Morwenna has told Tracey that her mother is constantly saying that she will turn out like her dad, who's now serving a sentence for GBH, and telling her how alike they are. This frightens and upsets Morwenna. Tracey works hard at bringing her out of herself, and persuaded her to come to Lenny Henry's talk. Afterwards they found themselves standing next to Lenny Henry, who gave Morwenna his megawatt smile, and to Tracey's amazement Morwenna smiled back at him. It was a small breakthrough for her, to respond to a stranger like that, and since then, Tracey says, she has been communicating more than she ever has before. Lenny Henry can have no idea of the difference he made to one very unhappy little girl.

But Morwenna's problems are profound and Ryan has referred her for psychiatric treatment, which she says she'll probably need for the rest of her life. Meanwhile we can only do our best to contain the situation, helping her to settle in class, finding quiet things for her to do when necessary away from the other children, supporting her mother, who's under immense strain, and trying to persuade her not to make things worse by comparing Morwenna to her father.

Ryan is with us every Friday now, and I wish already that she could give us more time. She has her work cut out at the moment dealing with disturbed children like Morwenna, and there's not much time yet for children with less pressing problems. Tracey and I discuss one difficult situation which must be familiar in any inner city school – parents who've been in this country for many years but still live very much in their own ethnic community, and daughters who've grown up here and are just old enough to start rebelling. The girls want to wear makeup and have boyfriends like other girls at school, and the crisis usually comes when they start staying out late at night and the parents panic.

One girl came to Tracey in a terrible state this week, saying she was leaving home. Tracey and I asked her to come and have a chat with us over a glass of Coca-Cola. I showed her the French prints I have around the walls of my office, which seemed to soothe her. Tracey pointed out to her that most parents worry when their daughters stay out until the early hours – especially if they don't know where they are – because London can be a dangerous place, and that it's all a matter of finding a balance.

'I think things are a little better at home now,' Tracey told me a few days later, 'but' – with a sigh – 'I suppose if all else fails, we could see if Ryan has time to have a word with her.'

Because Ryan's work is completely confidential I don't get involved in the detail. Tracey is Ryan's link with the school and she works well with Ryan to help those children who are especially vulnerable.

The more I see of Tracey, the more I admire her and realize how far in advance of the times she has always been in her teaching methods. It's an accepted idea now that children should assess their own work and set their own targets, but Tracey was doing this ten years ago. The booklets she produces for the teaching staff here, and for the pupils, are a wonderful combination of imaginative thinking, an understanding of how children learn, and practical down-to-earth advice, and I sometimes think they deserve wider publication.

We've just collaborated on one which we've called 'Sharing Good Practice at the Start of the Year' – not a title that's going to get into the bestseller lists perhaps, but something for the staff, especially the younger ones, to hold on to when confronted by a daunting-looking new class. It covers basic things that often get overlooked but which are vital in getting children on side, like remembering names and tips on how to do it, moving round the class so that there are opportunities to talk to children individually, smiling and using humour and making eye contact, and above all, being positive and giving children a sense of self-worth. A lot of it is about sensitivity and basic respect, about approaching children as people, and letting them see that you are human too. Of course we also emphasize the need for a structure to underpin all this – a clear, disciplined approach which is friendly but not familiar, good preparation of lessons, and clear targets set at the beginning of each lesson and reviewed at the end.

We've now also introduced a tracking system, with three

tracking periods a year. Teachers monitor attainment, effort and homework regularly, giving a mark for each, and working out the average grade at the end of the tracking period. The children discuss their grades with their form tutor, and set targets for themselves for the next period.

We have a system of regular academic checks, which children are invited to attend to check on their general organization, the progress made, the clubs and teams they belong to, the most recent piece of work they are proud of, and what they want to improve on next term.

All these checks help the children focus on their strengths and weaknesses, and give them the regular feedback and individual attention that enable them to develop. Our whole approach is based on personal interaction with every child. I think many of them aren't used to being treated in such a thoughtful way, and they do respond.

It's wonderful to have a staff who are so committed – I don't think I've ever worked with a more willing group of people. I've had few grumbles about the extra work involved in these kinds of initiatives, and I can see that the standard of teaching this year is going to be extremely high. They understand my concept of giving the children hyacinths as well as loaves. But we're very aware of the complexities of working at St George's, where a teacher usually has to deal not only with the class, but with support staff who may be interpreting for pupils, or supporting children who are having difficulties or have special educational needs. This is where Frances, and Sheila Young who is Head of Individual Learning, come in, and they've produced a booklet on working with support staff, which for an inexperienced teacher can be difficult at first.

Sheila has also helped us launch our programme for gifted and talented pupils. It may surprise some people to hear that we have such a programme at St George's, where expectations have been seen as so low, but we have some very gifted children. We already know from Gillian's workshops with dance professionals that we have some amazing dancers and actors, and from the little I've seen of the *Sister Act* rehearsals, it's going to be fantastic. And last year Miodrag, who won an independent school bursary, showed how brilliant at ICT a child can become, given the right resources. Whatever a child's special ability may be – writing, maths, sport, ICT, or academic ability in general – I want to see it developed.

Eddie Gaynor has been a valuable addition to our team. He has a quiet, thoughtful approach; he is genuinely delighted to be able to use his talents to help St George's, and has been unsparing with his time. He is in charge of literacy and he's already organized a reading week. We've joined in with a national sponsored Readathon, from which we've discovered that we have some enthusiastic readers, judging by the amount of money they've raised for two children's charities.

Like me, Eddie believes in bringing the message to the people, and each lunchtime Helen Vincent, a lively young English teacher, arranges for some pages from a book to be projected on to a screen in the cafeteria and scrolled slowly on to give the children a taste. It's certainly captured their interest – I put my head round the door the day *Lord of the Flies* was projected to be met by a hush as everybody silently ate their chips with their eyes glued to the screen. There's a competition to guess which favourite children's book has been chosen by which member of staff, with photographs and displays in the atrium. I chose Hilda Lewis's *The Ship that Flew*, a book I loved and which seems to have been a hit. 'I wish I could go back in time Miss,' one of the children said to me, waving his copy at me. 'It's the future I want to get to,' I laugh – 'Next March, when the Inspectors come.'

Eddie has also overseen the restocking of the book boxes in all the classrooms. It's been a considerable outlay, but it's important for children not to be dependent on the library alone. They're allowed to take books home, and if the odd one disappears because a child can't bear to give it back, that's all right with me. So many of these children have so little, and as long as the book is going to be read, I don't mind – though that's not the official line.

Eddie has produced *A Good Read*, a reading diary with notes which encourage the children to reflect on what they read and record their thoughts and feelings. I think it's beautifully done – lively and unpatronizing, helping them to form their own opinions.

It's so pleasant to see Eddie's tall figure at the school gates at the end of the day, seeing the children out of school in his friendly, courteous way. In my view good manners are the essence of teaching. If someone treats you politely you feel better about yourself and you copy their behaviour. Being a mother and a grandmother has convinced me of that – if you (playfully) put your tongue out at a baby it will try to do the same.

Eddie and Tracey get on like a house on fire – Sean and I sometimes laugh that we're feeling left out of their deep philosophical conversations – and they both have very much the same approach.

Tracey, I've noticed, is never afraid to apologize to a child if she feels she's in the wrong. I overheard her and a girl called Christina the other day in the corridor. 'I think you should apologize to me Miss,' Christina was saying in a rather whining way. 'I'm very upset with you, the way you spoke to me in the playground. You're always telling me not to get fired up, and you were very rude to me. I think you should say sorry, like you always make me do.'

Tracey said straightaway, 'You're quite right, Christina, and I do apologize. I was worried and I'm afraid I spoke in the heat of the moment, but I shouldn't have said what I did.'

'Oh, that's all right Miss,' Christina said with a generous smile, and the whole matter was closed. If Tracey hadn't done that there would have been grumbling behind her back and a feeling of resentment.

'What was all that about?' I asked.

'Oh, there was an incident in break. Someone got hit on the head, I'm not sure whether it was an accident or not, but it could have been nasty. The children were all crowding round, and I told Christina to get out of my way. I know I spoke to her rather sharply. She's right, we can't have one rule for her and another for me.'

Though the atmosphere is immeasurably better, St George's is still a bit like a tinderbox – a fire can break out at any moment. A lot of the children come from backgrounds where tempers are short and physical violence is the way you deal with frustration, so they've learned no strategies for controlling their anger. We all of us spend a lot of time trying to show them that there are other ways of dealing with things. I've so often heard Tracey saying quietly, over and over, to a child who is out of control: 'I want to hear what you're trying to tell me, but I can't if you shout.'

When the child is calmer, she'll say: 'Now what else can you do next time you feel you're losing your temper? You can walk away, or you can take a deep breath and try to speak calmly, or you can come and see me or another teacher.'

It's a constant struggle, and there are no easy solutions, but it's gratifying when you see a child making a real effort not to hit someone, or to apologize, or to own up to doing something – in other words, developing a moral universe and self-control.

I've always believed that it's better to give children a chance to own up rather than to inflict draconian punishments. I remember that when I was a young teacher I stupidly left my handbag in the classroom for a couple of minutes, and when I looked in it I found that £70 was missing. I'd been going to pay for something on my way home, and I was in a terrible state because it's a lot of money, and it was a huge amount to me then.

I thought I knew who the culprit was – a small boy in the class who was a real practical joker. So I said to the class: 'Someone has taken some money out of my handbag. I know no one would steal from a teacher, so it must be a practical joke, and it's a very silly one. I'm going to go out of the classroom and when I come back I expect to find the money back in my handbag.'

I held my breath, but when I came back after standing panic-stricken outside the door for five minutes, the money was in my bag. We had a discussion about stealing, and when and when not to play practical jokes, but I think they all knew that I knew what they knew . . . It certainly taught me never to put temptation in children's way, and I also learned that in serious situations it helps if you can give children a way out, rather than being confrontational. Fiona put her phone down for a moment when she was helping put up displays in the atrium and when she looked round it had disappeared. Tracey told the children who were around that she and Fiona were going away for two minutes and they'd expect the phone to be there when they came back. Magically it was.

There was a somewhat more serious incident recently. It was in a department where the staff sell school equipment to the children, and they had about £1,000 in a desk drawer. The money should have been brought to the office and banked, but the staff were pressed for time, and it had been allowed to accumulate. The missing money was quickly discovered, and there were about 40 youngsters potentially involved. Eve called Tracey and they decided it was probably a small group acting together.

First, they asked if anyone would admit to taking the money, but predictably no one did.

'All right,' said Tracey. 'I shall need to get the Headmistress to phone the police. But we can deal with it now if you want to, before I go to see her.'

Knowing that the culprits would probably stick together, she told the children to divide into groups. Then she left the room and waited outside for something to happen. After a while several boys came and admitted that they had been involved. It had all started as a game, but when it went too far everybody had got frightened and got rid of the evidence by throwing it out of the window. To everyone's immense relief the money was found down below in the carpark, under Eddie Gaynor's car.

Tracey contacted the parents of all the children she thought were involved. When they came in Tracey emphasized that although they'd done wrong, those who had come to her deserved credit for being prepared to own up. The others went on protesting their innocence in front of their parents, but Tracey made it clear to the parents that she believed they'd had a hand in it, whatever they said. It took many hours of staff time to resolve it all.

It was a worrying business and the staff involved were deeply embarrassed, since a cardinal school rule is: Don't put temptation in pupils' way. However, the money was retrieved, some people were brave enough to own up, the children concerned had a moral lesson, good relations with the teachers were developed further.

Thursday 21 September. 'What are you two doing? You're going to hurt each other,' I say to two small boys who are crossing the atrium, pushing and punching each other on the arms.

'We're not fighting. We're friends,' says one of them.

'Well, you've got a funny way of showing it.'

'He's my uncle really,' says one of them. 'But I'm older than him.'

'Your uncle? How do you work that out?' I know that they come from different homes and that one of them lives with foster-carers.

'Well, my grandad is his dad,' says one. 'So that makes him my uncle doesn't it?' And the two of them run off, laughing and punching one another.

Friday 29 September. I go past the Learning Resource Centre late in the afternoon after the children have gone, and see two figures at one of the computer screens. Miodrag has been using his IT talents to design a website for the school, and he's discussing it with Ariadne. Ariadne spent so much time helping Miodrag develop his skills and get his A Level bursary, and I know she's immensely proud of him. They're so intent that I don't disturb them.

Tuesday 3 October. I'm just about to go home and I meet Debbie coming away from the hall, looking flushed and furious.

'Going home Debbie? I say.

'I'm fed up,' she explodes. 'I'm not going to do it no more. Miss Rabie had such a go at me.'

'*Any* more, Debbie,' I say automatically. 'What for?'

'I wasn't really late,' she goes on. 'Only a few minutes. I didn't look at my watch, that's all. And then she gives me this lecture and tells me I'm late and kept everybody waiting.'

I know Gillian is producing *Sister Act* in a truly professional way. If anyone's consistently late for production meetings or rehearsals, they're out. It's an approach I applaud. Most of the children are totally committed and I gather even Debbie's been getting quite involved, but punctuality isn't her strong point.

'So has Miss Rabie told you you can't help any more?' I ask.

'No, *I've* said I'm not going to. I told her to . . .'

'Wait a minute,' I say. 'How about going back in there and apologizing to Miss Rabie. She's quite right. She can't put on a good production if people aren't going to take it seriously. She's a professional person. She told me you had some brilliant ideas. I'm sure she doesn't want to lose you.'

'Well, I'll *think* about it,' she says, stomping off towards the toilets. But I notice she's glancing back towards the hall to see what's going on.

Wednesday 11 October. During the lunch hour when I'm out in the playground I notice a group of boys over by the main gate, talking through the bars to someone outside, and I go over. It's Rory. He's given up his old grey coat and he's dressed in a navy-blue boiler suit. He's smoking a cigarette.

'Hello Rory,' I say.

'All right, then?' he says, looking away into the far distance.

'Still smoking I see. I won't say it, but you know what I'm thinking, don't you?' Rory grinds the butt of his cigarette into the ground with studied indifference. 'Are you on your lunch hour?'

''s right.'

'Enjoying the work? I hear you're doing well.'

'Yeah. 's OK' – on an up note.

'Would you like to come in and say hello to Mr Devlin? I'm sure he'd like to see you.'

'Na. 's alright.'

I'm struck by what a lonely figure he cuts, standing outside the school gate. Sean says he's seen him there before. Things went surprisingly well with his work experience, and the garage has agreed that he can stay on for another six months, with a view to a possible apprenticeship. I'm delighted he's found a place that suits him, but I think St George's is the only real security Rory's ever known.

Saturday 21 October. Half-term. It's an indication of how much more confident I feel now about St George's that I'm just back from a short trip to a conference in Washington on 'Turning Round Low Performing Schools', to which I was invited by Estelle Morris, the Schools Standards Minister. It certainly wasn't a holiday, and Sean and I were constantly in touch by phone, but it was extremely stimulating. It also gave me the chance to tell Estelle Morris how wonderful I felt it would be if the Government could find a way to recognize the special contribution of teachers in inner city schools by giving them some extra money and some kind of professional accolade – an idea to which she seemed very receptive.

During our four days we visited various schools in and around Washington, including a high school in a tough part of the city. It reminded me very much of St George's – the same vibrant mix of children from different ethnic backgrounds, the same kind of mobile school population, the same poverty and deprivation in the area around. I was extremely impressed by the head, who seemed to me to have that vital combination of real vision and business acumen. She was fascinated to hear about our heroes programme, and I was impressed by her idea of having 'parent helpers' – parents who are paid to come into school to supervise the children and help their learning in various ways, for example moving between classes, during lunch break and when they come out of school. The whole school had a very calm and welcoming feel and the parent helpers clearly contributed to that, relating to the children as parents rather than teachers, and being available to help new children, or ones who had problems.

One free evening I took myself off alone to wander round Washington. I spent some years in the United States as a young wife with small children, and I taught in schools in Arizona and California, so I have a great affection for it. As I stood among all those exciting buildings, looking down on the city, I experienced the same feeling of possibility that I had then, the sense that the world is a fountain of delight. How I want my St George's children to have the tools to engage with it, to be able to perceive what life is about.

As I go about my everyday tasks over half-term, restocking the freezer, getting my clothes cleaned and my shoes heeled, I think about my American experience, and decide to talk over with Canon John the idea of appointing parent ushers at St George's. If I come home from a conference with one good idea, I always reckon it's been worth it.

I also think, with a sigh, about all the monitoring visits and inspections that lie ahead of us this term. We've already had two monitoring visits from the LEA, one of them immediately before half-term. The idea of this visit, as stated in a letter from Paula Tansley, the Assistant Director of Schools for Westminster, was to 'avoid placing any additional burdens on the school' by 'focusing on the school's own action plan, supplemented by additional objective information which is readily available.' It sounds simple, but what it amounted to was having to produce a huge amount of data on attendance, behaviour, achievement, and other key issues at just over a week's notice, and Sean, Tracey and I were working flat out.

During this term we'll be having a visit from two specialist LEA inspectors who will drop in unannounced, a Diocesan RE inspection, another routine LEA Monitoring Board meeting, an LEA personnel review and an LEA finance review, not to mention another inspection by Ofsted. We're answerable to so many different people at St George's – the Diocese, the LEA, Nord Anglia, and Ofsted – that it's a wonder we have any time to teach.

I've been quite disturbed by the tone of some of the letters I've received recently from the LEA and the Diocese. Paula Tansley referred to the 'need to take a decision about the longer term future of St George's', and from the Diocesan office Tony Mackersie wrote of 'some crucial decisions being made during the next few weeks about the school's medium to long-term future'. Since it's been acknowledged that St George's is improving, and has every chance of getting off Special Measures, surely its 'long-term future' is to stay open as a Catholic school. Could there be people who would prefer to see it closed? I find the thought very unsettling. The site could easily be sold and a small estate of upmarket properties built on it, I mused.

Half-term is over with a vengeance. I'm sitting in my office after assembly on the first day back when there's a loud crash from the atrium followed by the most terrible swearing. It sounds as if furniture is being knocked over and I hurry out through Suzie's office to see two figures rolling on the floor, kicking out at the furniture as they skid about on the polished floor. Two Year 9s on reception duty are sitting wide-eyed behind the reception desk. It's a fight. We are equally surprised, after our successful campaign against fights. This one, however, doesn't look too bad, although it's noisy.

I can see at a glance who the culprits are – our friend Jason, and Juan, also from Year 10. Other people have heard the noise – it's impossible not to – and both Sean and Wendy are quickly on the scene. Jason is on top of Juan and trying to punch his face. Sean manages to take hold of one of Jason's arms, while I try to restrain Juan and get a kick on the shins from his flailing feet. They're both big, muscular boys, and when they're angry they're physically frightening, but I'm so angry myself I just hang on. Eventually the two let go, get up and stand breathing heavily, glaring unwaveringly at one another and emitting dire threats. Juan's nose is starting to bleed, but it doesn't look serious. Deirdre and Michelle, the two Year 9s on reception duty, are still huddling behind the reception desk, gazing at the scene. Fights of this kind are a rarity now and they look distinctly alarmed.

I can hardly breathe myself from annoyance. 'What disgusting behaviour!' I manage to say. 'Apologize to Deirdre and Michelle. *NOW!* Then I want to see you in my office, Jason. Juan, you go and wait in Mr Devlin's room.' I always feel it's better to see the parties to a fight separately – at least while they cool down.

I retreat to the sanctuary of my private toilet where I breathe deeply at the open window, run a comb through my hair and repair my lipstick.

When I get back to my office Suzie has made me a cup of tea. Jason is sitting on a chair, bent forward with his head down and his forearms on his knees. I ask him if he would like a glass of water, but he shakes his head.

'So what was that about?' I ask.

'Just fightin',' he manages to get out, barely opening his mouth.

'I know you were fighting Jason. You've done plenty of damage to prove it. I want to know why.'

Silence. Then his cheeks flame and he blurts out angrily: 'That tosser owes me money.'

'Don't use that kind of language please. What do you think he owes you money for?'

'I don't think. I know.'

'Speak politely please, or I'll end this interview,' I snap.

'Sorry Headmistress.'

'So what is it for?'

An even longer silence. I can see that I'm going to get nowhere with this line of questioning. His mouth is set in a sullen line, and he refuses to meet my eye.

'Whatever happened, that's no way to sort it out, and you know that,' I say eventually. 'I'm going to put you in detention. Go and see Mr Devlin about it at lunchbreak. It's a pity Jason, because you've been doing so much better this term.' This is true. Both Tracey and Sean have put in a great deal of work with Jason, encouraging him to come to school regularly, talking his antisocial behaviour over with him and trying to counteract some of the unhelpful messages he gets from home.

Sean, who has talked to Juan, tells me at break that Jason has a sideline outside school in second-hand electronic toys such as Gameboys, and this is what the trouble was about. 'I don't know where he gets them from,' Sean says, 'but it sounds like some kind of racket. Might not be a bad idea to have a quiet word with Simon, and get him to talk to Jason.'

We decide that the boys will clean up the playground after school for the next two days, and help Francisco with tidying and polishing the atrium. We don't have a blanket detention system, but try to design the punishment to fit the crime – or at any rate the child. Sometimes it's catching up with work they've missed, or making amends in some other way. Certainly no one wants to be in Mr Devlin's detentions. And woe betide anyone who comes late or doesn't turn up.

I decide to turn the tables on Jason's mum and ask her to come into school. Surprisingly she declines.

Jason is one of those who'll be doing work experience this term. I wonder what he's chosen, and which side of the Law his undoubted talents will eventually land him on. At least there are some challenging possibilities open to him, thanks to all the hard work Sean and Ariadne have put in on our careers and work experience programme, with heroic support from Jacques Delacave. As I told him the other day, he's like the proverbial good deed in what sometimes seems a very naughty world, as is our other great supporter, Professor Hakim.

I'm delighted to see that a lot of our children have real ambitions for work experience and Sean and Ariadne have spent hours sifting information, making sure that their choices will be relevant to them, and that as far as possible they get what they want. Law and accountancy are both popular, and the Distinguished Visitors Programme has given them other ideas too. They've had talks from an Inspector in the Metropolitan Police, a BBC producer,

Jamie Bowden of British Airways who was responsible for the London Eye, and a number of high-powered businesspeople including the Group Finance Director of Abbey National, who gave us a computer, with BT kindly providing three years' Internet access for the atrium. We even have an ambitious plan to invite Cherie Booth to speak next term.

It's late on an October Friday – a damp dreary evening. I've been drafting a difficult letter to one of the Governors who, like some of the others I'm afraid, doesn't seem to understand the etiquette involved in being on a school governing board. I point out that Governors are a corporate body, with no authority to act individually – something that was emphasized some years ago in the famous Auld Report on the scandals at the William Tyndale School in Islington. Eddie Gaynor was immensely upset to be questioned after the last Parents' Meeting about various matters to do with the running of St George's, and I had a similar experience when I discovered plans to talk about the school's past problems to a group of business people, with no reference whatever to me or anyone else. Fortunately I was present at the meeting, and was able to step in and provide another perspective, but after the episode with Eddie I feel I can't let the matter drop. I could do without this extra hassle, I groan to myself.

I finish drafting the letter and put it for typing into the folder in Suzie's drawer. There's still a light on in Sean and Tracey's office and I look in. Tracey is sitting thoughtfully with her elbow on her desk, her face resting on her hand.

'Still here?' I say. 'What are you doing?'

'I'm writing a letter to Social Services about that boy Mohammed,' she says. 'The one who's just turned up, you know?'

Mohammed is a malnourished-looking twelve-year-old who suddenly appeared in school on Wednesday with another child. We'd never seen him before and had no idea where he came from. He speaks very little English, but we eventually managed to establish that he's just arrived from Africa to live with a father he hasn't seen for about eight years, his father's present partner and her children. He looks the picture of desolation, and I'm not surprised – thrust into this unfriendly climate in a place where no one, apart from his father, speaks his language.

It's typical of the way children at St George's simply come and go. Julia, a Year 10 girl from one of the Balkan states whom I was mentoring last term, suddenly said to me when she brought her exercise book for marking: 'I won't be here next week.'

'Why not?' I asked.

She shook her head and looked down at the ground.

Is something the matter Julia?'

'I'm not supposed to tell anyone,' she said, her lip quivering.

'Whatever it is, you can tell me.'

'We're going away,' she said. 'We're going back. We're living in one room and my Mum and Dad think it will be better, but I don't want to go.'

'Why can't you tell anyone?'

'It's something about money Miss. I don't know.'

I didn't press her, and by the time we were able to discover anything, it was already too late. I still think about Julia – unable to speak the language when she first arrived, but so keen and quick to learn. Within a few months she was able to tell me that she thought England 'cool', and when I asked her what that meant I was impressed that she could give me both the literal and non-literal meanings of the word. She could have done so well given a bit more time, I think sadly, wondering what she and her family have gone back to.

'I've been talking to Alison about Mehra,' Tracey says, 'You know, in Year 11?'

'Oh yes, we have real hopes for her GCSEs don't we?'

'Well, we did. I don't know now. She hasn't been in school for a week. There's no one answering the phone, and according to her friends the whole family have gone.'

'Where?' I ask. 'Are they on holiday?'

'No, apparently they've taken their belongings. There are two stories from her friends – one is that they've gone to Bradford to live with an uncle, the other is that they've gone back to India.'

'What does Alison say?'

'She can't find out what's happened. She's reported it to the LEA Education Welfare Officer.'

Alison Toia is our new full-time attendance officer, a dedicated New Zealander who's with us on a temporary basis. She deals with children who are persistently absent from school, making contact with parents and carers, and trying to see what the underlying reasons for it are. Sometimes it's to do with the home, sometimes it's sorted out by something as simple as an eye test or a hearing test. Whatever the cause, Alison tries to plan ways to reintegrate the child. If it's a matter of bullying we tackle it, and make sure that when the child comes back into school he or she always has a friend at hand. Alison puts her heart and soul into her work. She can be formidable if crossed.

'Come on,' I say to Tracey at last. 'It's late. I think you should go home.'

'Don't worry, I'll soon be finished,' she says, and goes back to her papers.

It's eight o'clock and dark as I make my way towards the tube. Too late I see a figure materialize out of the shadows, I'm grabbed by the shoulder and a hand wrenches at my bag. I manage to hang on to the strap – probably unwisely because he might have a knife, but it's my favourite bag – and shout 'Oh no you *don't*! Give me that back!' I can feel all my Glaswegian hackles rising at the effrontery of it, and I go on shouting loudly for help. As we tussle, I catch a glimpse of a young frightened face and am relieved that I don't recognize it.

Someone is coming towards us on the other side of the road, and my attacker takes fright and runs off. I've still got my bag, but I feel shaky as I continue on towards the tube. I phone William on my mobile, and he tells me to take a taxi, but there isn't one around, and I continue home by train.

Later Fiona rings and when she hears what's happened she sighs. 'Oh Mum,' she says. 'Why are you doing all this? You should be having a nice relaxing retirement, enjoying your drawing class and going to the gym, not getting mugged in Maida Vale.' I can't help laughing at the contrast.

Why am I doing it? As I lie in a hot scented bath, trying to relax, I wonder myself. Yet somehow next day I'm up at 5.30 as usual, excited to be going into St George's. I actually look forward to staff briefings now. Because I know St George's isn't going to be my career for the next ten years, I realize I'm able to take more risks and show the staff more of myself than I ever could at Douay, where I always felt I had to be in role. In fact I sometimes see Sean or Tracey raise an amused eyebrow at one another when they feel I'm being uncharacteristically amenable.

I enjoy the quarter of an hour between 8.30 and 8.45, too, when my door is open for anyone who wants to drop in and chat over a tea or coffee. They talk and I listen and I pick up a lot of interesting things about where we're at, just as I do when I hang around talking to people in the corridors – I like to do what I call Management by Hanging About. Father George often pops in to see me at 8.30, or Candida might come bounding in with a cheerful 'Hello, I thought you'd like to know . . .'

Today it's Angela Camilleri, our new Head of Art who, with help from Tonya, is transforming the Art Department. It's like a wonderland in there now, with children's work beautifully displayed, and a great air of creative purpose about it. Norman Binch and Charles Salter, my two inspector friends who oversaw the creation of the new studio, have described Angela as an inspiration, remarking on the good relationships she has with pupils and the excellent painting and drawing work they are beginning to produce.

Angela wants to discuss the idea of having an 'artist of the month'. A child will be chosen each month to have his or her work framed by the Art Department and displayed in the atrium. I suppose some people might see this as invidious, but to me it's simply celebrating excellence, and I encourage Angela to go ahead.

The distant sound of singing drifts through my window from the Portakabin in the playground where Katerina is rehearsing a group for *Sister Act*, which now seems to be involving huge numbers of people and generating excitement all through the school. We've moved the Music Department from a room off the atrium into the two playground classrooms where the Individual Learning Centre used to be. It makes far more sense for it to be out there, where the children can toot and bang away to their heart's content without giving their ancient headmistress a headache. Like Angela, Katerina is an inspiration. I remember that at her interview we were somewhat concerned when she said that she had to protect her voice, but in fact she has such authority that she never even has to raise it. Children recognize real professionalism when they see it. I realized early on in my career that it's only weak teachers who have to shout, though we probably all have the occasional outburst under severe provocation.

William, Sean, Tracey and I had a wonderful experience this week when we attended a concert given by Katerina at the London Hellenic Centre. Katerina always looks attractive, but at school, of course, she dresses simply and professionally. What a transformation, then, when she appeared on stage, her pale shoulders rising from the most beautiful bronze chiffon dress, her hair curled delicately round her face – she made me think of Aphrodite rising from the waves. Her programme ranged from Mozart to *My Fair Lady* and we were all held spellbound by that exquisite soprano voice. I wonder if the children know quite what a privilege it is to be taught by Katerina. I have a feeling they do.

I'm just finishing assembly when Suzie appears beside me and hands me a note: 'Canon John is on the phone. He needs to talk to you.'

'Good morning John,' I say. 'You're bright and early.'

Canon John sounds puzzled. 'I've been called to a meeting,' he says, 'about problems at St George's.'

'A meeting with who? About *what* problems?'

'The Episcopal Vicar and Monsignor Barltrop.'

Warning bells begin to ring. Why should the Episcopal Vicar Mgr Turner and the Vicar-General want to see Canon John alone?

'I don't think you should go on your own,' I say. 'If there are problems at St George's, then I think I should be there to discuss them.'

I can feel Canon John's brow furrow for a moment. Then, 'Oh no,' he says. 'I don't think that's necessary Marie. I imagine this is purely a church matter. I don't think there's anything more to it. But I thought you ought to know.'

'But what can they want to talk about?' I persist. 'You know our report from the RE Inspectors this month was brilliant.'

'Oh, I'm sure it's nothing to worry about,' says Canon John again, reassuringly.

'When are you going to see them?'

'This morning around eleven. Much better probably if I go alone. It's just three priests getting together.'

I can see his mind is made up, although I think he's wrong. Something doesn't smell right about this. I see the world in darker terms than the good Canon.

'Well, tell me what happens, won't you?' I say. I think what a good, kind, conscientious man he is, always ready with his support, and anxious to do what's best for the school. I wish everyone in the Diocese were so straightforward.

It's a busy day, with an unannounced visit from an LEA Special Needs Inspector who arrives with another concerned with pupil welfare. From time to time I forget about the meeting, though it's always there like a shadow at the back of my mind. I think I know what may be behind Canon John's summons. There has already been trouble about the selection panel which will draw up a shortlist for the new Head. As the present Head, I can play no formal part in the proceedings, though of course I'm extremely concerned about an appointment on which the future of the school depends.

I did however assume that Canon John, as Chairman of Governors, would be chairman of the selection panel, and was disappointed to note that this was not so, and that the panel would be chaired by another member of the Governing Board. And Peter Brown, who has been invaluable in managing the school's finances, was not on the panel until Canon John intervened – a move which produced a reaction from the Vicar-General that I found bewildering: he believed that the actions of Canon John and me constituted 'illegal behaviour'. Canon John, I know, is anxious that when the Task Force leaves in the summer it could seriously affect staff morale. If Sean became Head, of course, there would be real continuity, and the staff would feel confident and secure. However, I suspect this is not how everyone sees the situation. Common sense is often ignored.

The two Inspectors spend a good deal of the day talking to pupils and staff, especially Maeliosa, Frances and Sheila, and observing work in St George's House and the Individual Learning Unit. I keep a weather eye out for where they are and see that they're kept well supplied with tea and coffee, but they have complete freedom to go where they like, and what they finally have to say is extremely appreciative and affirming. We're all a little calmer about these monitoring visits now I think, and if I see any child stepping out of line, I've only to give them one of my special looks and the behaviour stops.

It's late afternoon by the time the Inspectors leave and I'm just beginning to get my things together to go home when the telephone rings.

'Hello Marie,' a voice says. I realize it's Canon John, though his voice sounds unrecognizably faint.

'Hello John,' I say. 'How was the meeting?'

'It wasn't . . . well, it wasn't what I'd been expecting.'

I can tell from his tone, and from the unaccustomed hesitation, that Canon John is extremely disturbed.

'What happened?'

As he begins to tell me I sit down. What happened, it seems, was a sort of 'kangaroo court,' as Canon John describes it, aimed at getting him to resign as Chairman of Governors because he is 'out of his depth'. It was by no means simply a clerical meeting since, to his surprise, Tony Mackersie was also present. Canon John was told that the LEA 'had a problem with me', and I was described as 'conceited', 'stubborn', and 'colluding with the Chairman.'

By this time I find I'm holding the phone slightly away from my ear, as if it is infected. It comes back to me that when Canon John was elected Chairman, Tony Mackersie was seen by my colleagues to throw up his hands and raise his eyes to the ceiling.

'It's outrageous,' I say.

'It's worse than that Marie,' says Canon John, his voice trembling slightly. 'The aim, as I see it, is to drive a wedge between you and me. They didn't want me to tell you any of this, but I really felt I had to.'

'I'm not going to let this go,' I say. 'I'm going to write to Tony Mackersie and ask him to explain precisely how they have reached these conclusions. Will you confirm all this to me in a note?'

'How *could* they,' I think to myself after poor Canon John, greatly distressed, finally rings off. Canon John is the most dedicated of priests, and he has been put in an impossible position, caught between his devotion to the Church and his loyalty to the school.

I fume as I start packing up my things again, but I'm also aware that my position is different from Canon John's. However persecuted and furious I may feel, I'm well used to what I would describe as Diocesan politics, which to me have nothing whatever to do with true Catholicism or with Catholic education. I go to my bookshelf and take down *The Common Good in Education*, a wise document issued by the Catholic Bishops of England and Wales, and I read again a sentence that jumped out at me when it was first published in 1997. 'Education,' the Bishops write, 'is a service provided for society for the benefit of the most vulnerable and the most disadvantaged – those whom we have a sacred duty to serve.'

I do feel I have a sacred duty to serve the children of St George's, who are some of the most vulnerable and disadvantaged I've ever met. I'm *not* going to let petty politics and bureaucracy stand in my way, I tell myself, as I put on my coat and go out into the dark. Later, deeply troubled, I speak on the phone to Father Kit and Father George, and both these men of deep understanding promise to help in any way they can.

Whatever is going on behind the scenes, life at St George's itself continues on a distinctly up-note. Our three new parent ushers – one female and two male – are proving to be a great addition to the school and very popular with the children. Before we approached them with the idea, Sean, Tracey and I had gradually got to know and like them when we met them at parents' meetings and we were attracted by their lively, warm personalities. As well as helping in school, they give us a valuable link with the parents. They all seem delighted with their new role, and they have rather elegant yellow sashes emblazoned with the words 'Parent Usher.' They arrive at about 10.30 and stay until just after lunch, helping with lunchtime supervision, and making sure that everyone gets into classes on time.

The after-school homework club is flourishing – a lot of children now stay on to do their homework, and there's always someone in charge to answer questions – and so is the after-school cadet force, run by a splendid Territorial Army officer called Colonel Cox.

In fact the cadet force was using the school premises long before we arrived but no St George's children had ever joined, and it wasn't until Sean made friends with Colonel Cox that we realized what a resource was being wasted. It's a real revelation to see what it does for some of the really disaffected teenagers, and we're hoping to send some of them on a young people's camp organized by the TA in the spring, where they'll be able to do everything from caving to orienteering and mountain biking. Colonel Cox is kind but firm, and absolutely understanding and supportive of what we are trying to do. He's another example of a local person who has taken the sort of interest in the school we hoped for from the Governors.

In November we have a visit from two other very supportive people. I first met John and Frances Sorrell of the Sorrell Foundation through the Design Council and they're a delightful couple – top designers and genuine altruists with absolutely no side. Their foundation has come up with a clever project called 'Joinedupdesignforschools', and I've asked them to come to St George's to discuss the possibility of redesigning the dining area. We've done what we can with it, putting a nice green-striped awning over the part of the playground where the children queue for lunch – before that they had to queue in the open, whatever the weather – but what we really need is an extension, and a face-lift for our grim old multi-purpose school hall.

It's warming to talk to such a creative, positive couple who have only the children's interests at heart, and Tracey and I both feel that it's an extremely well-thought-out project. A group of our children would work with a designer, developing ideas with him for the new dining room and in fact briefing him as clients. 'I can think of lots of Year 10s who would really enjoy getting involved in this,' Tracey says, excited.

I'm as excited as she is. What is education, after all, but giving children interesting experiences. We'll just have to set about raising the money for the building itself – the Foundation will supply the designer.

I'm also thrilled that Cherie Booth has agreed to talk to the children next term. I've heard from her assistant, Fiona Millar, who says she'll be delighted to come on a private visit. She's coming as a lawyer, as Cherie Booth QC, and it's splendid to have such a role model, especially for the girls.

What's uppermost in our minds now, however, is how the school will appear to Ofsted when they visit us at the end of the

month. Our teaching has moved on by leaps and bounds, attendance is up, and manners and atmosphere have improved enormously – I can't imagine any of our children now saying 'Wot?'
when asked a question by an Inspector, as they might have done
when we first came. But we're still fighting a battle with the baseball caps and the chewing gum, though letters have been written
to parents and talks have been given in assembly.

'It's not going to give Graham Ranger a good impression,' I say
to Sean as we sit discussing Action Plan targets in my office. The
Years 9s seem to be the worst, and since we have a Year 9 Parents'
Evening coming up, we decide to try a new tactic.

'Can't I just have a caramel sweet or some nougat?' I ask Sean.

'No Marie, this is Method acting. You've got to have the real
thing,' he says, laughing and pushing a packet of Wrigleys
chewing gum across the desk towards me.

'Ugh!' I say, as I put it in my mouth. 'Let me just make sure I've
got a tissue, so I can get rid of it afterwards.

We walk towards the hall where a large group of Year 9 parents
are waiting to discuss their children's GCSE options. We're both
soberly dressed, Sean in a pinstripe suit, me in businesslike Marks
& Spencer – but as we mount the steps Sean clamps a baseball cap
on the back of his head, and slouches on to the stage, glowering,
while I very obviously chew the gum, rolling it around with my
mouth open, the way children do.

Still chewing, I welcome the parents and make the usual
announcements. They gaze at me wide-eyed. They clearly see
something is wrong, but they can't decide how to react.

'Parents and Carers,' I say eventually. 'Does it seem right to you
that Mr Devlin is wearing a baseball cap with his smart suit, and
that I am chewing gum while I'm speaking to you?' There's an
astonished pause. Then a titter begins to run round the room, and
soon everyone is laughing, including the Spanish and Arabic
translators as they translate.

'We're not saying that your children should never chew gum or wear baseball caps,' I tell them, 'but there's a time and place for everything, and chewing gum and baseball caps ruin the look of a smart school uniform. They are not appropriate in school, and when your children start work they may find that they are not appropriate then either. We have a visit from the Inspectors coming up and I know that you are as anxious as I am for the school to create a good impression and shake off its label as a failing school. So please, please, try to get this message through.' From the things many of the parents say to me as they leave I can see that they have got the point and are on my side.

I find I get on well with the vast majority of our parents. I see them – and always treat them – as key partners in their children's education and no matter how swamped by problems some of them are I find there is always interest when it comes to their children. I've recently come across a wonderful guide provided by the DFES which explains the national curriculum from the very first stage right up to public exams; it is produced in the principal languages for the large number of parents who don't speak English. It is very lively, and beautifully illustrated by Quentin Blake.

I try to make parents' evenings as welcoming as possible. There are always refreshments, and I hope that every one of them goes away feeling that there is something positive about their child – though this, I must admit, can be quite a challenge. But if parents go away with a totally negative view they can feel so disaffected they give up – or in some cases lash out at their child. If a child isn't behaving well, we try get the parents in to discuss the situation – to find out what time the child goes to bed at night, how much time he or she spends watching videos, who's there in the morning before the departure for school. It all has to be done very sensitively, because a lot of our families have extremely difficult lives.

*

The Inspectors arrive for their two-day visit. We're getting to know the two of them so well that it's almost like welcoming old friends as they come through the door, though I know that I mustn't fall into that trap, but must be constantly on the alert.

I like Kath Cross particularly. She seems to me to combine all the best qualities of a classic HMI with all the warmth and charm of a really nice human being. She has a friendly, cheerful way of dealing with everyone, including Graham Ranger, who can be slightly intimidating – though Khadija, for one, is not at all intimidated. 'Hello Graham,' I hear her say teasingly when she meets him in the atrium. 'Why do you keep inspecting this school? Are you short of money or something?' I hold my breath, but Graham Ranger simply laughs, obviously thawed by Khadija's elegant and outrageous charm.

Kath Cross is particularly interested in the school's spiritual life, but it is Graham Ranger this time who falls under Father George's spell. He finds him with a group of children in the chapel, discussing the Sacrament of Holy Orders, and typically, Father George has involved the children totally in a role play. Graham Ranger becomes absorbed too, and instead of staying for part of the lesson, stays right to the end.

There is another, unforgettable moment on the second day. It is the Thursday before Advent Sunday and Father George holds a special service in the atrium before school. It is a dark wintry day and all the lights are switched off. As children, staff and Inspectors stand silently waiting, a pure soprano voice pierces the gloom: 'Oh come, oh come, Emmanuel!', and Katerina and the choir enter, each carrying a candle, the choir joining their voices with Katerina's in a wonderful swelling sound that fills the whole atrium. Glancing round at everyone standing quietly together, the Muslim girls in their headscarves, the bigger boys with their heads awkwardly bowed, I have a sudden sense that, whatever the petty difficulties we're facing, 'All will be well, and all manner of things will be well.'

Later in the day we receive the Inspectors' verbal report, and it is certainly very encouraging, though it gives nothing away about how near we are to reaching the magic 'Off Special Measures'. But we are told that we have made 'good progress overall', and there is praise for the 'positive working atmosphere' and for the effectiveness of the senior management team. I'm also delighted that the Inspectors feel St George's is rapidly 'gaining a positive profile in the local area'.

Our 'positive profile' seems a little dented next day when I receive a strong letter from a local Councillor – with copy to John Harris, the Director of Education – complaining about the behaviour of four of our girls in a nearby shop. The shopkeeper has accused them of stealing cigarettes and chocolate, and of behaving towards him in an extremely rude and uncouth way. What a pity that this is the Councillor's first involvement with the school, I think. She's never visited us.

This is just the kind of incident we want to avoid, and Eddie immediately goes down to talk to the shopkeeper, returning with a grainy security video, which we peer at repeatedly for clues. It isn't possible to identify the culprits, though we have a shrewd idea of who they may be, but I talk very forcefully to all the children about the incident in Assembly, and I write to the Councillor, saying how seriously we take it. Eddie agrees to drop in regularly on the local shops so that the shopkeepers feel they have a channel of communication with us. They are friendly, hardworking people and I'm appalled at the thought that they should be subjected to abuse from badly behaved teenagers.

The queues waiting under the green-striped awning at lunchtime are suddenly sparser. The children are all given their own times for joining the lunch queue so that they can play in the playground or attend clubs, but a lot of them like to hang out with their friends, and the area outside the dining room is usually a heaving mass of children. For the Muslim children it's now Ramadan, and they are not permitted to eat during daylight hours. I notice that during the lunch hour most of them are just hanging about in the classrooms, separated from the rest of the school.

'Are you all right? Are you finding fasting difficult, with everyone else eating?' I ask Nekka, one of a group I meet on the top corridor.

'It's a bit hard . . . but we get used to it,' she says with a shy smile.

'It must be,' I say, 'but I'm so glad you are doing it. It's very important.'

I talk to Father George, and we decide the Muslim children need a room where they can go to pray and be quiet, and not be confronted by other children eating when they are fasting. The Technology Department offers a classroom, and we put a notice on the door during the lunch hour saying 'Quiet Please. Prayer Room' in Arabic and English. The girls especially, I notice, like to use it, praying or just sitting quietly together. Nearly one-third of the school is Muslim, and I feel this is an important gesture of respect and inclusiveness towards another faith.

For Christians this is an important time too, the beginning of Advent, a season of peace, joy and expectation. So how sadly ironic it is that I should be bogged down in a fruitless correspondence with the Church's representatives about the allegations of 'illegal behaviour' that have been made against me. One point at issue is whether I have sought to 'play any part' in the appointment of my successor, something that I am told 'regulations expressly forbid'. But, as I point out to Mgr Barltrop in a letter, though of course being a member of the Appointment Panel or taking part in a vote would be quite wrong, common sense suggests that I might have a useful view on the school's future development. No one from his office has ever asked my opinion on these matters, nor visited the school or ever asked me how it is developing.

As to the accusation that I have 'acted improperly' in attempting to influence the appointment of Foundation Governors, I again point out that for years it has been common practice for the Westminster Diocese to ask headteachers for the names of possible candidates to serve on the Boards of their schools. It may be that Mgr Barltrop is not aware of this, but if he is not, he should be, and should inform the appropriate Association of Headteachers so that their members may avoid the kind of accusations that are being levelled at me. After regretfully expressing my doubts that the Trustee's representative really understands what is being demanded of senior management at St George's, I end my letter by holding out an olive branch, inviting Mgr Barltrop as Episcopal Vicar to visit the school early next year to pray with us. I receive no reply to my letter.

Outwardly I appear positive and cheerful – I know I must – but I'm bewildered and deeply disturbed by the behaviour of the Diocese. Until quite recently what it amounted to was a spectacular and in my view unforgivable lack of support, but now I feel that those who should be supporting me are actually lined up against me, and it is very undermining. I don't think I could go on without the wonderful co-operation I get here at every level, not only from the teachers, but from the rest of the staff too – Francisco with his cheerful willingness to take on anything that's needed, Suzie with her ready smile and soothing cups of tea, Wendy, Maggie, all of them. These are the real Christians, to me.

Father George's presence, too, seems to put things immediately into another perspective. His wise counsel is available to everyone, and he's always in the chapel during breaks and lunch hours, ready to chat about something important or about nothing in particular – I rarely see Father George eat, he seems to live on air.

'Where are you going?' I heard one small girl say to a friend.

'Just gonna hang out with Father George,' came the casual reply. I smile, knowing that some children are keen to prepare for their First Communion and want to talk about this with him while still appearing cool.

Thanks to Father George's flawless taste, we have a beautiful new crib in the atrium. I wanted something that would give reality to the Christmas story for children to whom it's not familiar, so I commissioned him to go out and buy some figures. I should have known that Father George would never buy anything second-best, but I must confess I wasn't quite prepared for what arrived. The wooden figures are almost life-sized, beautifully carved and exquisitely painted – Mary, Joseph, the angels and shepherds, the ox and the ass, and of course Baby Jesus. The Technology Department has constructed a handsome wooden manger, and the whole thing is about half the width of the atrium. The children love it, and the younger ones can't resist moving the figures around – Baby Jesus tends to disappear from the front of the manger, but he's always there somewhere, tucked into the straw, and it's done with respect, nothing is ever damaged.

We nearly had a conflagration one morning, though. Some well-meaning member of staff had put a piece of pink cellophane over the bulb at the back to create a nice rosy light, and when Mick turned it on first thing it wasn't long before the cellophane got hot and began to smoke. Luckily Sean noticed it when he arrived at seven am, but I dread to think what would have happened if it had reached the hay.

Hanging in the atrium, also thanks to Father George, are two large and vividly coloured oil paintings of our Patron Saint, locked in mortal combat with a vast dragon – a gift from St James's, Spanish Place. I look at them thoughtfully these days as I go past.

As the end of term approaches, there's the lovely familiar feeling of anticipation. The choir is rehearsing for the end of term carol service, and snatches of carols old and new waft from the hall. Classrooms take on a Christmassy look, outings and class parties are planned – the dreaded karaoke parties, of course, being top favourite.

Christmas celebrations are a useful carrot to dangle in front of the children to keep them up to scratch.

'I'd love to come and see you doing your karaoke,' I tell the younger ones, not entirely truthfully, 'but I'll only be able to if you're all wearing your correct school uniform and looking very neat and tidy for the next few days.'

'I don't think you'll be able to go ice skating if all your work isn't handed in and all your books aren't marked,' I overhear Sean telling another class.

'We can certainly have a very *small* celebration for Christmas,' I say to the whole school in assembly, 'but we can't do anything very exciting unless everybody's on their best behaviour, and we've got a tidy school.'

As the end of term approaches, the school looks sparkling. Noticeboards are tidied, Christmas displays pinned up in class-rooms, decorations hung in the atrium. 'I got glubbs,' says Ali to me happily, holding up small hands in enormous plastic gloves as he joins the playground litter patrol.

Walking briskly up Lanark Road at around 7.30 am on the day of the carol service, I'm aware of the loud clack of my heels on the icy pavement, my breath hangs in the air, and the road under the streetlights glistens with a heavy white frost. As I approach the school, I'm conscious that something is different. Tracey appears simultaneously from the carpark, wrapped warmly in woolly hat and scarf.

'Where are the lights?' she says immediately.

Of course! The whole school is in darkness. We find Sean already in.

'The power's off,' he says. 'I've been trying to get through to the LEA for emergency help, but there's no one answering.'

The building's freezing and we stumble about with our coats on. 'Oh well,' I say, 'the power will probably come on soon. It usually does.'

'The problem is, though, it's only us,' says Sean, looking out of the window. 'The lights are on everywhere else.'

It's 8.30 by now and the day has dawned, grey and uninviting.

The staff are beginning to arrive and several of them make it clear that they think it's much too dark and cold to work. It is, and I rack my brains to think how we're going to cope as the children start to appear. Sean keeps trying the LEA, but still can't get an answer.

Father George appears from the chapel carrying some large church candles which we place round the atrium, with Maggie and Mick standing guard. Ironically, after months of telling the children to take off their coats in class, we now go round making sure they've got them on.

'Don't you know that it's illegal to keep us here when it's so cold? You've got no right to do it you know. We can sue you.'

Predictably Peta appears at my door to berate me about the situation. She's in a state of high anxiety, but we manage to persuade her back into her classroom. I'm in a state of fairly high anxiety myself by the time the electricians finally arrive.

'It's yer circuit switch,' they tell us with the gloomy satisfaction of people who have made a terminal diagnosis.

'How soon can you fix it?'

'It'll be tomorrow now. The power'll be off most of the day and you do know, don't you, that once the boiler's fixed the building's not going to warm up straightaway.'

This is terrible. Clearly I've no option but to close the school for forty-eight hours and postpone the carol service. Sean hastens down to Prontaprint to copy a handwritten note to that effect for parents, while I go and see Barbara – I can't send the children who have free school meals out with no lunch and no money on a freezing day like this. Fortunately Barbara has some gas ovens and rings, and she sets about preparing a hot snack for them. Meantime the admin and welfare staff start phoning parents, asking them to collect their children or give permission for them to go home, while I phone Canon John.

He understands the situation and trusts my judgement – unlike the LEA apparently. I'm closely questioned on the phone about my reasons for closing the school and we're instructed to attend a meeting with them tomorrow, as if we might be planning a couple of days' illicit holiday. What kind of world are they living in, I wonder . . . Actually, I know only too well.

'I must go. I've got children to see to here,' I say briskly, cutting short the conversation.

We line the children up in the hall, year group by year group, to check that all their homes have been contacted and that everyone who needs it has had something to eat. Even with so many people in the building it's bitterly cold, and teeth are chattering. Some parents arrive to collect their children, and we send the rest off in small groups.

Sean, Tracey, Eddie and David stand by the gates with the three parent ushers, making sure that all the children have their letters. After a while one of the parent ushers comes back into school holding the little African boy Mohammed by the hand. Mohammed seems on the verge of tears. We already know that he's having problems fitting in with his father's new family. 'I think he doesn't want to go back home because his dad's not there in the day,' Tracey tells me.

Wendy makes another call to Mohammed's home, and the parent usher offers to walk back with him, which seems to cheer him up a little. I thank my lucky stars for the parent ushers. The effect they have on the school is far greater than the actual time they spend here, and they all seem to have an instinct for picking out the children who are a bit isolated, as well as knowing how to jolly the difficult ones along.

Inside, Barbara is handing out hot drinks to the staff, and gradually they leave, lugging heavy bags and briefcases of marking and preparation work to do at home.

Next day, well muffled up, I go into school to see how things are progressing. The boiler men are there and hard at work, as Mick, recovered now from his accident, reports when I meet him in the atrium.

'It's freezing, Mick,' I say. I'm still wearing my coat, thick scarf and woollen gloves.

'It certainly is that, Lady Stubbs,' says Mick cheerfully.

Still wearing my gloves, I have another brisk conversation with the LEA from my icy office, this time with the Assistant Director of Education who rings to enquire what is happening. After hearing what I have to say, she agrees that there is really no need for a meeting, and I go home thankfully to make some last-minute additions to the school Christmas card list and other administrative chores in the warmth of my home.

Monday 18 December. We've had the karaoke parties, the quizzes, and the outings. We've had Christmas charades, where the children's written descriptions of the staff were often illuminating. 'Makes you feel comfutable' is one verdict on Tracey. 'She always says what is on her mind. She has taken us on a lot of trips' sums up our enthusiastic PE teacher, Eve Churchward, and I am 'very fashionable' with 'a good sence of humour', I'm pleased to learn.

Now, at last, we're having the carol service. The parents have arrived in large numbers, the choir are in place on stage, the shepherds are ready and waiting outside the hall, dressed in an assortment of sheets and knotted handkerchiefs, and so are the wise men, looking particularly exotic and impressive. Every Christmas since I've known her Tracey has been finding costumes for nativity plays, and this one is no exception. It's all part of the touching and familiar ritual that makes up Christmas in a school, especially a Catholic one.

What distinguishes this occasion is the sheer quality of the music, and of the short but affecting nativity scenes produced by Gillian who has been working hard with Katerina, Carol Goodridge, our new Head of Music, and her assistant Justin. Children of every religion sing in the senior and junior choirs, and the carols, some old, some new, are drawn from various different cultures and many parts of the world. It is a Catholic service in the true sense of the word, bringing us all together in a spirit of peace and goodwill. One by one, children of different nationalities rise and go to the lectern, some of them to read aloud the magical

210

words of the Bible story, some to read poems. All of them do it clearly and earnestly and when Barrie from Year 9 gives us a touching solo there's barely a dry eye in the house.

Finally we raise the roof with 'O Come, All Ye Faithful', Canon John gives us a Christmas blessing and we all troop out for a seasonal drink and a mince-pie. How nice our parents are, I think to myself afterwards. So many are so genuinely and openly appreciative that I go home feeling warmed.

By the time the last day of term arrives, as usual the staff and I feel as if we're barely on our feet we're so exhausted, but we get together in the staff room when the children have left to drink a glass and wish one another a merry Christmas. It's a delight to me to see that Ariadne, though she is tired like the rest of us, is looking so much more relaxed. 'Well,' I say, raising my glass. 'Here's to 2001 and coming off Special Measures.'

'Hear, hear,' says everyone.

'And on that theme,' announces Sean. 'I can now reveal that attendance figures for this term are up to 89 per cent. So we've only one per cent to go before we can be classed as normal.'

There's clapping and a lot of laughter and joking about whether any of us can be considered normal any more.

'What about "Moving Forward Together in 2000"? It will be 2001 next term. We'll have to get everything reprinted,' Ariadne points out.

She's right. But then I have an inspiration. 'Well, how about simplifying it to "Moving Forward Together"? It's long-term and positive, and it would be an economy because we could just trim the posters.'

'How Scottish!' says someone.

We take one down from the noticeboard and trim it to see how it looks, and we all agree that it works.

'Well,' I say, raising my glass again. 'Here's to Moving Forward Together then.'

'Moving Forward Together,' everyone choruses.

The atmosphere is warm and united, and as I finally make my way home on the tube with the crowds of late-night Christmas shoppers, I think how much like a happy family the staff room feels.

7

Christmas

My own family, I know, are the ones who need my attention now. They have all supported me loyally, but in the run-up to Christmas, when I would normally be organizing outings and helping out with shopping and babysitting, they've been getting a little plaintive. I make a resolution that I won't even mention St George's over Christmas. I can't promise myself not to think about it – that would be unrealistic – but I decide that I'm just going to bite my tongue.

I've always done the catering for our big family gatherings and I've let everyone know that this year's going to be no different – it's partly habit, but this time it also feels like a matter of pride. Fortunately I've managed to buy all my presents on late-night trips to the West End, but on the first weekend of the holidays the shock of doing a huge Christmas food shop makes me feel as if I've been shot from a cannon, straight into Sainsbury's. Arriving home I look at the wreckage of my domestic arrangements, scrabble about in the airing cupboard searching for tablecloths and table napkins, wonder where that thing called an iron is, and dream a little of a time when I'll be able to manage these things properly, when I won't wake exhausted every morning and fall into bed exhausted every night.

Perhaps, subconsciously, I'm beginning to prepare myself for my parting from St George's. Tracey, Sean and I went out together for a simple meal just before the end of term, and we all agreed that we had no idea, on that grim day when we started, how bonded to St George's we would all become. I suppose I might have known it would happen. Taking on a school is like taking on a child – you get terribly interested in it, and you begin to want to look after it and protect it. I want to see the little toddler that St George's still is grow up and flourish. I feel a responsibility to it, and I know that the hands I want to leave it in are Sean's.

I think about all my lovely staff. We've moulded ourselves into such a close and happy team, but I know that very gradually I must begin to withdraw from them, so that they won't miss me when I go. To me that's part of the job and very important, a way of freeing them to bond with the new Head, whoever that may be, or to get on with whatever else they choose. I think you must do that with children too. I've always felt exasperated with teachers who have pupils weeping and wailing when they leave. When you're young and you want to finish with a boyfriend, you tend to make yourself slightly unpleasant, to withdraw, so that it's easier for him to let go, and that's how I think it should be.

As I wrap presents and decorate the tree, I can't get the situation with the Diocese out of my mind. I think admiringly of Father George who manages, with his usual good judgement, to stay well clear of local church politics. Father George's connections, he says, are at the top – not because he's ambitious or wants to make use of them in any way, I'm sure, but simply because people are attracted by his style and by the kind of person he is. Typically he's gone off to Rome this Christmas, where he hopes to attend the Pope's private Mass. I'm not clear about how all this works, but am just grateful to have him on board.

On Christmas Eve we go to Midnight Mass ourselves, driving under clear stars through the frosty, silent countryside. On Christmas morning the whole family arrives for lunch, though we miss my mother who finds the journey down from Glasgow too tiring nowadays. We all chat to her on the phone, and as I'm putting the receiver down I have a sudden urge to ring Sean about something that's worrying me in the Action Plan. Secretly, I'm also longing to hear whether he's finally decided to apply for the headship. However, I know it's more than my life is worth to open my mouth on the subject of St George's – the family quite reasonably want a break – so I suppress the thought, and return to the kitchen, where Fiona and Hilary, with a lot of laughter, are making the bread sauce.

Nadine's little daughter Sophie is four now, curious about everything. I watch her as she sits on the floor, in a sea of Christmas wrappings, examining something. It's a little box, and when you press the catch in the right way it springs open. She's fascinated – you can almost hear her imagination working.

> I buried the key of a sardine tin.
> Resurrected, I thought it might unlock the universe.

Those lovely lines by one of my favourite poets, the Australian Judith Wright, sum up for me the hopefulness of childhood. They feel somehow an appropriate thought with which to begin the new millennium.

8

The Inspection

Spring Term, 8 January to 6 April

'**W**ho was that nun I saw disappearing down the corridor just now? Was it someone to see Father George?' I say to Tracey when she looks into my office on the first Friday afternoon of term.

Tracey looks blank for a moment, then she starts laughing. 'I think it might have been Sister Mary Clarence. Or it could have been Sister Mary Lazarus. I'm quite not sure.'

'Sister Mary Clarence?' I say, puzzled. 'Who's she . . .?' Then the penny drops.

'Gillian's having a costume fitting – I think it's the nuns this afternoon,' says Tracey. 'She says you have no idea how difficult it is to get their habits right. And with people like Father George around of course, they've got to be.'

'I can't imagine Gillian allowing anything through that's not absolutely correct,' I say.

It's less than a month now to the first night of *Sister Act*. As soon as Gillian had the go-ahead, she called a staff meeting to discuss what help she needed, and since the autumn *Sister Act* has been like an electric current running through all our lives. Every department seems to have become involved. Art and Technology are constructing and painting the scenery, Carol and Katerina are helping with music, Father George is supplying the ecclesiastical extras and everyone's pitching in to help with props and costumes, which are being made, borrowed or hired.

216

Urgent appeals are appearing on noticeboards. 'More rosaries needed for *Sister Act*.' 'Has anyone got an old-looking/antique table or desk they could lend?' 'Front of house – please encourage your year group to volunteer.'

It really is a team effort, and it looks as if it's going to be a sell-out. Tickets are on sale every lunchtime from a desk in the atrium and Gillian has made sure that there are professional-looking posters with pictures of the cast, just as in a real theatre. As for the children, I've never known them to be so caught up in anything – except perhaps football. They're approaching it all like real professionals, checking the rehearsal schedule in the atrium for last-minute changes, making sure they're word-perfect, and turning up on time.

What pleases me most is that Gillian has managed to involve some of our more difficult characters like Debbie – who apparently thought better of walking out – Jason, and even Jo.

Jo and I have had several encounters since the day when her parents came to my office to confront Jeanie's parents about the set-to the girls had had. I managed to mediate then, and both girls made all kinds of promises, but Jo's behaviour hasn't changed. She's like a nervous little cat with her claws always at the ready. Last term she was involved in another particularly unpleasant episode in the playground, and I made the decision then to exclude her for a few days. It's not something I ever do lightly, and permanent exclusion is something I go out of my way to avoid. You are, after all, telling a child you've given up on them and wasting any work you may have done, and it's an extremely serious matter for a head. But occasionally, as in this case, a temporary exclusion seems justified. The staff were at the end of their tether with Jo, and this demonstrated to them – and her – that it could be done.

Jo's father came to see me, and he was extremely angry. 'Why do you always pick on *her*?' he kept repeating. 'She's only standing up for herself. If she hits out at someone it's because they've given her grief.'

I observed that Jo really does need to learn that there are other ways of dealing with people who annoy her.

'No she doesn't,' he said. 'Not down where we live. She needs to be able to look after herself. That's was she needs.'

I could understand his anxieties. They live on a tough estate.

'But if Jo thinks biting and scratching is the only way to approach a problem, she's going to be in serious trouble one day. She could even end up in court,' I pointed out.

In the end Jo's father calmed down, and we had a useful discussion. We agreed it might help to channel Jo's energies into some activity that would make her feel calmer and more physically confident about herself. Gillian and Tracey persuaded her to join the dance club, and I'm delighted that she'll be dancing in *Sister Act*. I'm genuinely surprised at the range of children who are either acting in it or participating in some other way. It's a clever choice of Gillian's. The boys aren't embarrassed to be cast as American cops and gangsters – in fact it seems quite macho.

'That was a really nice piece of writing Mandy, and you got it in on time!' Tracey has stopped on the stairs to speak to a stocky, untidy-looking Year 10 with bleached hair growing out at the roots and enormous hoop earrings.

'Thanks Mandy!' Angela Camilleri, laden with big art folders, hurries through a door ahead of Mandy and turns to give her a special smile.

'Well done Mandy,' I say when I meet her in the atrium. Mandy looks at me with some surprise.

'Na,' she says, tossing her head so that her big earrings swing to and fro. 'You don't mean that. I'm crap, I am.' She's holding a big untidy-looking sheaf of papers clutched to her chest and I see that her nails are chipped and bitten.

'I don't believe that. I'm hearing good things about you,' I say.

'Yeah?' she says uncertainly, casting a half-smile at me over her shoulder as she goes into the classroom, her pile of papers disintegrating all over the floor as she sits down, which makes the whole class laugh.

There are a number of children like Mandy in many schools. She's always late with her work and late for lessons, the last in after break, the first to attract attention by giving a silly answer in class, and generally an unhelpful influence on her group of friends. If there's an accident in the Technology Room or the Art Department, Mandy's quite likely to be behind it. She's careless and slapdash and never has the right equipment with her, and we all agree that she's got stuck in her role as the class clown, someone who's dim and thoroughly disorganized.

In fact she's an interesting girl with potential, though she's doing her best to hide it. 'She did a really imaginative piece of writing for me a few weeks ago,' says Tracey, at the meeting we convene to discuss the problem.

'Yes, when she takes the trouble her art work is very original,' adds Angela.

'It's just that she's a pain in the neck,' says someone else ruefully, and we all laugh.

We want to try to give Mandy a new image of herself, so that's why we're bombarding her with positive comments. Everyone on the staff is looking for opportunities to build her up and find things to praise her for. It can go a long way to changing behaviour, and so can the reverse. Sometimes we decide we all need to be extremely firm for a while with a child who's behaving badly. It all depends on the nature of the child. Horses for courses.

'*Bonjour*, Lady Stubbs.' An earnest little Year 8 girl looks up from her book.

'*Bonjour*, Anna.'

'Would they call you "Lady Stubbs" in France, Lady Stubbs?'

'No, I think they would just call me "Madame Stubbs".'

'They chopped titled people's heads off, didn't they? In that resolution they had.'

We're talking in the library, which has acquired a distinctly Gallic air, with prints by Matisse and Magritte on the walls, and evocative photographs of Paris by well-known French photographers. We're in the midst of French week, and Khadija and the Modern Languages Department have managed to inject a French element into almost every part of the curriculum. The theme in the Design Department is 'French Fashion since 1850', with wall displays about Yves St Laurent and other French couturiers. In Science, the children are finding out about the work of Pasteur and Marie Curie, in music they're listening to Bizet, and the Video Club is showing a Truffaut film.

Not to be outdone, the canteen is offering a 'French breakfast' of orange juice and croissants, with Barbara and the rest of the staff in typical French aprons and a French flag flying over the food area. Most popular of all, the Modern Languages staff are handing out French chocolates at morning break and after lunch.

To our delight, the redesign of the canteen is under review. We've just heard that we are one of seven schools selected to take part in the Sorrells' 'joinedupdesignforschools' project. The projects chosen by the other schools are interestingly varied, ranging from a tree house for a school in Glasgow which is short of space, to a new summer uniform for a school in Nottingham, on which they'll be working with the designer Paul Smith.

We've chosen fifteen Year 10s to work on our dining area – seven boys and eight girls, right across the ability range. It isn't only the brightest or best-behaved children who get chosen for special projects or outings – Tracey always talks to the year head and tries to include children who would benefit, perhaps because they're discouraged, or have very low expectations of themselves, and need a boost. The designer Ben Kelly, who will be working with the children, has come into school to meet Tracey, Angela Camilleri, and Hannah Sakyi from Food Technology and they've decided they need to include some lively characters who have plenty of chutzpah and strong opinions. There's no shortage of those in Year 10.

The children start by carrying out a time and motion study to find out what exactly goes on at lunchtime, and for a couple of weeks we're accosted at all points by Year 10s carrying clipboards and filling in impressive-looking questionnaires. The exercise reveals a high level of dissatisfaction – 'It's like being in a factory and being pushed towards your food,' says someone – and most pupils complain they have very little free time in the lunchbreak because they spend so much time queuing. The next stage is to canvass everyone's opinions on improvements they would like to see. Barbara sensibly suggests that we need more tills to speed up serving and paying for food, and other requests are for better tables and more light.

Ben Kelly strikes just the right note with the children – encouraging, open-minded and respectful of their suggestions. They spend a happy day with him, John and Frances, touring restaurants and cafés in the West End, looking at design features that work well. Afterwards they go to the Design Centre to see examples of Ben's work. They are followed around by a television crew who are filming the project for a series of programmes to be screened in 2002, and Frances is impressed by the sensible way the children deal with it.

The proposal that emerges is for a new double-height, top-lit foyer connected to our existing hall, and there is an idea for lightweight dining tables and seats that can be raised and stored flat against the wall to make the space we have more flexible. As they work with Ben the children's confidence grows and their written reports are full of enthusiasm. 'The designers are really up-front people. They have taken our ideas and improved them in many different ways. I think this project is great, especially telling everybody "I'm helping to design the lunch hall for you lot",' writes one. 'It feels like the school is actually putting your ideas forward,' writes another.

As fourteen-year-old Melissa concludes: 'It just goes to show that design is more than Ikea furniture.' Secretly, however, I give thanks for Ikea, whose nice-looking furniture has given a lot of areas in the school a facelift at a very modest price.

Monday 5 February. I'm not sure how we're going to survive all this week's excitements. On Tuesday we have the first performance of *Sister Act* – a matinée we're putting on for local primary schools. On Wednesday afternoon Cherie Blair is visiting St George's, and on Wednesday and Thursday we have evening performances of *Sister Act*. Today is the first full dress rehearsal, and the hall is stacked up with furniture, props and scenery. The leading actors are in a state of nervous excitement, someone vital is away ill, there are anxieties about a costume that's gone missing, and the whole school is behaving rather as if it's the end of term. I have to give everyone a sober reminder in assembly that we have an extremely important inspection coming up in just over a month and we haven't got room to let things slide.

'We're a busy, happy school,' I tell them, 'with no time for, or interest in, irresponsible behaviour.'

I'm sitting in my office mid-morning when Suzie buzzes me to say that the Westminster Council Press Office is on the line. I was the school's press officer for thirteen years at The Douay Martyrs, and for me dealing with the press has become something to enjoy. The conversation goes something like this.

'Oh hello Lady Stubbs. This is just to say that we'll be dealing with all the publicity for Mrs Blair's visit on Wednesday, so there's nothing you need to do.'

'Mrs Blair's not coming,' I say mischievously.

'I'm sorry . . .?'

'I think you've been given the wrong information. It's not Mrs Blair who's coming. It's Cherie Booth QC, and we have everything arranged already.'

'I'm afraid you can't do that. This is an important visit. It's election year and this is the Prime Minister's wife. There's no question about who should handle it – it's much too politically loaded for the school to deal with.'

'Look,' I say, beginning to lose patience. 'Cherie Booth is a top QC who is coming to talk to the children here about careers in the law. It's a private visit. Her assistant Fiona Millar has sorted everything out.'

There's a silence. 'Well, I'll have to consult about this,' the voice on the other end says finally, before ringing off.

For a moment I see the whole visit fading away if they get involved. 'I think there's been a misunderstanding and the wool's got a bit tangled,' I say tactfully in answer to a phone call about the arrangements.

Sorting things out is easier said than done, but I put my foot down and make it quite clear that I'm keeping numbers small and don't want a formal occasion, though I'm very happy for Councillor Joiner, who has been a good friend to us, to attend.

When Cherie Blair does arrive, accompanied by Fiona Millar, she is warm and utterly natural, and we are all very taken with her dashing purple pants suit and little high-heeled boots. Canon John, Peter Brown and Jacques Delacave have all joined us for the occasion, and it's amusing to see how completely they all succumb to her charm, twinkling away at her as she chats unself-consciously with them in the atrium.

She speaks to the young people in the packed library not just as a lawyer but as a mother, answering their concerns in a very warm and human way, encouraging them to stick at the more boring work in order to enjoy an interesting career later on, and giving a realistic picture of what it's like to work in the law, particularly for women. She admits honestly that she is very busy, and doesn't always know how she is going to cope. Despite her razor-sharp intelligence, she comes across as the kind of friendly, approachable woman you could enjoy chatting to.

Paula Pryke has made up a lovely scented nosegay for the children to present to her, such as was carried by judges in olden times. Cherie Booth is obviously touched by this imaginative gesture as well as by the donation the children have collected for CAFOD's emergency appeal for the terrible earthquake in Gujerat, a disaster that affects a number of our children's families.

I too am touched that she should have found time in her packed schedule to come to St George's, and the effect on the children of someone so warm, glamorous *and* successful is tremendous. We all agree that her photographs don't do her justice.

Martina sums up her appeal as we watch her car departing: 'She's really brainy, and I liked her boots.'

Exhausted by the social demands of the day and by the prospect of a long evening ahead, I slip off at six o'clock for a soothing hour at Persis, leaving Sean and Tracey to hold the fort. By the time I get back the audience is already beginning to arrive. The excitement everywhere is palpable – it's as if everyone's nerves have been wound up a notch or two, including the parents', many of whom must have been living with *Sister Act* for months. There's a lot of chatter and laughter in the auditorium, though no one, I think, knows quite what to expect.

Backstage, and in the classrooms where the cast is getting made up and ready, staff are zipping cabaret singers into figure-hugging satin dresses, gangsters in sharp suits are slapping on hair gel and having their ties adjusted, and nuns are wrestling with voluminous black habits. Gillian is everywhere, calming, encouraging, dealing with last-minute emergencies, clear and professional as always, but never losing her sense of humour.

As I take my place in the audience with Canon John, I spot a few other Governors settling into their seats. I realize I'm a bit nervous too, rather as if I'm watching members of the family perform. The matinée apparently went off very well, but this is when the children will be on show for the first time to their families and friends. Everyone has put so much into this production, not just the children and the teaching staff – especially Katerina who has put in long hours on the music – but people like Mick and Francisco. Everyone's lent a hand.

But when the curtain rises on a nightclub scene in Reno I soon forget my nerves. This isn't just any school production – it's the most professional thing I've ever seen on a school stage, and the children's confidence and delivery is amazing. It's as if some of them have been just waiting for this in order to come into their own.

It's a gorgeously schmaltzy story. Glamorous cabaret singer Dolores agrees to testify against her Mafia boyfriend after she witnesses a murder. With a price on her head, she's hidden by the police in a convent disguised as 'Sister Mary Clarence', where she changes the nuns' lives for ever and transforms the hopeless choir into the biggest attraction in town. It has all the right ingredients – fun and humour, plenty of action with cops and gangster chases, and great singing and dancing opportunities, as 'Sister Mary Clarence' rehearses her fellow Sisters in wonderful gospel numbers like 'I will follow Him' that have us all tapping our feet. And when the Sisters perform for the Pope, by special request, the final chorus simply brings the house down.

It's a very moral story, too. The gangsters are brought to justice, worldly Dolores discovers her own spiritual values, and under her influence the sisters face reality and begin to help the local community – so I need have had no worries on that score. And I like the dénouement, which seems singularly appropriate – the failing convent, which had lost its way and was soon to be closed, is saved by Dolores' efforts, with contributions from the Police Department. The only difference, I reflect rather sadly, is the enthusiastic support she gets from the local Monsignor.

The second night is just as successful, and after the final curtain the beaming cast are called back on stage time after time until the audience is exhausted with clapping. Everybody is knocked sideways by this outpouring of joyful high spirits and natural talent and by the sheer professionalism of what they've just seen. There's a special curtain call and a thank-you for all the backstage helpers, and I'm touched to see Debbie taking her bow. And Jason, as one of the Mafia henchmen, was an inspired piece of casting.

The person to whom we owe everything, of course, is Gillian, and it's an emotional moment when I thank her and the cast present her with an enormous bouquet of flowers, especially as her mother has come all the way from South Africa to see the production and is sitting in the front row.

'I've never seen anything like it – anywhere,' says Sean, as we're finally packing up to go home.

'Neither have I,' I say. 'I think we can take a little of the credit, don't you Mr Devlin, for spotting Gillian and persuading her to stay?'

Tracey, who has just come in, nods. 'She's brought the whole school together. Who would have thought a year ago that we'd ever see that?'

Who could have imagined any of this a year ago, I think, as I doze fitfully on the way home in the taxi I've allowed myself for once. I've sat through umpteen school productions, some of them very good, but nothing has been in the same league as what I've just seen at St George's, done by a group of 'kids' who were once written off as unmanageable.

The whole school is as high as a kite afterwards, and enthusiastic letters flood in from Peter Brown and other Governors, and from a primary school headteacher and local residents we invited to see the show. We're all on Cloud Nine for weeks and Carol, a delightful, bubbly version of Bonnie Langford, who played the convent's autocratic Mother Superior, was so convincing that we can't resist greeting her as 'Reverend Mother' and deferring to her when we go through doors.

I have a revealing exchange with another member of the cast when I stop to congratulate her in the corridor.

'Can I ask you something, Headmistress?'

'Of course you can.'

'Were we really good? I mean properly good. People aren't just being nice because everyone behaved and there wasn't no trouble?'

I see the insecurity in her eyes. 'You weren't just good,' I say,

'You were absolutely magnificent. There isn't a school in the country that wouldn't have been proud of a production like that.'

Her smile is radiant. 'Oh that's all right then,' she says. 'Thanks, Headmistress.' Then, as she walks off down the corridor, she turns and smiles again. 'We had a really good time, didn't we?'

Much less fun is the thought of all we have to do before the Inspection on 14 March, which is approaching fast. Over the years I've developed my own system for dealing with inspections, and this one is not materially different from any other. It's just that so much hangs on it – the whole future of the school in fact, which means the future of the children and the staff. I'm aware every day of the threat to St George's if we don't manage to get off Special Measures this time round. Time is running out for the Task Force.

I know we have a clear conscience. We've tackled all the targets set in the Action Plan, and analysed our progress rigorously and regularly. In most areas it's been huge, and it's my job to communicate this to the Inspectors in the best possible way. The staff have been brilliant, working hard and willingly and accepting my sometimes rather unusual approach with friendly good humour. Early in the term I produced a special staff bulletin called 'Off Special Measures', with a drawing of a skeleton on the cover. Inside, under the heading 'Nitty Gritties: The Skeleton that Holds Everything Together', I listed the basic things we must attend to if we are to get off Special Measures – the kind of things Inspectors look for but that can easily be allowed to slip under the pressure of events.

These include making sure that corridor duties and lunch duties are always covered, arriving on time for lessons, keeping up to date with marking, and making sure that there are lively displays on classroom walls. I also included basic pastoral duties for the staff – following up parental enquiries and unauthorized absences without delay, completing registers, and – just as important – programming some fun into the time spent with their forms. We do all of this, but we have to be *seen* to be doing it. The bulletin also defines each staff member's particular responsibilities because in my book having a clear picture of your role is an important part of doing it well.

I can imagine that this time last year there might have been some sniffy reactions to such a 'childish' presentation and to being offered such basic advice, but fortunately by and large these staff are mature enough to accept help in the spirit in which it is given. The skeleton was immediately nicknamed George, and 'George Says . . .', a parody of that favourite game 'O'Grady Says . . .', has become a catchphrase in the staff room when something needs to be done.

We have gradually developed a format that makes lesson-planning easier and interpreting lessons more straightforward for anyone who is observing. Staff have become so confident and skilful that lesson plans can now be briefer and more flexible, and teachers are involving the children in creating their own learning aims for the next lesson.

Tracey has done some helpful team-teaching with younger members of staff, who have worked in the classroom beside her, learning at first hand from her experience and her imaginative approach. This, on occasion, includes videoing the class discussing a particular topic and playing the video back to them the next week. It's a kind of instant revision, it shows the children how they learn and interact, and they love it.

Modest and ever-willing to learn, Tracey acknowledges that working with younger staff has been a learning experience for her too. The young staff themselves suggested the idea, and I was delighted that they felt able to. It showed me that we are now a real learning community, where people feel able to be open about their difficulties and their mistakes. As I always tell my staff, I don't mind anyone making a mistake, provided they are willing to learn from it.

The children who are taking GCSEs this year are somewhat better prepared than last, but it's a slow process, improving pass-rates. The target we've been set by the LEA through Nord Anglia is for 30 per cent of all pupils to have five or more A*–C grade passes. It's unrealistic we know, but it's important to do as well as we can. Frankly, if we manage 20 per cent it will be miracle. Sean and Ariadne have organized extra revision sessions for this year's GCSE pupils, and we're going to be ruthless in chasing up non-attenders. But they've had only one uninterrupted year to catch up in.

So many of our children arrive in school with little or no English that they are naturally a couple of years or more behind children who have grown up speaking the language. Quite a few will probably go on and get their GCSEs or other qualifications later at college, which is fine. But unfortunately this does nothing for our figures.

From the moment we finished the last Inspection I began collecting together relevant documents for this one in a series of box files, and the staff have been bringing me anything that is evidence of our achievements. I do this for each Inspection, and this time I'm going to burn the midnight oil transferring the documents into plastic sleeves and ring binders, with an index of key issues at the front which Suzie is going to type. At the last inspection I noticed a certain irritation on Graham Ranger's face when he was confronted with box files of loose papers, even though they were carefully arranged and ordered, and this time I'm determined everything is going to be perfect.

I believe in giving Inspectors all the help I can, and over half-term Sean and Tracey and I meet in school to put together the detailed analysis I always provide before an Inspection. We sit in my office chewing our pens and drinking coffee while Francisco whistles cheerfully outside in the atrium as he paints away, giving it a facelift in preparation for the big event ('Do you want yellow, or yellow, or yellow, Marie? – let me guess!').

It's a nice bright day, and the pale February sunlight brings a glow to the brightly coloured statue of St George, who has survived a serious accident when blown off the shelf by the wind and a major repair job to remain at his post on the shelf beside the Action Plan. We too feel quite a glow as we discuss the ways in which we have pursued our targets and addressed the key issues raised in Graham Ranger's last report – improving the quality of teaching and learning, improving attainment at Key Stages 3 and 4, improving the ethos of the school, and improving our links with the community – virtually zero when we arrived.

'Don't forget Leroy Logan and Hendon,' Tracey reminds me.

Leroy Logan, a well-known black officer in the Metropolitan Police, ran a popular seminar for our children on careers in the police force. About 90 per cent of St George's children are not white, so he had something very realistic and inspiring to offer. He also told us about a leadership course run for youngsters during the summer holidays at the Police College in Hendon, and we've arranged for eighteen children to go on it this year.

'And Colonel Cox and the cadets. Mustn't forget them,' says Sean with a smile. 'I wonder how they're getting on.' I wonder too. Numbers joining the cadet force from the three top years are now in double figures, and at this very moment six of our children are in the Brecon Beacons with a party of other cadets for four days of adventure training – and a couple of those boys are quite a challenge. Colonel Cox and his colleagues in the TA are great with the children, and absolutely indomitable, but I hope they are not being put too severely to the test.

There are many other things to list – our contact with the nearby home for the elderly, our good close relations with the local police and, last but perhaps most important of all, our Careers and Work Experience Programme, which is extending all the time, thanks very largely to the imaginative help of Jacques Delacave.

'What are we going to say about the Governors?' asks Sean as we come to the end of the report.

Hm, the Governors. In December the Inspectors noted that 'disputes between the headteacher and members of the governing body are an unhelpful diversion to the school's development'.

I'm not surprised that Graham Ranger picked up on the friction between us and the Governors, and this observation seems to call for some sort of response. I can't claim that we have made great strides, but we have made huge efforts to explain to the Governors what we are trying to do and to encourage them to come to the school to see how we are doing it. Some of them have taken up our invitation, and I had a particularly nice letter from Audrey Millar, a long-standing Governor, saying how much she had enjoyed her visit and how impressed she was by Tracey's work. So I can point to at least some positive developments in my report.

'Do you remember how we sat here night after night last year doing the Action Plan?' says Sean as we get ready to leave.

'Will I ever forget it?' I say. I recall how Sean looked then, grey with exhaustion, and the tension on Tracey's face, and I recall those nights when I often lay awake with my mind churning into the small hours and the mornings when I set off for school with a terrible sinking feeling. We're not out of the woods yet, I think, but thank goodness it's a very different scene.

We stand for a moment at the door discussing the weekend ahead. I'm planning to go to ground in the country, catch up with the family, and take some nice long walks, Sean and Dorothy have a full social programme in London, and Tracey is off to the Midlands. We stroll with her to the carpark, she hops into her little sports car, revs up and we wave until she disappears out of sight in the direction of Edgware Road. As Sean and I walk together to the tube I notice that there are buds on the weary London trees, and in one of the back gardens there is a blackbird singing.

Wednesday 28 February. It's the first day of Lent and Father George holds a special Ash Wednesday service in the atrium, which most of the school attends. He reminds us all of what Lent is about – prayer for the good of the soul, fasting for the good of the body, and alms-giving for the good of our neighbour – and he points to the similarities between Lent and Ramadan, and the practices of other world religions. I think, yet again, what a genius he has for drawing everyone in, whatever their beliefs. There is a great deal of talk about 'inclusiveness' these days, but Father George does it naturally, with no need for theorizing.

Afterwards, two little Year 7 girls come to tell me they've decided to give something up for Lent and to put the pennies they save in the collection box 'because we'd like to help someone else.' One is going to stop having crisps at break, and the other is going to give up her favourite Twix bars. What a long spiritual journey St George's has made in the past twelve months, I think. If I'd suggested giving something up for Lent this time last year, the idea would have been so incomprehensible to most of the children that I might as well have been talking Serbo-Croat. I also reflect that many of our children have so little that they may well be giving money to people who have more than they do.

Yet it's the movement of the spirit that counts. I know that this is what our task is really about: creating the foundations of a good Catholic school – a good school in general, and helping the children find a moral framework for their lives. Get that right, I tell myself, and the rest will follow. Getting off Special Measures is only part of the story.

But I am nervous about the Inspection. It's only a fortnight away now, and we're all beginning to get edgy. I know it's my job to bolster the staff and to help them lighten up – nobody ever appears to best advantage when they are tense and anxious. In our morning briefings I try to make them laugh.

'It's natural to be worried,' I tell them. 'And I can tell just how worried Mr Hearn here is because he's wearing that bright yellow shirt again. It looks like some sort of signal. Look at me, I'm a complete wreck. One of my problems is that I can't do up this jacket because of all the chocolate I've had to eat supporting you people.'

Tracey, Sean, Eddie and I find opportunities to talk to individual members of staff, making sure they feel professionally content, confident that they and we have done everything we can to prepare them for the coming Inspection. I express my confidence and trust in them, and my words are genuine. Without exception they've put their best foot forward. Every one of them is competent and professional, and we have some teachers who are so outstanding that any school would be proud to have them.

I'm aware that the children, too, are very tuned in to this huge moment, and anxious to do their best, and I make the most of this with little pep talks in assembly.

'When an Inspector calls, what would make him happy?' I ask rhetorically. 'Do you think he'd be happy to see people chewing gum and wearing baseball caps in school?'

A resounding shout of 'No!'

'Do you think he'd be happy to see people pushing and slamming doors?'

'No!'

'Do you think there's any possibility that he'd ever see things like that in this school?'

'NO!'

In fact the majority of children have long moved on from this sort of behaviour, but it never hurts to be reminded.

'I want you to look happy and smiling for the Inspectors,' I tell the children. 'because the teachers will probably be much too worried to smile.'

The staff and I discuss possible problem areas. We all agree that behaviour in the library needs watching, and we decide to give the librarian extra support. Everyone takes a slot for popping in and Father George mentions that he will be on duty there for some of the time when the Inspectors come as he enjoys the library.

On the day before the Inspection we have a full staff meeting, and, as always, I issue everyone with sheets of paper on which to make notes about each lesson and record how long the Inspectors stayed in the room. If my staff are to be judged, I want to ensure they are judged fairly, not just on the basis of a five-minute observation.

We have one last look at 'The Knowledge', the chart that Sean, Tracey, Eddie and I created, showing clearly the main areas for staff to revisit before the Inspection – good practice in preparing and conducting lessons, basic information about the school and its intake, and what we have done to improve its morale and ethos.

'I know you've all done your revision,' I tell them. 'And you've really got nothing to worry about. Anyone can have the odd blip on the day, but *I* know how good you are, the Inspectors will have my assessments of your teaching, and you need have no worries about your grades.'

At half-term I came across a tray of little South American 'worry people' in a shop in Covent Garden and before we disband I offer the tiny cotton figures to every member of staff.

'Tell him all your worries,' I say, 'then forget everything, put him under your pillow and sleep the sleep of the just.'

Some of them look at me rather quizzically, but I can see most of them are tickled by the idea, and they laughingly tuck the little figures away in pockets and briefcases. I suspect they see it as another example of the Head's incipient insanity.

I insist everyone leaves on time today, even Sean and Tracey, but it's later than I intend when I finally leave school myself. I just can't seem to let go. Yet again I check through the files we've prepared for Graham Ranger to make sure there's nothing missing, though I know I've been through them over and over again. Finally I get a call from Nadine, who's been trying to get me at home. 'I thought you were getting back early today,' she says in exasperation. 'You're going to be exhausted tomorrow you know.'

'I'm leaving now,' I say. I take one last walk through the corridors and classrooms to make sure everything's clean and in order. There's a light still on in the chapel, and I'm about to turn it off when I realize there's someone in there. Father George rises to greet me. I know he has been offering up special prayers for all of us during the past few weeks.

'Just a last-minute reminder to the Almighty,' he says, with a mischievous smile. 'But I've no doubt He's on our side.'

'Do you think everyone else who should be is on our side?' I can't help asking.

'Who knows, Marie,' says Father George with a sigh. 'Who knows.'

Tuesday 13 March. I don't sleep much, and I'm up at crack of dawn. My most businesslike navy suit is hanging ready, fresh from the dry-cleaners, and I decide on my highest heels to give myself a lift. Once in uniform I feel better, but I'm horribly aware of the way my suit jacket strains when I do up the buttons, and I apply my eyeliner with a shaky hand.

As I try to swallow some breakfast, I remind myself what life is going to be like when all this is over. I'm going to go to the gym and get fit again. I'm going to lose weight because I'm not going to need to eat comfort foods. I'm going to have time to enjoy the family, start going to concerts and the theatre again, and I shall begin my botanical drawing class. I try to conjure up soothing images of plants and trees and beautiful gardens, but it's no good. This is The Day, and there's absolutely no escaping it. My daughters all ring to wish me luck before I leave, despite the ungodly hour – 'We've got the champagne on ice, Mum. We all know you're going to do it,' says Nadine – and the warm feeling this gives me lasts me all the way to school.

Everyone else is in early too. By 7.30 Mick is giving the atrium floor one final polish, and Maggie, whose white ensemble today really is delightful, is watering the plants hanging on the stairs and in the atrium, and wielding her eco-friendly bug spray. The school plants seem to have become Maggie's special responsibility and she is particularly proud of a vast palm in the entrance hall, which she insists I view with her now. I'm also invited to view the sparkling cleanliness of my private toilet, which I shall be sharing with the Inspectors.

'Dazzling, Maggie,' I say. 'It's perfect. We've really got to look after them, haven't we.'

'Keep 'em sweet, eh?' she says with a conspiratorial wink.

Suzie and Wendy are checking the parents' room, which will be the Inspectors' base. Suzie has laid out the vital files, and Wendy, calm and efficient as ever, is setting out trays with teabags, instant coffee and biscuits.

'Have we got plain biscuits as well as those ones with cream?' I say anxiously. 'Oh, and we must give them decaf as well.'

'We've got it,' says Wendy soothingly. 'It's all here.'

'And what about that notice for the door saying "Ofsted Base". It'll remind the children not to make a noise.'

'It's on the computer. I'll print it out now,' says Suzie, with her usual cheerful smile.

At 7.45 Sean, Tracey, Eddie and I have one last chat to check nothing's been overlooked, and then go to wish the staff good luck. Everyone's looking smart today. Khadija is her usual exuberant self, joking and laughing with Father George – she's seen it all so many times before that nothing can faze her – but there are some very pale, serious faces among the younger staff. I feel like the commander of an army unit that's about to go over the top, and I post a member of the artillery to keep watch for the approaching enemy. It's tempting to put a stirring military march on the PA system, but we've already made our choice, and by 7.55 Bob Marley is telling us that 'every little t'ing's gonna be all right.'

Just after eight am the message is passed down the line: 'They're here! They're coming up Lanark Road!'

'They're early!' I mutter. Bob Marley is discreetly replaced by *Panis angelicus*, I straighten my jacket, take a deep breath, and go out to greet the Inspectors, fixing a welcoming smile on my face, which is met by an equally fixed smile from Graham Ranger. Neither of us is fooled. We're on opposite sides today, and their judgement of us will be unsparing, pleasant though they are.

As ever, they are courteous and businesslike as we show them to the parents' room, where they set down their things and prepare to go into conclave. Suzie, wearing her most warm and caring expression, immediately offers them a cup of coffee, which is politely accepted. Then the door is firmly shut.

Now they're actually here, we all begin to feel a little better, though there's a moment of panic when one member of staff arrives with something to be copied that she'd overlooked. While Suzie sees to it, I offer the flustered teacher a cup of tea and boost her with a compliment about her outfit, and she goes away looking slightly less wild-eyed.

The children start arriving – 'Calm down please, you remember who's here's today, don't you?' – adrenalin starts to flow, and it begins to feel more like the Blitz, with everyone rallying round and pulling together. Nothing makes such a bond as a common enemy, and the children enter wholeheartedly into the wartime spirit. 'I think they looked like they enjoyed that Miss,' a Year 9 whispers conspiratorially to me after assembly – a model event, with special prayers by Father George. 'They've gone upstairs now,' someone else warns me. 'Don't run,' I hear the prefects telling everyone. I don't think I've ever been in a school where I felt such a will for an Inspection to succeed. It is totally unique in my experience.

The jungle drums are in action, and I am kept discreetly informed of where the Inspectors are. Sean and Tracey are everywhere, supporting, affirming, listening to worries from staff who feel they haven't done themselves justice, making sure that children like Peta, who are easily upset by an unfamiliar atmosphere, have adequate support.

The Inspectors have already called in umpteen exercise books and lesson schemes, but there is another nail-biting moment mid-morning when they ask to see punctuality data for Year 10, and I have to find Sean to locate the most up-to-date version. 'They want it *now*,' I hiss. Mr Ranger seems quite snappy in fact, since he'd asked for it earlier. The whole thing takes a matter of minutes, but it feels like hours, and I apologize profusely for the delay as I hand the figures over. When Ofsted asks for something, you produce it at the double.

By lunchtime the Inspectors have already been plied with so many cups of coffee by Suzie, who leaps to her feet every time she sees them returning to the parents' room, that I think they must be in danger of becoming overcaffeinated. They have lunch in the canteen, and I see them in earnest conversation with several of the children, including Debbie. I long to eavesdrop but know that I mustn't. They stroll round the playground, chatting with various groups, their sharp eyes missing nothing.

I'm standing near the door to the playground as they come in again when I hear a loud voice at my elbow.

'Two days before the gun, eh Miss!'

I turn to see Ian, a cheeky, dark-haired boy from Year 8 with a stentorian voice, who is grinning cheerfully at me.

'I'm sure we'll get a good report,' I hear myself say in an unusually formal voice, 'since you're all behaving so well.' I catch Kath Cross's eye and she gazes back, professionally enigmatic.

As for me, I feel rather useless. We're so well prepared that there's almost nothing for me to do, and sitting in my office, plied with numerous cups of tea and coffee by a concerned and thoughtful Suzie, or venturing out for a short recce through the corridors, I feel rather like the superannuated butler in *The Remains of the Day*.

When the Inspectors finally leave at 4.30, I search their faces for some kind of reaction, but they are inscrutable. I suppose in my arrogant heart of hearts I think we've done all right, but they give no indication at all of what they're thinking. It's true there seem to have been no major disasters, but as Sean says when the three of us meet for a post-mortem, 'You might as well be talking to the terracotta army for all they give away.'

I have a sense though, as they leave us with a courteous 'Thank you. We'll see you at the same time tomorrow', that they've pretty much made their minds up, whatever the verdict is going to be.

'How did it go Mum? How did it go?' Fiona is on the line as soon as I arrive home.

'Nothing terrible so far,' I say. 'I'm sure we'll get a good report, but off Special Measures? – I don't know. It's a huge jump in a very short time. Maybe we'll be given a "Serious Weaknesses" designation.'

'What are you doing now?' asks Fiona.

'Trying not to have a gin and tonic.'

I feel as if my reserves are running low with all the relentless giving, giving, giving. But it's Lent, and the thought of my St George's children and their crisps is very strengthening. So orange juice it is.

William is out at an official dinner, but he manages to phone for a report, and finds me in bed at 9.30. Such a thing has barely been heard of before. I speak to both Sean and Tracey, just to make sure there's nothing worrying either of them, and they both tell me they feel as if they're running on empty, or words to that effect.

Next morning I gaze in horror at the face in the bathroom mirror – unhealthy-looking skin, bags under the eyes, lines on the forehead and crow's-feet that seem to have suddenly turned into crevasses. Makeup doesn't seem to help much either. It's all just the strain, I tell myself as I apply another coat of mascara, which adds to the Morticia Adams look.

The first person I meet when I get to school is Francisco, who is placing the chairs in the atrium where they belong with mathematical precision, whistling cheerfully the while.

'All tidy for the Inspectors,' he greets me with his usual sunny smile. 'We do good yesterday. No?'

'Yes, I think we've done fine, Francisco,' I say confidently. 'And this all looks perfect. You did a great job on these walls.'

'And today, all over?'

'Yes, today's the day.'

What if it really is all over, I think. I feel as if the fate of St George's is literally hanging in the balance. I can imagine the press coverage: 'Task Force Fails Lawrence School'.

Sean and Tracey are in already, and we confer in my office

before going to see the staff. We don't know what the Inspectors' plan is for today, but we suspect they'll be finished by the end of the morning, to allow time for their deliberations.

'I think they've already made their minds up,' says Tracey. 'There was something about the way Graham Ranger smiled . . .'

'The smile on the face of the tiger,' says Sean.

'We don't want everyone to relax and think it's all over,' I say anxiously. 'Knowing our Mr Ranger, there could well be some last-minute surprises.' We decide simply to tell the staff that today is flexible – the Inspectors may be finished early, but then again they may not.

Everyone's doing their best to be optimistic in the staff room. Candida bounds in with her usual merry smile, Eddie and David appear philosophical, and Khadija is teasing everyone, as always. Maeliosa tells me she has just lit a candle for us.

A few people agonize.

'I just feel I could have done better . . .'

'How could I have made such a stupid mistake . . . ?'

'I'd got it all mapped out in my mind beforehand . . .'

'You and the rest of the universe,' I comfort them. 'In any case, you're not going to be judged just on that one lesson.'

When the Inspectors do arrive, this time to some uplifting Gregorian chant, they give no indication how long our ordeal is going to last. Glancing through their half-open door as I pass casually by, I note that they are already deep in discussion over their coffee – a good sign perhaps? 'Oh, stop trying to read the runes, you idiot,' I tell myself crossly.

Before long there are requests for yet more data, and Ariadne and Sean fall over one another in the school office in their rush to provide it.

'They've gone upstairs again,' Sean hisses, putting his head round my door.

'Where are they?'

'I'm not sure. I think they're in the Art Room.'

240

'Oh, good. They've got some fantastic work on the walls up there.'

Maggie, resplendent in her highest heels and her best spring outfit, pops her head round the door from time to time to keep me posted about where the Inspectors are, with a wink and an expressive movement of her head.

At lunchtime, as usual, the school is busy with club activities, and the Inspectors wander round freely, talking to the children, whom I'm delighted to see responding in a polite, open and friendly way.

From time to time I overhear snatches of conversation round the school: 'We're going to get this great new dining room . . .' 'This big posh school called Harrow lets us go on their playing fields . . .' Tracey reports that the Inspectors are keen to hear more about out-of-school activities, and one boy has waxed enthusiastic about his half-term trip to the Brecon Beacons, and all the climbing and mountain biking he did.

I notice again what a warm and encouraging manner Kath Cross has, and how good she is at communicating with the less articulate children, and with those whose English is poor. But I can't help hoping she doesn't get buttonholed by Peta, who is always at the ready with a long-winded list of complaints.

Soon after lunch Canon John appears in my office, ready, as Chairman of Governors, to receive the Inspectors' report. He is clearly as apprehensive as I am, pacing restlessly up and down and gazing anxiously out of the window.

'A cup of tea – a coffee?' I suggest.

'Oh, no thank you, Marie.'

Poor Canon John, what did I get him into here, I ask myself. He has been through hell and high water in the cause of St George's, and he is by no means the only one.

Half an hour later I hear familiar voices in the atrium, and the representatives of the Diocese, the LEA and Nord Anglia are ushered in. I haven't spoken to Tony Mackersie directly since our disturbing exchange of letters, but he, Phyl Crawford and Karen

Lynch are clearly very much aware of their roles on this important occasion. They are all carrying themselves upright and a little stiffly – perhaps they are nervous too.

Suzie has laid out tea, coffee and biscuits, and we all sit around the table in my office making rather stilted conversation. Soon we are joined by Sean and Tracey. They both look weary and somewhat apprehensive and I'm reminded of the time, a year ago, when we three stood together outside the hall, before that first staff meeting. These are the people who have staked everything on St George's and have worked themselves into the ground to make it succeed.

After what feels like hours Suzie buzzes me. 'The Inspectors are ready. Shall I ask them to come in?'

We all gaze fixedly at the Inspectors. As usual they take their time seating themselves and arranging their papers on the table. I steal a look at Tony Mackersie, trying to work out what he is thinking, but he is fiddling with his papers.

Graham Ranger clears his throat. 'First of all, on behalf of us both, I would like to thank you for your generous hospitality. We have been made extremely welcome at St George's, and have been given every assistance in arriving at an opinion about the school and how it has progessed since our last visit.' He smiles graciously in my direction.

'So what *is* your opinion? Come on, Graham, tell us, quick,' I'm begging him silently. I incline my head and smile back as cheerfully as I can.

Graham Ranger consults some written notes. Then 'In accordance with Section 14 of the Schools Inspection Act 1996,' he reads in formal tones, 'I am of the opinion that the school no longer requires Special Measures since it is now providing an acceptable standard of education for its pupils.'

I hear a sharp intake of breath somewhere to my left, but for a moment no one says anything. Now Graham Ranger has spoken the words, we can none of us, I think, quite believe them. Tracey looks stunned, Sean grins from ear to ear, and Canon John turns to me immediately, his face wreathed in smiles.

The pleasure and relief is so great I do something I've never done before. 'Would you mind moving a little?' I ask a surprised Canon John who is sitting next to me. 'I have to do this, Mr Ranger, the staff expect it,' and I lean over and give Graham Ranger a quick peck on the cheek.

The tension evaporates. Sean, Tracey and Canon John all burst out laughing. Tony Mackersie looks on expressionless, Karen Lynch smiles, and Phyl Crawford looks bemused. Graham Ranger, obviously taken by surprise, twinkles back at me. I don't think being kissed by heads is part of normal Inspection procedure. 'I'll probably read about this in the papers,' he smiles.

I've come back to earth a little now, and I wait for Graham Ranger's next words, which I know will be 'But there are still serious weaknesses. . . .' It's most unusual for a school to be taken off Special Measures without any provisos or qualifications.

'You have transformed this school,' he says simply, with genuine feeling, going on to read his full formal report aloud in careful, measured tones. We sit engrossed for a good forty minutes or so.

Kath Cross goes round the table congratulating everyone in her friendly way, and Graham Ranger begins to gather up his papers.

I glance at Tony Mackersie, who is leaning over to speak to Karen Lynch. Our eyes meet, and he says some dutiful words.

But nothing can spoil this moment of triumph, and I'm longing to tell the staff. Graham Ranger rises. 'Well, I'm sure you'll be wanting to pass on the good news,' he says. 'I shall, of course, be sending you our full report.'

Sean, Tracey and I see the Inspectors to the door and as we shake hands I say: 'I hope you won't take this personally Mr Ranger, but I hope never to see you again, except perhaps at some gathering.'

There are more laughs and congratulations, and we watch their departing backs as they walk briskly off down Lanark Road.

When I go back into my office, Phyl Crawford and Karen Lynch are putting on their coats, but I have missed Tony Mackersie, who must have a pressing engagement.

Sean, Tracey, Canon John and I hurry towards the staff room. 'Don't give anything away!' I say. As we open the door the chatter dies. The staff are sitting round in tense little groups, nursing cups of tea and coffee. People leap up as we come in, crying: 'What's happened? Have we done it? Quick, what's the verdict.'

We all stand looking at them for a second or two, without expression. Then I turn to Canon John as Chairman of Governors, who announces in solemn and measured tones: 'Colleagues, I am here to formally congratulate all of you. The school was today removed from Special Measures . . .'

Almost before he can finish the room erupts. People are jumping, hugging, laughing, crying, clapping. There are cries of 'We really did it then!' and 'I can't believe it!'. Eddie comes over in his quiet, thoughtful way and shakes my hand, Khadija is gesticulating in Gallic fashion, and Ariadne simply stands beaming with joy and taking in the news.

When the rumpus dies down Canon John leads us in a prayer of thanksgiving. Then it's my turn to speak.

'My very sincere congratulations to the best teaching team in the world,' I say. 'I just can't tell you how much this means to me. It's you who did it – you and the children. So I want to propose a special toast to you, the staff – the nicest, funniest, most gifted and most willing crowd of people I have ever had the pleasure to work with.'

And I'm going to join in this toast, I think. I've already decided that I'm going to count today as my Laetare Sunday – that day of relaxation the Church allows us in the middle of Lent.

Soft drinks and wine appear from the fridge. 'I see you were anticipating a celebration,' I say, laughing.

'I reckoned we deserved it after all our hard work, whatever the outcome,' says Sean, pouring me some wine.

I raise my glass. 'To St George's,' I say.

'To St George's,' everyone echoes.

More clapping. 'When are we going to tell the children?' asks Tracey. It's typical of her to be thinking of them.

A year ago, I remember, I shook hands with every one of them, searching each face for some hopeful sign that we could work together. It was a very personal moment, though I knew nothing about any of them, and I know that now I want to give them this terrific news personally, not in a big assembly, but year group by year group as we did then.

'Let's wait till tomorrow,' I say, 'There's not much time left this afternoon, and I'd like to tell every year group separately, myself.'

We stay for a moment or two longer, laughing and chatting, congratulating one another, remembering the small mishaps, reliving the hair-raising moments – then it's time to get back to work.

I can't wait to get home and celebrate with the family, but there's so much to be done – a press release to organize, with a statement from Councillor Joiner, a letter to write to the parents, another to the Governors and a third to all the innumerable friends, supporters and celebrities who've given us such sterling help during the year.

I give silent thanks, too, to all the legions of unseen people who have helped St George's – understanding, supportive wives like Sean's Dorothy, and all the other husbands, partners, friends and parents who have been there in the background, unacknowledged, putting up with St George's unusual demands. I also think of Philip Lawrence, and how proud he'd be of his school.

Finally, we decide that we'll make this Friday a special day for the children by allowing them to come to school in their own choice of clothes and leave at 2.30.

'It's Red Nose Day too,' Tracey reminds us, 'so it will be nice if they can go off and join in at home.'

'We can call it an 'Early St George's Day,' suggests Canon John.

It's 7.30 by the time I literally totter the few steps from the lift to my door. As I approach, the door opens, and there are William, Nadine, Hilary and the children, all laughing.

After the hugs and congratulations, I'm told we're all going round to Fiona's.

'Why?' I ask several times. 'We're all here now. Why can't she and Mark come here?'

'Fiona's got the champagne on ice,' I'm told.

We all get into the car and drive the few minutes to Fiona's house, where she and my sons-in-law are waiting. I'm led to a place of honour in the sitting room and a glass of champagne is put into my hand. I feel as if I'm on champagne already. I'm in a kind of haze, partly tiredness, partly relief, and partly excitement, which lends an unreality to the proceedings.

After a toast to 'Mum, we always knew you'd do it', the big curtains in the sitting room are drawn aside to reveal – 'Whatever is it?' I say. 'It looks like one of those things they stand on at the Olympic Games.'

Everyone roars with laughter. 'You've got it in one, Mum,' says Fiona, taking me by the hand and leading me over to stand on the highest step of what I now see clearly is an Olympic-style plinth with places for the three medallists, bronze, silver and gold.

'You *are* a winner, Mum,' she says. 'You sprinted for gold and you got it. I had this made in Clerkenwell. It's ash. Do you like it?'

'You had it *made*?' I say incredulously. 'What would you have done with it if things hadn't worked out, if we'd failed?'

'Used it as a plant stand,' says Fiona, with a shriek of laughter. 'But we always knew you'd do it.'

I can't speak . . .

Everyone seems to be smiling next morning at staff briefing, though I suspect some of the younger staff were out celebrating last night because there are a few suppressed yawns as we discuss plans for the rest of the week.

Sean, who never rests, has been in early, and the first thing the children see is a poster saying 'Congratulations!'. During the first periods of morning school, I meet each year group in the hall to tell them what the Inspectors have said and congratulate them properly. I want them to remember this day, and I want to impress upon them that this has happened because of their own efforts.

'We knew already, didn't we, that St George's was doing well, because we've all been working so hard this year to improve it,' I say to them. 'Now the Inspectors have told us they agree with us. It's official.' Loud clapping bursts forth and there are big grins all round. 'You can be very proud of St George's and very proud of yourselves. Don't sit back and think it's all done, though. We've still got lots of hard work ahead of us. But let's enjoy today. Three cheers for us. Hip-hip-hooray!' And the roof is almost blown off by the mighty cheers.

When I explain that we are no longer on Special Measures because the Inspectors feel that we are now a successful school, the children are thrilled, though I think some of the younger ones find the concept a bit difficult to understand. 'What did they measure us *for*?' I hear a puzzled eleven-year-old asking a friend afterwards.

All through the school there's a carnival atmosphere, and there are beaming faces everywhere, from the team in the canteen to the teaching staff as they move from class to class, and the children I meet in the corridors. There's such a wonderful sense of pride and achievement – everyone's walking tall.

And everyone's so willing today. Children offer to carry things for me, Maggie keeps popping her head round the door to ask if I need anything, and upstairs I actually find Sherry putting up a new display on one of the noticeboards.

'Oh Miss, innit great?' cries Debbie, rushing up to me in break. 'You'll be getting that champagne bottle for your bracelet now, won't ya!'

'I certainly will, Debbie,' I say with a smile.

At lunchtime the familiar BBC television news van is at the school gates once more, and Suzie appears with a copy of the *Evening*

Standard, which has a news report ('Dark days are over at murdered head's school') and an editorial on St George's 'resurrection'. On Friday *The Times* devotes several columns to our story and the *Independent* welcomes the 'rehabilitation of one of Britain's most notorious comprehensive schools.'

Soon my desk is deep in letters and cards – kind, generous messages from old friends and past colleagues, from new friends of the school like Paula Pryke and Professor Hakim, from people who knew St George's before its dark days, from people who have read or heard about us and tell me they have been praying for us. Other headteachers send warm supportive messages and there's a letter from David Blunkett, expressing his personal gratitude to us for turning St George's round.

There are no excited phone calls from the Diocese, but eventually a formal letter arrives from Monsignor Barltrop, congratulating me on the 'wonderful news'. 'I am well aware,' Mgr Barltrop writes, 'of the extraordinary demands the school and its agenda have placed on you and your colleagues over the past year.' Perhaps my tiredness has made me ungracious. What a pity, I reflect, that this valuable support was not available to Sean, Tracey and me earlier. Mm, I reflect, 'agenda' is a word I have been conscious of quite a lot in the last year or so.

Some of the messages I find most affecting are from the staff. They've been here with me at the coalface, and they know better than anyone what an achievement this is. The following week we have a little ceremony, and I give each of them a home-made card saying 'Thank you for taking the plunge with the Task Force' under a picture of the glamorous 1950s bathing beauty Esther Williams launching herself off a diving-board. As well as thanking them I want to make them laugh, to remind them of the fun we've had together, as well as the hard work.

We organize a special school photo to commemorate the occasion. Correctly uniformed and smiling broadly, everyone lines up in the playground, and it appears to go without a hitch. When the photograph arrives, however, we gaze at it in dismay.

'What on earth is he doing?' I ask.

'Looks like a dubious gesture to me,' says Tracey.

Whatever happened, I think it was probably just high spirits and over-excitement, but Tracey is understandably furious. The culprit is hauled in for questioning, and several days later she receives the following letter:

To Miss O'Leary

I apologize for ruining the school photo. I did not think anyone would notice my hand. I thought the picture would be taken from a far angle not a close-up. I again apologize for what I have done and I promise it will never happen again. I also have a few suggestions that might help.

1. Use the photo anyway
2. Use the first photo
3. Use a computer to scan the photo and remove my arm
4. Ask the Government for a payment for the new photo.

'Oh well,' I say to Tracey, 'it wouldn't be St George's, would it, if it had all gone entirely according to plan. We'll airbrush it out.' And we do.

When the written Ofsted report arrives, Sean, Tracey, Eddie and I sit down with it in my office, and I can't resist getting out the notes on Graham Ranger's visit a year ago.

As I glance through today's glowing phrases I remember the school we came into then, a place of fear, despair and low expectations, a school that had given up hope.

'Do you remember that awful phrase Graham Ranger used, "at the bottom end of limited progress",' Tracey says, shaking her head.

'"The headteacher has led a rapid programme of school improvement over the past 12 months." That sounds a bit better doesn't it?' says Sean, quoting from the new report.

'Even though she totters on her high heels,' I laugh to lighten the atmosphere.

Everyone relaxes a little and we go over the report together, revelling in its findings:

> The pupils' response to their teaching and learning is very good. They are willing, eager to succeed and are gaining in confidence as learners. The pupils respect the teachers' authority and show an increasing willingness to participate in the life of the school.
>
> They value the clear expectations of good behaviour, the ordered environment and the extra trust and responsibility they are given. Universally they are in praise of the improvements made to the school over the last 12 months and are proud of the school's achievement. The school has a greater sense of Catholicity and has a positive ethos for learning.

How could I ever have reached this point without Sean and Tracey? It would have been an impossible mountain to scale. They have given their hearts and minds and soul to this project. I shall never be able to repay them.

Of course it's not a perfect picture. The report notes that two-thirds of our pupils have reading ages below their chronological ages when they arrive, and their attainment levels are low, so our standards are below the national average. But 'rates of progress are now satisfactory overall.' I think again how much we need Sean to press on with this school.

The bottom line is that teaching and learning have immeasurably improved. Four lessons in five are now satisfactory or better and one-third of all teaching is good or very good. Last spring, the Inspectors observed that in one-third of all lessons the pupils dictated the pace, not the teachers, only 20 per cent of teaching was good, and in some subjects there was no good teaching at all.

Last year our Literacy and Special Needs programme was classed as 'poor', whereas now our English as an Additional

Language work is highly praised. Then there were 'severe problems with attendance,' now it is just over 90 per cent, and approaching national averages.

What pleases me most, perhaps, is the children's own reaction. Last month the *Evening Standard* interviewed some of our fourteen- and fifteen-year-olds, and I've put their comments on my noticeboard.

'Before, I wouldn't have classed this as a school,' said one. 'It was more like a youth club. People just came to school to socialize with their friends and they talked to the teachers however they wanted. Now they show more respect. People outside see the school differently as well.'

'The most important thing is the teachers,' said someone else. 'Before they didn't have the same attitude towards us. Now they really make us believe we can do it.'

'We have more subjects to choose from and more activities,' was another comment, 'and we have been going on lots of trips. That makes you happy, knowing that if you do your work there's something to look forward to at the end of it.'

It's the children's opinion that matters, and I'm delighted by their enthusiasm and their articulate remarks. But I'm aware that these are all bright, well-motivated pupils, who I know are going to do well. There are others who start at such a disadvantage, I think as I gather up my things, that whatever we offer them will never seem enough.

At the end of the afternoon we stand at the door saying goodbye to the children and giving them each a chocolate bar to round off a successful week. 'Coo, thanks Miss.' 'Bye Miss.' 'Wicked, Miss!' 'Bye Miss O'Leary.' 'Bye Mr Gaynor.' 'Bye Mr Devlin.' 'Bye . . .' They drift off in groups, some towards the bus stop, some to the tube, some in the direction of Kilburn High Road.

When they've all gone there's still a small figure rummaging about in his rucksack in the playground.

'Aren't you going home Ali?' I say. I know Ali hasn't much to go home to, and he's often one of the last to leave.

Ali smiles his crooked smile as he does up the buckle on his rucksack. 'Eez good,' he says, nodding back towards the school. 'We learn. Eez ver' good!' Then 'Bye Meez.'

And with this endorsement, Ali picks up his rucksack and trots jauntily out of the school gates and down the road.

9

Afterwards

Summer 2001

The Inspection was not, of course, the end of this particular story – the Task Force remained at St George's until the end of the summer term. Meantime there were GCSEs to prepare for, school trips to arrange and another May Ball to organize – this time a wholly joyful event for both staff and leavers that went without a hitch. Debbie was the surprise of the evening, looking amazingly sophisticated in a tasteful black dress, with her hair swept up. She even managed to keep her voice down, and was met by a very handsome and well-dressed boy after the ball.

One glorious sunny morning towards the end of May our helpful Councillor Joiner, Jacques Delacave and a representative of the Rotary Club were there to see the school take official delivery of a smart new seventeen-seater minibus decorated with the St George's and Rotary Club logos. Jacques had not forgotten his promise, and for months he had been quietly fundraising – though I suspect he also dug deep into his own pocket. Cheers rang out as he cut the ribbon, and then the bus was blessed by Father George.

The minibus opened a whole new era for the rugby and soccer teams, who now had transport to away matches and to their practice grounds on Saturdays, and they began to improve almost literally by leaps and bounds. In fact during the spring and summer our whole sports programme took off. Teamwork training sessions were arranged with the army, who also put on an impressive fitness display in the playground, and in June St George's held a highly successful Sports Day at the Paddington Recreation Ground – an enjoyable afternoon with high jump, track events, relay races, and the presentation of many cups and prizes.

Inside school, improvements began to the dining area and the children were thrilled to see their own ideas and suggestions become reality. The improved layout speeded up the lunch queues, a salad bar was installed, and the whole area was transformed with fresh paint and attractive modern posters. John and Francis Sorrell presented the plans for the new extension to the Governors and so charmed and inspired them that it was agreed that they would go ahead and raise money for the second stage of work.

We continued 'planting the golden seed'. The careers and work experience programme expanded, and it was heartening to see how high some of our youngsters were now setting their sights. It wasn't just in traditional areas such as the law, accounting and medicine. One pupil wanted to work in an art gallery, several were interested in dance, and another in journalism. St George's also took part in a project to encourage youngsters from Inner City schools to apply to Oxbridge. Some of our fourteen- and fifteen-year-olds spent two days visiting Oxford and Cambridge colleges, attending introductory sessions, and to their general surprise – 'The students weren't a bit snobbish. I met one who lived in Kilburn' – having the time of their lives.

Towards the end of the summer term I received a letter from a government body, the Audit Commission, telling me that Ofsted had recommended the school as a national example of good practice. The Audit Commission promotes the best use of public money by monitoring how it is spent, so this was immensely flattering. The conclusion of their case study was that our success depended on a 'strict, positive regime with clear expectations, grounded on a strong set of values' and 'relentless vigour in implementation'. Sean, Tracey and I agreed that we couldn't have put it better ourselves.

That summer I received two singular honours. I was named one of four Catholic Women of the Year, and I was made a Dame of the

Order of St Gregory, a Papal decoration for outstanding service to the Catholic Church. The first was celebrated at a big formal luncheon at the Hotel Russell – an inspiring occasion to which all the family came, as well as Sean, Tracey, Canon John, Peter Brown, our Governor Audrey Millar, Father George and Jacques Delacave.

The second was announced by the Archbishop of Westminster, Cardinal Cormac Murphy-O'Connor, when he visited the school in June. It was a truly happy visit. As the Cardinal, a tall and imposing figure in his scarlet robes, stepped from his official car in Lanark Road, he was greeted by a group of brushed and shining Year 7s enthusiastically waving flags of St George. He met and spoke to groups of children in the atrium and then proceeded to the hall, where the choir, conducted by Katerina, sang a lovely Irish lullaby and 'Trottin' to the Fair', the words of which I found were still lodged in my memory from my days in the Glasgow Children's Choir.

The Cardinal showed the staff and children my decoration and spoke very sensitively about it, telling them that it may have been presented to their Headmistress, but that it was really for the whole school. He was gracious, friendly and I felt his genuine support – an impression reinforced later by an article he wrote in the *Financial Times* in which he chose St Catherine of Siena as his favourite Saint. It was she who famously said to God: 'It is my will that you do not delay any longer.' 'Luckily we can boast a few Catherines in the Church of England and Wales today,' the Cardinal wrote. At least the Cardinal feels there is a place for strong women in the work of the church, I thought. How I empathize with the author of the Patience Prayer: 'God grant me patience . . . and I want it *now*!'

Later we marked my St Gregory award with a quiet family ceremony in the crypt at St Etheldreda's, conducted by Father Kit who had been my spiritual guide and mainstay and one of my most loyal supporters throughout all my time at St George's. It was with Father Kit that I had celebrated my retirement from

Douay, and as he laughingly told me afterwards, he had never expected to be celebrating my retirement a second time.

There was, however, one big disappointment. On the second day of interviews for the new Head, the staff learned that Sean's application had not been successful. The Selection Panel had chosen Philip Jakszta, the Acting Head of a Diocesan school in Tower Hamlets, Blessed John Roche, which was closing in a year.

Personally I was astonished by this decision. I had nothing whatever against the pleasant Philip Jakszta, since I knew very little about him, but the idea of throwing away all the knowledge and experience of St George's that Sean had built up during the past year, the personal qualities that made the staff and children trust him, and the stability and continuity that he would bring to the school, to me simply didn't make sense. St George's had a lot of developing still to do.

I remembered the long and dedicated hours Sean had spent on unpicking and putting to rights St George's desperate finances, analysing its dire attendance figures, and on numerous other highly skilled and labour-intensive tasks. Without Sean's vision for the children, his ability and meticulous attention to detail, I thought sadly, St George's would still be in chaos and the Selection Panel wouldn't be in the position of appointing a new Head at all.

I have never admired Sean more than I did at this time. If we were upset, I can only imagine how he must have felt, but he was clearly determined not to show any bitterness, or allow the decision to affect his work. He simply carried on, giving the school all his energies as he had every day since we came. And I was delighted for him when, two weeks after the interviews, he heard that he had passed the new National Professional Qualification for Headteachers, which he had been studying hard for in his spare time.

'You'll make a truly great head,' I said to him. 'Everyone here knows that. I'm just sorry it's not going to be at St George's.'

Sean looked steadily at me for a moment. 'Well Marie,' he said. 'So am I. But in the end we're here until the summer to do what's best for the children, and we've got to do everything we can for them.'

And as professionals, of course, that is what we did, working with the new Head, and doing our best to ensure as much continuity as possible. We knew, too, that as the summer wore on it was our duty to withdraw, to let their new Head get to know the children and to leave him a clean, fresh school. As term ended we carefully took down all the photos and Wendy passed them to the children who were in them; we left the noticeboards empty and ready for whatever 'Moving Forward Together' messages the new Head might choose to put on them at the beginning of the autumn term.

I had been looking forward to continuing to play some role for the school after my retirement in August, advising and providing continuity for staff and pupils, perhaps as a Governor, as I know I would have done if Sean had become Head. But this could have been problematic for the new Head. My vision was not to be. I had not imagined that I would be – as Shakespeare puts it – 'untimely ripped' from St George's in this way. Saying goodbye to the children was especially painful. It was sad, too, to part from my wonderful staff.

'I used to feel excited every single day I came to work at St George's,' one of them told me. 'I can't imagine ever having such fun again.'

'Get down to that gym now,' said Maggie, with a wink as she clasped my hand.

'All the very best. We'll be wid' you in spirit,' said Mick.

To Francisco I gave a framed photograph of the two of us, looking at paint charts. 'Some of my happiest times Marie,' he said, looking away. 'It will be on my mantelpiece.'

I was determined that we would end the term on a positive note, and we finished with a beautiful service of thanksgiving conducted by Father George. As the choir, with Katerina, sang the anthem, and I looked round at the children and staff standing quietly together, I thought of how much healing had gone on during our year at St George's.

After the service I was handed a pink envelope containing a carefully typed letter:

To all members of Staff.
Thank you for everything that you have done for our school. For those teachers leaving our school, every single person in the school'll miss you. We appreciate your concern, taking it out of special measures. We highly appreciate your presence in the school. Hope you find joy and happiness in the future. Good luck. Have a wonderful holiday. Miss you. Love you lots.
  Anastasia

So that was how our time at St George's ended. Well, not quite. The school received 140 applications for 120 places for September 2001 – double the number it had received the year before. And when the GCSE results arrived, they had materially improved on the previous year, a quick estimate suggested. Whereas the previous year many of the children had had no passes at all, now nearly every child who had taken GCSEs had at least one pass, so everyone had something to take away with them.

Some of the results were impressive by any standards. Tariq had eleven A*–C grade passes, and had won a scholarship to an independent school. Suzi, still bent on a career in medicine, had seven, and was off to a good neighbouring sixth form, along with another star pupil, Rayan, who had achieved eight.

Rory stayed on at the garage and got his apprenticeship. Jason, to everyone's astonishment, caught the acting bug and decided that he was going to try for theatre school, and it even looks as if Jo might follow in his footsteps. And to our relief, poor displaced Mohammed returned to his family in Africa – one of the many wandering souls to whom for a short while St George's was a kind of home.

And Debbie? 'I fink I might get married,' she told me cheerfully.

'Well, you can't get married yet,' I said. 'You want to do your exams and get some proper qualifications. What do you think you'd like to do?'

'I'd like to be a manager,' she said with a grin, 'and boss people around.'

'Yes Headmistress,' I said, and we both started laughing. 'Chill man,' I added, at which Debbie gave a shriek, and loosened her hold on the new St George and the Dragon charm on my bracelet.

'If you'd known at the beginning what you know now, would you have taken it on?' asked Sean, pouring me another glass of wine.

He, Tracey and I had met at a little Italian restaurant in Victoria to say our farewells, or rather our *au revoirs*. After an experience like St George's it's as if you've been in a war together, and I knew we'd always keep in touch. In a few weeks' time Sean and Dorothy were off to Worcester, where Sean had a new job as Head of a good Catholic school. It was the first post he'd applied for after being turned down for St George's, and he was selected against a strong field of candidates. I was delighted and not at all surprised. He'd been called to interviews for seven other head-ships. Lucky Worcester got him first.

Tracey, looking more relaxed than I'd seen her for a long time, was clearly excited about her new job as Deputy Head of a school in Birmingham. I hope they know what a gift they're getting, I thought.

We'd already exchanged presents – a hip flask from me for Sean to use on his beloved golf course, and for Tracey a little hand-crafted egg that opened to reveal a flower. It was a symbol of growth and I knew it would have meaning for her. They'd pre-sented me with a tiny pair of silver boxing gloves to put on my charm bracelet – another memento of St George's to add to the champagne bottle the family had already given me. Sean had given me an elegant pen with 'Superhead' inscribed on it, and Tracey had given me a humane spider-catcher, a wonderful, soft contraption which was guaranteed not to harm the spider – both of us were nervous of spiders.

'Probably,' I said, in answer to Sean's question. 'Because as you know, I can't resist a challenge – however, foolhardy.' We all laughed.

But how much more joyfully might I have succeeded if I had not had to be fuelled by anger, as I gradually discovered the depths of what seemed the betrayal of the children by those who should have supported me? As George Sand said, indignation is the highest form of love.

'I think you should write about it,' said Sean.

I remembered his words as I stood alone a few days later in the Philip Lawrence Memorial Garden. I had just handed my keys to Mick, at the same time checking that he had posted the precious personal items and photographs back to Mrs Lawrence.

'Yes, I thought, 'I *should* write about it – for Ali and Debbie and Jason and Jo and Alexa and Mohammed, and all the children whose talents are being thrown away, and who often get blamed when it's the adults who've failed them. They can't speak for themselves because they don't have the words, and a lot of them don't even speak English.'

I took one last look at the Memorial Garden, then closed the black gate and turned into the roar of Maida Vale.

Next day, out of the blue, came a letter from a literary agent, suggesting I write a book . . .